Abdullahi Y. Shehu

# Elections in
# NIGERIA

## THE LONG ROAD TO DEMOCRACY

MEREO

![Mereo logo]

Mereo Books

1A The Wool Market Dyer Street Cirencester Gloucestershire GL7 2PR
An imprint of Memoirs Publishing www.mereobooks.com

Elections in Nigeria: the Long Road to Democracy: 978-1-86151-917-7

First published in Great Britain in 2019
by Mereo Books, an imprint of Memoirs Publishing

The address for Memoirs Publishing Group Limited can be
found at www.memoirspublishing.com

The Memoirs Publishing Group Ltd Reg. No. 7834348

Typeset in 10/13pt Times
by Wiltshire Associates Publisher Services Ltd.
Printed and bound in Great Britain by Biddles Books

# CONTENTS

Introduction

Preface

Acknowledgments

# INTRODUCTION

Election is the bedrock of democratic governments. All modern democracies hold or conduct elections, but not all elections are truly democratic. The measure of a democratic election is that it is transparent, fair, credible, and acceptable to the people. The problem however is who determines these outcomes in an election – and that is where the concern about a sustainable democracy arises. Every contestant in any election hopes to win, thus making election essentially competitive. While the competitors do not have to like each other, they must tolerate each other and acknowledge that each has a legitimate right and an important role to play in national development.

One may ask, can there be democracy without elections? Yes, it is possible to have a democracy without free, fair and credible elections, and that is why some right-wing dictatorships or single-party governments stage what they also call 'elections'. In such situations, the process may offer genuine choices, but such choices may only be within the ruling or governing party. In a sense, that is selection, but the machinery operated under such systems claims to be democratic. In reality these cannot be democratic elections.

To put in perspective what a democratic election is, Jeane Kirkpatrick, a former US Ambassador to the United Nations, observed that 'democratic elections are not merely symbolic... They are competitive, periodic, inclusive, definitive elections in which the chief decision-makers in a government are selected by citizens who enjoy broad freedom to criticize government, to publish their criticism and to present alternatives.' By this, Kirkpatrick meant that opposition parties and candidates must have the freedom of speech, assembly and movement necessary to voice their criticisms of the government openly and to present alternative policies and candidates to the electorate. Merely giving the opposition access to the ballot box is not enough for a democratic election. Democratic elections are periodic, that is, held at intervals; but it is crucial that they are also inclusive enough to present at least a semblance of democracy. It should also be noted that democratic elections are not limited to the choice of candidates. Sometimes the electorate or the people in general may be asked to decide on a certain State policy through referenda or other electoral processes. All these are important in elections that should inform our understanding of the issues to be addressed in this book.

As democracy allows every citizen to participate in the debate and political processes through the writings of scholars, or by joining a political party, every individual is thus a politician of some sort, except that while some are involved in active campaigns and canvassing of support for their preferred parties or candidates, others may choose to influence the political processes through other means. I am the latter kind of politician. My goal in this book is simply to appraise the practice of democracy in Nigeria, and highlight some key issues that have either informed electoral choices in the past or are likely to influence choices of candidates for better or for worse in the 2019 elections in Nigeria.

My intention, therefore, is not to indulge in an intellectual exercise or a discussion of the political economy of elections and democracy, but to contribute to a better understanding of the challenges of democracy and development and how elections can serve as a panacea for the myriad problems confronting Nigeria in the 21st century. To do that, I will attempt a short discussion on the concept of democracy and look at the practice of democracy in Nigeria with a focus on the Fourth Republic, which began in 1999.

## What is Democracy?

It would appear too elementary to waste time here on defining democracy, but that is necessary in order for interested readers to have at least a basic appreciation of democracy before understanding how it is practised in Nigeria. Every society practises one form of government or another, such as oligarchy, aristocracy, theocracy, monarchy, fascism, socialism, authoritarian or dictatorships in form of military rule, and democratic regimes.

The emergence and development of the elite theory of democracy is credited to prominent classical theorists Gaetano Mosca (1858-1941), Vilfredo Pareto (1848-1923) and Robert Michels (1876-1936).The word 'democracy' comes from the Greek *demokratia*, literally meaning 'rule of the people' (Greek *demos*, 'people', and *kratos,* 'rule').[1] The theory of rule by the elite is therefore seen as a composite sociological theory which seeks to explain power relations in contemporary society. Based on this, 'democratic government originated from the Greek city-states, where democratic ideals started and were transferred to other societies'. Nevertheless,

1 N.A. David, Y.A. Manu and A. Musa, 'Elections, electoral Process and the Challenges of Democratization in Nigeria's Fourth Republic', *Research on Humanities and Social Sciences* 4(17) 2014, pp. 94-95.

David and his colleagues observed that even though democracy might have originated from the Greek practice of government, the Greeks did not provide a useful or realistic model 'as only a small minority of the adult population were granted the right of political participation which was achieved through direct vote on issues and these ideals are quite different from the modern democratic system which is based on majority rule and representative government'. According to these scholars, democracy in its modern form emerged in the 19th century, when representatives were chosen through free competitive elections and with most citizens having the right to vote. This type of government was established in Britain and the United States between 1860 and 1890 and later spread to other European countries, as well as the developing regions of the world, including Africa and Nigeria, in the second half of the 20th century. In democracy, 'the supreme, absolute and uncontrolled power remains in the people'.

Former American President Abraham Lincoln described democracy as 'Government of the People, by the People and for the People'. The 'people' refers to the entire citizenry, but the electorate consists only of those who are eligible to vote.[2] In most countries where true democracy is practised, the citizens or electorate have freedom of choice of who their leaders should be in the electoral process. There are different forms of democracy or systems of government, including the parliamentary system practised in the United Kingdom and the presidential system practised in the United States and many other countries. There are also other systems of government in other countries: the Chinese system, the Russian system, even the Dynastic system of government in some Arab countries. A few of these are also considered democracies because of their uniqueness.

It is important to mention that although election is an element

2. In Nigeria, the eligibility age is 18 years with residency requirement.See section 12 of the Electoral Act 2010 as amended.

of democracy, not all democracies conduct elections, and so long as such societies are able to run an effective system of governance that includes other elements of democracy such as the rule of law, respect for human rights, freedom of speech and association, they can be regarded as democratic.

By far the most important elements of democracy are the rule of law and national security, without which there would be no freedom and no human rights. In Nigeria there have been public discourses on whether the rule of law takes precedence over national security and human rights. That is not a major concern here and I will not delve into the polemics of that.

## Democracy in Nigeria

Every society has some semblance of democracy, but true democracy depends on broadly acceptable ingredients of popular participation, rule of law, freedom of choice and association, etc. Before the advent of colonialism, though Nigeria was considered a 'primitive society' simply because it had not embraced any so-called civilization, it nevertheless had some elements of democracy, especially through its many ethnic and cultural groups. Following the British exploration, annexation, occupation and final amalgamation of Nigeria in 1914, the country was under British colonial rule, which presumably emanated from the British type of democracy. But the real feeling for democracy began with the agitation for self-rule or self-government with the struggle for independence in the 1950s.

Constitutional development in Nigeria can be divided into four phases. The first, which some people refer to as the 'the imposition phase', led to the Clifford Constitution (1922) and the Richards Constitution (1946). The second, the 'negotiation phase', produced the MacPherson Constitution (1951), the Lyttleton

(Federal) Constitution (1954) and the Independence Constitution (1960). The third, what some people also called 'the civil phase', led to the First Republican Constitution (1963), and the fourth, 'the militarised phase', produced the Second Republican Constitution (1979), the 1989 Constitution and the 1999 Constitution. Despite all these constitutional developments, Nigeria has not institutionalised democracy.[3] Some people refer to the current stage of democratic governance in Nigeria as not truly democratic but 'civil' rule, because the building blocks of a true democracy have not been set in place. Were these building blocks properly established, separation of powers between the three arms of government would have been obvious and respected.

The various Constitutional Conferences that were held as part of the processes of negotiating for political independence in Nigeria and its ultimate granting by the British in October 1960 were all experiences in democratic development. That explains why Nigeria adopted the British parliamentary type of democracy after independence.

With an approximate population of 200 million, Nigeria is a key regional power in West Africa and accounts for 50 per cent of the region's population. It also has one of the largest youth populations in the world. Nigeria is a federation of 36 autonomous States, and it is a multi-ethnic, multi-religious and culturally diverse country with several complexities. Nigeria is endowed with largely untapped resources. It is not only the largest oil exporter in Africa, but also has the largest natural gas reserves on the continent. Talking about complexities, ethnicity apart, only Nigeria can be described metaphorically as a religious society with too many beliefs and yet no religion. Ironically, no country can succeed with such complexity except Nigeria because no country in the world has the kind of experience that Nigeria has. That Nigeria is still what it is and is

3. A.T. Ajayi and E.O. Ojo,'Democracy in Nigeria: Practice, Problems and Prospects',*Developing Country Studies*, ISSN 2225-0565 (online), 4(2) 2014.

trying to rebuild a 'fractured' nation means that God has not done with Nigeria yet.

Over the years, Nigeria has made significant progress in different aspects of human development. However, the country is still faced with monumental challenges, including security, poverty, unemployment, reducing dependence on oil and diversifying the economy, addressing insufficient infrastructure, and building strong and effective institutions, as well as governance issues:public financial management systems and the capacity for human development.

In the First Republic (1960-1966), elections were considered free, fair and credible, not only because of the way they were conducted, but also because of the pedigree of the politicians who contested and won elections. At that time, presumably, corruption was minimal in Nigeria. But the dismantling of that republic by a group of military officers introduced a new dimension which made corruption inherent in the polity of Nigeria. The perennial military rule created conditions for corruption to germinate and grow, with its attendant consequences on the political system. By the end of the Second Republic in December 1983, corruption was obviously the greatest threat to democracy and the political stability of Nigeria, thus warranting another military destruction of the foundation of democracy. Between 1960 and 1969, Sub-Saharan Africa witnessed 27 coups; 30 between 1970 and 1979 and 22 between 1980 and 1989. By 1989, about 60% of Africa's democratically elected governments had been toppled by the military.[4]

## Nigeria's Fractured Democracy

To chronicle Nigeria's political transition, one may recall that a significant part of the political system was dominated by the military. Nigeria became independent on 1 October 1960, with a high expectation of political development. Following the transition

4. Ibid., p. 112.

from colonial rule to political independence, *TIME Magazine* of 5 December 1960 in its caption 'The other Africa: Independence Without Chaos'[5] eulogised Nigeria and made Sir Abuabakar Tafawa Balewa, Nigeria's first Prime Minister, its cover person to celebrate him and Nigeria on that historic occasion. According to Kukah, the article read in part as follows:

> In the hurly burly of the 1960s' African avalanche of freedom, Nigeria's impressive demonstration of democracy's workability in Africa is too often overlooked... Nigeria entered the world community without noisy birth pangs or ominous warnings of its determination to avenge ancient wrongs. Since moderation and commonsense are not the stuff that headlines are made of, the world's eyes slid past Nigeria to focus worriedly on the imperialistic elbowing of Ghana's Nkrumah... In the long run, the most important and enduring face of Africa might well prove to be that (face) presented by Nigeria...Where so many of its neighbours have shaken off colonialism only to sink into strong man rule, Nigeria not only preaches but practices the dignity of the individual.

Alas, this was not to last long. This nascent democratic experience was truncated by the intervention by some young army officers led by Major Chukwuma Kaduna Nzeogwu, which overthrew the Tafawa Balewa government by a military coup on 15 January 1966. The configuration of the major actors of the coup and the eventual leader who emerged thereafter (General Aguiyi Ironsi) were Igbos and their targets were mainly northern political leaders, which portrayed the military action as tribalistic, thus leading to a counter coup on 15 July 1966, which overthrew the Ironsi junta and replaced it with General Yakubu Gowon, a northerner, as Head of State. In short, this was the beginning of ethnic politics which has

5. Mathew Hassan Kukah, Catholic Bishop of Sokoto Diocese, 'To Heal A Fractured Nigeria', Convocation Lecture delivered at the University of Uyo, Akwa Ibom State, November 2014.

divided Nigeria ever since. Gowon was the longest military Head of State. He ruled for nine years from 1966 to 1975, when he was overthrown by General Murtala Mohammed; whose tenure as Head of State was short-lived, thanks to yet another military coup, led by officers perceived to have been ethnically motivated. Murtala was assassinated, which led to General Olusegun Obasanjo taking over as Head of State. This, in brief, is the chronicle of earliest military interruption of the democratic process in Nigeria.

General Obasanjo initiated a process which culminated in the promulgation of a new constitution in 1979, thus replacing the Westminster system of government which was practised during the First Republic.[6] His government organised a successful transition from military to civilian democratic rule, which culminated in the swearing in of Alhaji Shehu Shagari of the National Party of Nigeria (NPN) as the first Executive President on 1 October 1979 under a presidential system of government. Thus, Obasanjo became the first military head of state in Nigeria's political history who voluntarily handed over power to a civilian government; and this singular act of keeping to the transition timetable and eventual handover of leadership of the country to a democratically-elected President earned Obasanjo widespread credibility and respect both within and outside Nigeria. Former President Shagari won a landslide victory in the general elections conducted in August 1983, with a majority of seats in the National Assembly, thus marking the first experiment of conducting successful elections by a civilian administration.

Unfortunately, the democratic government was again interrupted by another military coup led by Major General Muhammadu Buhari (as he was then), who became Head of State and ruled from January 1984 to 25 August 1985, when he was also overthrown in a 'palace coup' led by General Ibrahim Babangida, who declared himself a military President.

6. The non-inclusive limitation of being elected by only federal constituency as in the case of Tafawa Balewa, elected as a member of federal parliament and only elected Prime Minister and Head of Government by other parliamentarians, was the rationale for discarding the parliamentary system and replacing it with the presidential system of government in 1979.

Upon assuming office, the issue of handing over power to a democratically-elected government was not a priority for the Babangida regime. Nevertheless, the regime announced a political transition programme which was to terminate in 1992. However, after several cancellations of different transition programmes, and after being pressured to relinquish power in 1993, Babangida announced the longest political transition programme in the history of Nigeria when he eventually promulgated the Transition to Civil Rule (Political Programme) Decree Number 57, on 28 July 1987 and announced a transition programme to end in the fourth quarter of 1992. This transition programme was to progress in several 'guided' stages.

The Babangida transition programme was characterised by numerous signposts that could serve as important lessons for military transition in Africa, but this is not the place to discuss that in detail. Suffice it to say that this country learned some lessons in political transition from the adoption of two major political parties (one a little to the right and another a little to the left), the Option A4 Method of election which provided transparency and credibility in the electoral process, and most importantly the outcome of the 12 June 1993 presidential election, which led to the emergence of Chief M.K.O. Abiola and Ambassador Baba Gana Kingibe (both Muslims)[7] as President and Vice President elect.

General Babangida was forced out of office and he 'stepped aside' in August 1993, handing over power to Chief Ernest Shonekan, who was not an elected politician. Shonekan chose to manage a political transition under a certain arrangement that was clearly set to fail within a short time when General Sani Abacha staged a coup d'état and seized power from him on 17 November 1993 after only three months.

7. It is hard to contemplate that such an arrangement would succeed in Nigeria nowadays, as ethnicity and religious biases have influenced leadership choices.

Abacha was among the military officers who had tested power and was predicted to be Head of State, and when he took over power, in order to pacify the political class and allow some peace to reign, he immediately announced the convocation of a Constitutional Conference to discuss the modalities of a political transition programme, including the drafting of a new constitution. Following the adoption of the report of this Constitutional Conference, Abacha announced a 'multi-phase' transition programme that would usher in a civilian democratically-elected government in 1998. The main features of the Abacha transition programme included the creation of additional states[8] and local government areas, local government elections on zero party bases, lifting the ban on political activities, and the formation of political parties and phased elections at all three tiers of government.

Unknown to many people, including the politicians who were struggling for power and relevance before Abacha, he had planned to transform himself from a 'military dictator' to a civilian president through a guided transition programme. Unfortunately, or fortunately, he died mysteriously on 8 June 1998, leading to the emergence of General Abdulsalami Abubakar as new military Head of State on 9 June 1998.

It was obvious that the country no longer needed either a military regime or an elongated political transition programme. Thus, reading the mood of the nation, as well as the pressure from the international community, and particularly to ease the tension occasioned by the successive deaths of Abacha and Abiola, the acclaimed winner of the 1993 presidential election, General Abubakar, after consultations, announced a 10-month transition programme on 20 July 1998. This was diligently implemented, culminating in the election and swearing in of Chief Olusegun Obasanjo under the platform of

8. Indeed, Abacha created six new states proportionally across the six geopolitical zones, namely, Zamfara State in the north-west; Gombe State in the north-east; Nasarawa State in the north-central; Osun State in the south-west; Ebonyi State in the south-east; and Bayelsa State in south-south, with several local government areas across the federation.

the People'sDemocratic Party (PDP) as President of the Federal Republic of Nigeria on 29 May 1999. Thus ended the long history of military incursion in the political system in Nigeria.

The key features of Abubakar's transition programme were that it was short and looked into not only the mysterious deaths of Abacha and Abiola, but most importantly the eagerness to return the military to the barracks as military rule had become unfashionable. He promised to conduct a credible election, and therefore set up the Independent National Electoral Commission (INEC) and appointed a former Justice of the Supreme Court, Ephraim Akpata, as its Chairman and gave it the independence to conduct a free, fair and credible election.

Perhaps the most important feature of General Abdul-Salami Abubakar's transition programme is the promulgation of the 1999 Constitution, which is being operated today with ongoing amendments as these become necessary. Although the Constitution has been criticised in several ways and there has been agitation for the adumbration of what some people refer to as a 'truly civilian constitution', it is enough to note that no constitution is perfect.

I have given this brief chronicle of the history of political transition in order to give the reader the necessary background information on the fractured experience Nigeria has had and how democratic government was finally re-established in 1999.

## The Return to Democracy

By the 1980s, most African countries were still under military dictatorships, but from the early 1990s, military rule had become unacceptable or unfashionable, and Nigeria could not be spared by the winds of change. Without going into the political struggles that led to the restoration of democracy in 1999, the 1999 elections, though conducted under military surveillance, marked the beginning of a renewed democratic history for Nigeria. Since then, Nigeria has experienced a relatively stable democracy, even if a fledgling one. Elections were conducted, though not without some skirmishes or violence, in 2003, 2007, 2011 and 2015. In all the elections except the last in 2015, the People's Democratic Party emerged as the winner and strongest party and ruled for 16 years from 1999 until 2015 when it was replaced by an alliance of smaller parties that formed a formidable force under the banner of the All Progressives' Congress (APC). The circumstances that led to this dramatic change will be discussed in later chapters.

The fifth national election in 2015 signposted the first peaceful transfer of power in Nigeria from one political party to another, and while there were allegations of malpractice, including vote-rigging and other forms of electoral fraud in all the elections, the 2015 election in particular was considered free and fair, partly because the electoral process was transparent, fair and credible, and the incumbent President must be given the credit for accepting defeat, which had never happened before in the history of Nigeria.

The campaign issues of the APC in 2015 were based on a tripod of security, anti-corruption and economic revival. These issues were considered the most critical for Nigerians,who gave resounding support to the APC, which led to the emergence of Muhammadu Buhari as President of Nigeria. Three and half years into the APC administration, another election is set for February 2019. It should be recalled that the PDP lost the 2015 election not because it did not have an agenda but because Nigerians had lost confidence in the leadership of the PDP and needed a radical change, which they thought the APC might provide. Many people believed it was unthinkable for an incumbent government to lose an election, since that had not happened before in Nigeria.

Between 1999 and 2018, the political microscope has expanded, just as politics itself has become more sophisticated, despite the prevalence of corruption. It is against this background that we should see the contours of politics and elections through a different prism that is objective, forward-looking and issue-based. That is precisely what I will attempt to do in this book.

## Summary of the book

Against this background, and in order to provide more information on the issues and options in the 2019 elections, my concern is primarily with the presidential election. Although the state and local government elections are equally important, the real issues pertain to the federal, and particularly the presidential, election. Understanding the elections and electoral processes is crucial in order to place the issues in a proper perspective, and so I will begin in the first chapter with a discussion on election and electoral process.

We cannot understand the dynamics of the 2019 elections without appraising the very important election of 2015, which was considered the first transparent, free, fair and credible election and led to a peaceful transition from one political party to another – for the first time in the history of Nigeria. I shall therefore in Chapter 2 review the key issues that shaped the 2015 event as background to the 2019 elections. Specifically, this chapter will examine the high expectations during the election of the President, the outcome and where we are in terms of managing the expectations. That will naturally lead to the very important issue of how the APC managed victory, which is examined in Chapter 3. This discusses the APC Manifesto and the promises made to the electorate during the 2015 presidential election, the main campaign issues that characterised that election and how the ruling party fulfilled the promises it made to the citizens. This is certainly not a critique, nor is it intended to spite or promote any party, but to attempt to predict the outcome of the forthcoming 2019 presidential election.

Chapter 4 will form the climax of the book. It attempts a comparative analysis of the campaign policy documents of the two leading parties, the APC and the PDP. It examines the strengths and weaknesses of each candidate and attempts to predict the outcome of the election based on the analysis.

The future of democracy and good governance in Nigeria is discussed in Chapter 5, which also briefly examines the salient question of whether democracy must first take root before good governance can follow or whether good governance comes first. The chapter identifies some potential risks and threats to the 2019 elections and concludes with the role of the international community.

Chapter 6 is concerned with the future of Nigeria. It examines the challenges and crises of nation building and proffers some recommendations which entrench democracy and good governance. The conclusion is a summary of the issues discussed in the book.

# PREFACE

Nigeria has practised uninterrupted democracy since 1999. Although some people say that Nigeria's democracy is not true democracy but civilian rule, there is no perfect democracy; therefore Nigeria's fledgling democracy is work in progress.

After a series of military guided transition programmes spanning over three decades, Nigeria finally returned to civil democratic rule on 29 May 1999. Since then there have been five successful elections, in 1999, 2003, 2007, 2011 and 2015. The 2015 presidential election was particularly remarkable because it was the first undisputed election and also the first time an incumbent was defeated and conceded defeat in a free, fair, transparent and credible election in Nigeria. That election left significant lessons for strengthening democracy and good governance.

The Peoples' Democracy Party (PDP), which had been in power since 1999, was replaced by the All Progressives' Congress (APC). In 2015, the records of performance of the PDP were the main campaign issues, namely, deteriorating security, widespread corruption and a declining economy. These were the major campaign issues for the APC. Nigerians voted massively for the APC with the expectations of better living conditions, especially in these three areas.

Election at intervals is one of the key elements of democracy and it represents the covenant between the people and those they choose to govern them. The next elections are scheduled for February and March 2019. In the forthcoming presidential election, there will be about 73 contestants for the post of the President of Nigeria under different political parties, but to all practical purposes, it will be a contest between the ruling APC and the major opposition PDP. In that regard, there will two chapters open for the electorate: one is the APC's 'Next Level' and the second is the PDP's 'Let's Get Nigeria Working Again'.

A review of the two policy documents of the parties reveals little difference. There is also no clear difference in terms of ideology, and moreover, it is hard to distinguish between the two parties since most of the *dramatis personae* have changed membership between the two parties. Ideally, enlightened voters, in making their choices, should ask themselves – has the present level been satisfactory to deserve another level for consolidation, or was Nigeria working before the change from PDP to APC to warrant another change back to that status quo? If there was going to be second title for this book, perhaps it would be appropriate to say it is between the "Next Level" and "Let's Get Nigeria Working Again".

As a conscious effort towards political education and awareness, this book is about issues and options for the electorate. It reviews the political transition programmes in Nigeria and discusses elections and the electoral processes. It examines why and how the PDP lost the 2015 election and how the APC has (mis)managed its victory since coming to power. Most importantly, the book interrogates the campaign policy documents of the two parties and provides some prognoses on the strengths and weaknesses of the two candidates

– President Muhammadu Buhari for the APC and Alhaji Atiku Abubakar (former Vice President) for the PDP. It attempts to predict their chances of winning the election, but ultimately concludes that the outcomes of elections are not necessarily determined by objective factors and records of performance, but by the sentiments of the voters.

The book concludes by drawing attention to some potential risks and threats to the elections and to the future of democracy and good governance in Nigeria. It will be interesting reading for those who would like to know more about the political history of Nigeria and the strenuous efforts being made to entrench a truly participatory and sustainable democracy. It is commended for politicians, policy makers, diplomats and administrators, as well as researchers and students of comparative politics.

ATY

February 2019

# ACKNOWLEDGEMENTS

This book was inspired by the vibrant political activities towards the 2019 Presidential election in Nigeria, and in particular the launch of the campaign policy documents of the APC and PDP in November 2019. Through my personal interactions with friends and monitoring of public commentaries in the media and social media, I was motivated to write this book as part of my intellectual contribution to the political history of Nigeria, and in particular, to better raise awareness about the issues the electioneering campaigns should be based on and the options for the electorate in making their choices.

Writing and publishing this book would not have been possible without the immense contributions and support I received from many people and from various sources. I cannot mention all by name in this acknowledgement for lack of space. Nevertheless, I must acknowledge, not in any special order, the valuable contributions of my friend Brigadier General Ibrahim Umar Babangida (Rtd), who, within a short time read through the manuscript and made useful comments; my adopted mother and editor, Venetia Sommerset; my editor Chris Newton of Mereo Books; Ambassador Abdul-Kader Rimdap, who introduced me to Chris and who facilitate the rapid work on the book; and my two very close, reliable, supportive and dependable brothers and former colleagues – Babacar Ndiaye and Mu'azu Umar, respectively.

Most importantly, I appreciate all those who take their time to read this book.

# CHAPTER 1

# Elections and Electoral Processes in Nigeria

Election is the choice of a person to occupy a public office and to perform certain functions prescribed by law over a specified period of time, while the method of selecting such a person is the process. Election is one of the key elements of a democratic society: the social contract between the people and their representatives in governance. In this regard, election is what distinguishes democracy from other forms of government, while election with integrity is the *sine qua non* of a truly democratic system. Periodic election as a feature of democracy is also a process through which the level of participation in governance, the performance of a government, its credibility and acceptability can be tested.

Every democratic society has devised a process through which leaders are elected, and Nigeria is no exception. Accordingly, Chapter II section 14 of the Constitution of the Federal Republic of Nigeria (1999) provides that:

*(1) The Federal Republic of Nigeria shall be a State based on the principles of democracy and social justice.*

*(2) It is hereby, accordingly, declared that:*

*(a) sovereignty belongs to the people of Nigeria from whom government through this Constitution derives all its powers and authority;*

*(b) the security and welfare of the people shall be the primary purpose of government: and*

*(c) the participation by the people in their government shall be ensured in accordance with the provisions of this Constitution.*

The Constitution in section 130 states that: (1) There shall be for the Federation a President; and (2) The President shall be the Head of State, the Chief Executive of the Federation and Commander-in-Chief of the Armed Forces of the Federation. And section 132 provides that: (1) An election to the office of the President shall be held on a date to be appointed by the Independent National Electoral Commission; and (2) An election to the said office shall be held on a date not earlier than sixty days and not later than thirty days before the expiration of the term of office of the last holder of that office.

Furthermore, section 135 of the Constitution says:

(1) Subject to the provisions of this Constitution, a person shall hold the office of President until –

(a) when his successor in office takes the oath of that office;

(b) he dies whilst holding such office; or

(c) the date when his resignation from office takes effect;

or

(d) he otherwise ceases to hold office in accordance with the provisions of this Constitution.

(2) Subject to the provisions of subsection (1) of this section, the President shall vacate his office at the expiration of a period of four years commencing from the date, when –

(a) in the case of a person first elected as President under this Constitution, he took the Oath of Allegiance and the oath of office; and

(b) in any other case, the person last elected to that office under this Constitution took the Oath of Allegiance and Oath of Office or would, but for his death, have taken such Oaths.

The Constitution in Section 153 further established certain Federal Executive Bodies, including the Independent National Electoral Commission. Consequently, the INEC has been established under Section 14 of the Third Schedule of the Constitution and section 15 of the same Schedule provides that the Commission shall have power to –

(a) organise, undertake and supervise all elections to the offices of the President and Vice-President, the Governor and Deputy Governor of a State, and to the membership of the Senate, the House of Representatives and the House of Assembly of each State of the Federation;

(b) register political parties in accordance with the provisions of this Constitution and an Act of the National Assembly;

(c) monitor the organisation and operation of the political parties, including their finances;

(d) arrange for the annual examination and auditing of the funds and accounts of political parties, and publish a report on such examination and audit for public information;

(e) arrange and conduct the registration of persons qualified to vote and prepare, maintain and revise the register of voters for the purpose of any election under this Constitution;

(f)  monitor political campaigns and provide rules and regulations which shall govern the political parties;

(g) ensure that all Electoral Commissioners, Electoral and Returning Officers take and subscribe to the Oath of Office prescribed by law;

(h) delegate any of its powers to any Resident Electoral Commissioner; and

(i)  carry out such other functions as may be conferred upon it by an Act of the National Assembly.

I have given this constitutional framework so that readers can understand the very foundation upon which elections and the electoral processes have been established in Nigeria. There is no denying that through its electoral laws and processes, Nigeria seems to seek for perfection, yet it is not itself perfect in any way. This is precisely why I wish to discuss the Electoral Act, as well as Election Guidelines, with reference to the Presidential election since my focus here is on that election. The dynamics of election and electoral processes are in the formation and funding of political parties, internal democracy in the parties and party politics, as well as intra- and inter-party issues; all these form the substance of this chapter. The chapter will discuss the experiences of the past elections in other to draw some lessons for the 2019 elections.

## The Electoral Act 2010

Drawing from its powers to make laws for the Federal Republic of Nigeria as enshrined in the 1999 Constitution, the National Assembly (NASS) passed into Law an Electoral Act for the conduct of elections. The Electoral Act 2010 draws inspiration from section 153(1)(f) and Third Schedule Paragraph 15(f) of the

1999 Constitution. The Act repealed the Electoral Act No. 2 of 2006 and the Electoral Commission Act, CAP 15, Laws of the Federal Republic of Nigeria (LFRN), 2004 and enacted the Electoral Act 2010. It aims to regulate the conduct of elections and other matters, and is a reflection of the lessons learned in conducting elections and electioneering processes in Nigeria. It is therefore the principal subsidiary legislation derived from the Constitution for the purposes of elections and so cannot be ignored. The Electoral Act 2010 (as amended) is in annex 'A'.

Conducting an election is a routine activity, but conducting one with integrity is a function of true democracy. To meet the aspirations of Nigerians in this regard, and in accordance with the law, the Electoral Act provides comprehensive measures for conducting elections. In summary:

1. Part I of the Electoral Act provides for the Establishment of the Independent National Electoral Commission as an independent body charged with the responsibility of conducting national and state elections.

2. Part II lays out the staff recruitment procedure and other matters.

3. Part III deals with the National Register of Voters and Voters' Registration, and section 23 specifically says 'Buying and Selling Voters' Cards' are serious offences punishable under the law.

4. Part IV consists of procedure at elections, and this is where the INEC derives its power to issue guidelines for the good conduct of elections.

5. Part V deals with political parties, their composition and candidacy for elections.

6. Part VI lays out Procedure for Elections to Area Council of the Federal Capital Territory (FCT).[9]

9. Local Government elections in the states are conducted by State Electoral Bodies.

7. Part VII specifies various electoral offences.

8. Part VIII addresses issues regarding determination of election petitions arising from elections, including constitution of electoral tribunals and appeals; while

9. Part IX contains miscellaneous provisions pertaining to elections.

Since 2010, the Electoral Act has undergone amendments, including in October 2018, with the aim of strengthening the Act and improving the electoral processes. Chief among these is the introduction of the 'Card Reader or any Other Electronic Device'. It would be recalled that the card reader, despite its failures in some cases, was the main factor behind the transparency and credibility of the 2015 elections.[10]Section 52 of the Electoral Act had prohibited the INEC from using any electronic device for election until the NASS passed the Electoral Amendment Bill and former President Jonathan signed it into law on 20 March 2015.

Most of the petitions that went to the tribunals after the elections were on the legality or otherwise of the use of the card reader. Curiously, the INEC submitted during the proceedings that 'the directive on accreditation of voters with aid of card reader machines was not backed by any law. And that failure to comply with the

10. According to Ade Adesomoju in a report, 'PVC better than US voter card – Ambassador', *Punch*, 30 March 2015, 'The Ambassador of the United States to Nigeria, Mr. James Entwistle, applauded the decision of the Independent National Electoral Commission to use the Permanent Voter Card in the general elections. The ambassador, who spoke with journalists at the International Conference Centre, venue of the National Collation Centre of the election results said Nigeria's PVC involved superior technology which his state of Virginia in the US needed to copy. According to him, 'I am very impressed by the decision of INEC to use technology in this election. The Permanent Voter Cards are very high-tech...'They are more high tech than my voter card from the state of Virginia in the US. My voter card does not have biometric. It does not have my fingerprint. The high-tech gives the process more integrity...I congratulate INEC on taking the part of High-tech. I think we need to come and study it so that we can use it in my country.'

directive could not vitiate any election conducted by INEC.'[11] The Supreme Court, in a lead judgement delivered by Justice Cletus Nweze, JSC, had held that

> Indeed, since the Guidelines and Manual, which authorized the use and deployment of the electronic Card Reader Machine, were made in exercise of the powers conferred by the Electoral Act, the said Card Reader cannot logically, depose or dethrone the Voters' Register whose judicial roots are, firmly embedded and entrenched in the selfsame Electoral Act from it (the Voters' Register) directly, derives it sustenance and currency… since the National Assembly has not deleted the provision of Section 49 of the Electoral Act (2010), which allows manual accreditation. It would be wrong for any Petitioner to seek to rely on the report of the Card Reader (which is intended as a supplementary measure to the already provided means of accreditation) to prove over-voting.

This judgment, according to legal practitioners, has not in any way declared the card reader machine illegal.[12]

## 2018 Amendment Controversy

The new amendments proposed in 2018 included mainly amendment of 'sections 49 and 52 to allow INEC use card reader to authenticate voters' card, use total number of voters authenticated with the card reader as actual figure of voters that voted in a particular unit, and transmit the votes electronically'.

On 7 December 2018, President Muhammadu Buhari (PMB) refused to assent to the amendments proposed by the NASS, saying they were too close to the 2019 elections and could create confusion with regard to which laws were applicable for the elections. This

---

11. Femi Falana, Guest Columnist,'The Legality of the Card Reader',*Thisday* newspaper, 5 April 2015.

12. Ibid.

generated mixed reactions, including some calls on the NASS to override the President in the 'national interest'. After all the discussions on the President's refusal to assent to the amendments, the NASS could not override the president; hence the electoral law remains as its last amendments in 2015.

## Election Manual and Guidelines

Section 153 of the Electoral Act, 2010 (as amended) gives power to the INEC to issue regulations, guidelines and manuals for the conduct of any elections in Nigeria. In furtherance to the Electoral Act, the INEC has also issued Guidelines and Manual as part of efforts to strengthen the electoral process.

Based on Part IV of the Electoral Act, the INEC issued the Guidelines for the 2019 elections on 14 January 2019 (see annex 'B'). One of the innovations in the new guidelines is that accreditation and voting will be done simultaneously, unlike in the previous elections when accreditation of voters was done separately between 8 a.m. and 2 p.m. This innovation may have been informed by the experience of the past, when some voters after accreditation did not come back to vote after 2 p.m[13]. Despite this, some political parties had threatened to take the INEC to court for issuing the guidelines without consulting them.[14]

All this suggests that the necessary legal framework for free, fair and credible elections is in place through the above instruments. It must be pointed out, however, that despite these legal instruments, election rigging remains one of the major challenges in conducting elections with integrity in Nigeria

13. In justifying this modification, INEC revealed that over 2 million voters who were accredited during the 2015 elections did not turn up to vote.

14. It should be noted that the Act did not require INEC to consult the political parties in drafting and issuing such guidelines.

## Election Rigging and Other Malpractice

Democracy has become a universal aspiration and a transnational norm. However, elections are undermined by several malpractices, including rigging. Election rigging simply is the corruption of the election process and this takes many dimensions. These include:

1.  Illegal printing of voters' cards
2.  Illegal possession of ballot boxes
3.  Stuffing of ballot boxes
4.  Falsification of election results
5.  Illegal thumb-printing of ballot papers
6.  Infant or underage voting
7.  Compilation of fictitious names on voters' lists
8.  Illegal compilation of separate voters' lists
9.  Illegal printing of forms used for collection and declaration of election results
10. Deliberate refusal to supply election materials to certain areas
11. Announcing results in places where no elections were held
12. Unauthorised announcement of election results
13. Harassment of candidates, agents, and voters to divert attention to rig election
14. Change of list of electoral officials
15. Box-switching and inflation of figures[15]
16. Vote buying.

The preponderance of rigging or other malpractice in the election processes in Nigeria has been well documented, but one that portends a serious threat to the 2019 elections is vote buying and selling of a voter's card. Vote buying and selling involves the offer of financial inducement to potential voters. During the gubernatorial election

15. See Nwokeke P. Osinakachukwu and Jayum A.Jawan,'The Electoral Process and Democratic Consolidation in Nigeria',*Journal of Politics and Law*4(2), 2011.

in Ekiti State in August 2018, it was alleged that both the APC and PDP were involved in this unwholesome electoral malpractice and predictably, only the highest bidder would emerge victorious. Yet the electoral umpire did not issue a statement to say whether or not it was investigating the veracity of this allegation, nor has anybody been reportedly arrested or prosecuted for such an electoral offence.

Further, apart from inducements of party officials by their members seeking to be presented as candidates of their parties in the forthcoming elections, the media were awash with allegations that most of the outcomes of the party primaries in October 2018 were determined by who paid what. While the nomination of the presidential candidate of the APC was manipulated and skewed in favour of one candidate, the nomination of that of the PDP was alleged to have been influenced by financial inducement to the delegates. Overall, this portends a great danger to the efficiency and credibility of the electoral process, and considering how this has affected previous elections and may affect subsequent ones, we shall discuss this further in Chapter 5 in regard to the future of democracy in Nigeria.

The report of the United States Institute of Peace (USIP) on an electoral violence risk assessment on Nigeria, released in November 2018, alleged that the ruling APC may use 'intimidating tactics' to shore up the votes, as well as to 'deter large turnout of electorate in the opposition strongholds'. There is already a possibility of voter apathy as a result of the way in which the campaigns are getting 'dirty', and any intention to rig the election will take advantage of such apathy. The USIP report indicated that states such as Adamawa, Anambra, Ekiti, Kaduna, Kano, Lagos, Plateau and Rivers are at greater risk of election violence.

The evidence is already building up that the APC might create confusion and rig the elections because of the partisanship shown by the security agencies during the conduct of the Ekiti and Osun States 2018 gubernatorial elections, as well as National Assembly by-elections conducted in Bauchi and Kwara States.[16]

16. 'Quick Facts',*Thisday* newspaper, 10 December 2018, p. 18.

## Election with Integrity

We learnt earlier on that election is an important aspect of democracy, but only election with integrity can guarantee the credibility of elections and reinforce the confidence of the electorate in the process. It is the integrity of the election that legitimises the political leadership and also makes it accountable to the electorate. In this regard, elections can further enhance security, democracy, human rights and freedoms, and develop or undermine these aspirations. Partly as a result of globalisation and economic equality, countries are being compelled to show concern about their citizens' interests in free, fair and credible elections. The notable roles of civil society organisations and international observer groups should be acknowledged. Credible elections are important and complementary to the values espoused by the international community, including the Universal Declaration on Human Rights and the International Covenant on Civil and Political Rights, as well as freedom to participate in the electoral processes.

Nigeria aspires to consolidate the gains of democracy by strengthening the electoral processes. The Global Commission on Elections defined an election with integrity as 'any election that is based on the democratic principles of universal suffrage and political equality as reflected in international standards and agreements, and is professional, impartial, and transparent in its preparation and administration throughout the electoral cycle.'[17]

Despite the modest improvements and successes in elections and electoral processes in Nigeria over the years, there are nevertheless potential threats and challenges to the entrenchment of election with integrity. Addressing all the challenges would require some far-reaching reforms in the entire body politic. That may not be as easy as it is assumed, but for practical purposes the Global Commission on Elections, Democracy and Security identified the

17. See 'Deepening Democracy: A Strategy for Improving the Integrity of Elections World-wide'. Report of the Global Commission Elections, Democracy and Security, September 2012.

major challenges and how to address them in seeking to entrench election with integrity, and these include:

First, the foundation of every democracy is to cater for the wellbeing of the citizenry by providing them with specific rights, including freedoms, and the rule of law is the pillar for ensuring that these rights are guaranteed. To this end, the Commission recommends that building the rule of law to substantiate claims to human rights and electoral justice is the first step towards promoting the credibility of election and strengthening confidence in the process and the legitimacy of the outcome of elections.

Second, elections are conducted by competent authorities, such as the Electoral Commission. Thus, the outcome and credibility of any election can be affected by the bias, partisanship, compromise or incompetence of the electoral body. Needless to recall that the success and credibility of the 2015 elections in Nigeria was attributed largely to the professionalism of the electoral body, particularly the Chief Electoral umpire, Professor Attahiru Muhammadu Jega, who was seen to be neutral, transparent and fair but firm. However, in Kenya, the outcome of the 2007 presidential election was disputed, leading to the most egregious violence in the history of that country because the electorate questioned the impartiality of the Electoral Commission members, who were perceived to have been handpicked by President Moi Kibakiin order to ensure his re-election. The lack of integrity of that election led to serious violence, and it remains a sore point in the electoral history of that country. For developing countries that are struggling to strengthen their electoral systems and processes and entrench sustainable democracy, therefore, it is necessary to build professional, competent electoral management bodies (EMBs) with full independence of action to administer elections that are transparent and merit public confidence. And as we shall see in the analysis to follow in Chapter 5, Nigeria faces a potential threat in this regard during the 2019 elections.

Third, creating the enabling 'level playing field' for all

contenders in the electoral processes is essential for sustainable democracy, yet from the analysis of the formation of political parties, their funding, as well as party politics and internal democracy, this appears to be another challenge in the electoral process in Nigeria. In order to address this challenge, part of the recommendations of the Global Commission is for countries to create 'institutions and norms of multiparty competition and division of power that bolster democracy as a mutual security system among political contenders'. Again, one of the issues to be interrogated in this book is whether or not the current party structure and electoral processes can guarantee a successful, credible and acceptable outcome of the presidential election in Nigeria in 2019.

Fourth, the credibility of elections depends on the legal frameworks put in place, not only to guarantee freedom and equality of participation in the electoral process, but also to protect the contenders from the victimisation of the outcomes of elections. Such framework should include the removal of 'barriers – legal, administrative, political, economic, and social – to universal and equal political participation'.

The fifth major challenge to entrenching electoral integrity has to do with regulating the sources and extent of political party financing. There have been instances where states were 'captured' by organised crime groups through illicit financing, and this has significant consequences for the security and stability of the political system.[18] Thus, one of the recommended strategies for ensuring the integrity of elections is by 'regulating uncontrolled, undisclosed, and opaque political finance'.

A sixth major challenge in elections and electoral processes in Nigeria is the issue of violence. Leading up to the 2019 elections, there is a serious concern about hate speech and fake news, and

18. Citing the example of Costa Rica in managing illicit political party financing, the Global Commission on Elections, 2012 observed that 'Illicit money has found its way into politics in countries throughout Latin America, and Costa Rica, despite its performance as a strong democracy with good governance, is no exception. In the late 1980s and early 1990s, investigations into drug trafficking found that both of the major parties in the country had accepted contributions from suspicious sources, including General Manuel Noriega of Panama and numerous other individuals later linked to drug smuggling and other illicit activities', p. 32.

new technology has the potential of aggravating this challenge. The fireworks have already started through the social media and sponsored campaigns of calumny. If one recalls the dirty campaigns orchestrated by the PDP against the APC candidate (General Muhammadu Buhari), including the uncharitable prediction about his health in 2015, it is likely that the same tactics may be adopted by the APC if care is not taken. Unfortunately, the electoral umpire, the INEC, seems to be handicapped in regulating such practices, either from lack of resources or general incapacity.

The pattern and effects of electoral violence in Nigeria have been documented in a case study by the Global Commission on Elections (2012:32), which observed that:

Nigeria has experienced chronic electoral violence since its transition to democracy and civilian rule in 1999, including more than 15,700 election-related deaths. High stakes combine with readily available guns for hire in the form of organized crime gangs and a historic lack of prosecution of perpetrators to make electoral violence a relatively attractive tool of electoral competition – even within political parties.

Important progress was made in the 2011 elections towards professionalizing the country's Independent National Electoral Commission (INEC), most importantly through the appointment of a respected academic as chairman. Professor Attahiru M. Jega, who became known as 'Mr Integrity', revamped the voter registration process, improved transparency at the Commission and for the first time prosecuted electoral violence since its transition to democracy and civilian rule in 1999, including more than 15,700 election-related deaths.

Unfortunately, improved electoral administration and transparency were not sufficient to achieve major reductions in violence in some regions. During the run-up to the election, 165 people were killed in violence related to political campaigns and voter registration. Another 800 to 1,000 died after widespread protests broke out in the north on the announcement of incumbent President Goodluck Jonathan's victory. More than 65,000 were displaced.

This violence represents a political failure in the face of what was largely a technical and administrative success. Losing candidates and party leaders failed to meet their responsibilities to restrain their supporters and accept the election results.

## Formation of Political Parties

Political parties are the main pillars of democracy in Nigeria. There is no provision for independent candidature. Nothing is wrong with that except that the politics of party formation, administration and funding make it almost impossible for Nigeria to attain its desired perfection in elections by getting the right candidates, because the right candidates may not be fielded by the political parties. To understand the contradictions in the electoral processes, an overview of party formation and other aspects would show how the processes are manipulated for selfish interests and personal aggrandisement and often with impunity.

In 2014, the APC emerged as an alliance to seize power from the PDP.[19] The APC became formidable and through its campaign and programmes, including the promise of restructuring Nigeria, which persuaded a lot of voters from the South-West, the party set a record of defeating the incumbent government in 2015. I shall discuss in detail how the party has managed its victory in Chapter 3.

No sooner had the party assumed office than the cracks of major divisions in the alliance began to appear, suggesting that the alliance was merely an alliance of convenience to seize power and not to develop a sustainable party structure based on ideology and credible programmes. But one thing that is clear from the fragmentation of

19. The alliance was formed by the major opposition parties, namely, the Action Congress of Nigeria (ACN), the All Nigeria Peoples' Party (ANPP), and the Congress for Progressive Change (CPC).

both the PDP and the APC is not only the party politics, but the lack of transparency and accountability – better described as lack of internal democracy within the parties. This naturally leads to a discussion of the issues of party politics and internal democracy in the electoral process in Nigeria.

## Political Party Financing

One area where elections and electoral processes can be undermined is through the financing of political parties. In Nigeria the Electoral Act provides for public and private contributions to a political party, but it aims to regulate such funding in order to minimise the undue influence of certain financiers.

The Electoral Act has pegged the maximum party expenditure for each candidate contesting the position of President at 1 billion naira, and lays down that no political party should spend more than 5 billion in a presidential election. The problem is that it is very difficult, if not impossible, to ascertain and verify effective compliance with such regulations, and the parties have devised various ways of concealing their true financial status. While the Electoral Act obliges the INEC to verify and report the financial status of each registered political party to the NASS at least once a year, such reporting has never attracted any headline news to show that the monitoring is effective.

But it is still the case that in most, if not all, the political parties, those who pay the piper often dictate the tone of party leadership and even candidates to be presented for election. Recently, during the party primaries to select candidates for the 2019 elections, this became obvious when it was alleged that Akinwunmi Ambodewas denied the APC ticket for a second term as governor of Lagos as a result of the decision of the Party Leader, Bola Tinubu. Thus, Ambode will set the record as the first governor of the state not to be given a second chance to contest for the governorship under the APC.

One cannot conclude discussion on influencing the party machinery without mentioning the role of the state governors, who are so powerful that they practically determine who gets what in their states. This started during the PDP era (1999-2015), but it seems it is getting even messier under the APC, with allegations of nepotism and flagrant abuse of acceptable standards of decency. Classic examples are the selecting of the gubernatorial candidates in the ruling APC in Imo and Ogun States, which generated accusations between the two state governors and the APC National Chairman.

In seeking for ways to effectively regulate political party funding with a view to improving the electoral processes in Nigeria, therefore, article 7 of the United Nations Convention against Corruption (UNCAC, 2003) and the African Union Convention on Corruption (2003) provide a framework for regulating party financing consistent with acceptable international standards. Other ways of regulating the funding of political parties may include balancing the public and private contributions and enforcing compliance without reservation, restricting the abuse of state resources, including the use of the presidential airplane for political party campaigns, controlling the campaigns expenditure through effective audit and independent monitoring and oversight.

## Party Politics and Internal Democracy

As earlier stated, democracy, and elections in particular, are a struggle among the elite class. We cannot understand what party politics is without first seeking to understand that a political party is a platform in a democratic process that allows a group of people with common understanding and interests to state how they seek for election and governance in a democracy. Party politics, on the other hand, is the processes and internal manoeuvres within and/

or between political parties for the purpose of canvassing votes, winning elections and administering a political system. In that sense, if the political party is formed by good people, chances are that the policies of that party will also be good and acceptable. But how do we measure what is good or bad? The measurement of good or bad in a political party is how the actors play politics, either in the national interest[20] or in their own personal or class interests.

In Nigeria, experience has shown that whereas every politician seeking election claims to do so to serve the country, in reality most politicians seek public office to serve their selfish interests rather than the national interest. This is one of the main reasons for instability in the parties and the political system as a whole. The revelations or allegations of corruption against almost all political office holders after the overthrow of the Second Republic are evidence of this. But the general view that in politics there is no integrity and politicians deceive the electorate in order to win elections makes party politics appear a dirty game. In fact there are good and honest politicians, but the manner in which politics is being played would hardly give opportunity for such people to make real change.

While there is room for improvement in the practice of party politics in Nigeria, the emerging trend of lack of internal democracy within the parties has been the main reason for the instability of the political parties themselves and the body politic as whole.

Basically, what is described as lack of internal democracy is manifested in several ways and may include:

1. Manipulation of the constitution of the political party based on personal considerations, including edging out, disqualifying or denying some people certain rights within the party or for seeking elections under the party.
2. The invention of 'zoning' of political offices since the

20. By national interest its meant putting the interest of the collective whole or country first before any other thing, including taking or accepting decisions that may be against one's personal interest.

restoration of democracy and party politics in Nigeria since 1999, though presumably helpful in ensuring some fairness and stability in a party, may be undemocratic even if party members are compelled to abide by it. This process has been challenged in a few instances, and that has put the credibility of the practice in question.

3.  The manipulation of the process of nomination of candidates is also one of the reflections of undemocratic practice in party politics. Over the years, this has been a problem and has led to several contestants, such as Goodluck Jonathan, to lose re-election. It may be recalled that it was the insistence of Jonathan to re-contest in 2015 that caused the northern stalwarts in the PDP, including seven governors, to defect to the APC, giving it additional strength and eventual victory.[21]

4.  Perhaps the most egregious dimension of lack of internal democracy is that some powerful people decide to impose candidates against the wishes of the majority.

The many ways in which political parties organise themselves, including intra- and inter-party relations, are all important in sustaining an enduring electoral process and the political processes as a whole. I have only given an elementary explanation here in order to lay the foundation for understanding how this will play out in the 2019 elections. In other words, what lessons can the electorate learn from the defections of major political figures from one party to another and the amalgamation of political gladiators in the struggle for power and influence? But one thing is sure in our analysis of all defections in the politics of Nigeria, and that is that every politician is seeking for relevance and recognition, and one can afford to set principles (if there are any) aside in order to gain such relevance and influence in the political equation at any level. For example, there

---

21. There are of course other reasons why PDP lost the elections, including issues of corruption, insecurity, etc, which will be discussed in the next chapter.

are some self-seeking politicians who would pretend to be in one political party yet are taking the ostrich attitude described as 'anti-party activities', simply because their interest was not met in the choice of a candidate produced by the party to seek election. One of the leaders of the defunct National Party of Nigeria (NPN) from one of the north-central states told the NPN Working Committee that a particular candidate, though seen as popular, would not win the gubernatorial election in his state, and went further to undermine his winning despite his popularity. One can only agree that anti-party activities is a common trait in Nigerian party politics and electoral processes.

Even in the APC of today, some former governors decided to remain in the party not because they are truly committed to it, but simply because they would exercise influence as party leaders where their governors are in the other party. The same thing applies to some PDP stalwarts.

I have earlier stated that it may not be wrong or even unethical to shift from one party to another, but the frequency of that and its ultimate outcomes have certain impacts on elections and the electoral processes in Nigeria. Whether such defections and realignment of forces will fundamentally shape the 2019 elections remains to be seen. But what is important is to sensitise the electorate on the key issues, rather than personalities that should determine their choices in the elections.

## Conclusion

In conclusion, due to the obvious issues affecting elections and electoral processes, there is a serious concern regarding the future of democracy and the credibility of the forthcoming elections in 2019. It thus seems that Nigerians are eager to see that the electoral processes are improved and the right candidates emerge as leaders of the country. Unfortunately, it is unlikely that 'ethical' and credible candidates will emerge as party flag-bearers, because it is the party that provides the platform to a candidate to seek election to any office in the land. The INEC has registered over 90 political parties, but most of them are only in name, without any significant presence across the country. During the Third Republic, the electoral rule provided that a political party must have had at least a 5% victory in state and local government elections before it could present a candidate for the office of president. That was good practice to ensure that the number of political parties was manageable by the electoral body. Despite the multitude of registered political parties, the 2019 presidential election, it appears, will be mainly a contest between the ruling APC and the main opposition PDP. This is not because there are no credible candidates in the other parties, but because of the unfortunate fact is that electioneering processes are so expensive in Nigeria that only the very rich can play an active part.

It is against this background that I shall now proceed to examine how these concerns actually played out in 2015 and how there may still be important issues for the electorate to contend with in the 2019 elections.

# CHAPTER 2

# Before 2019, there was 2015

To understand the dynamics of the possible scenario in the 2019 elections, it is necessary to recall some background information from the 2015 elections. We can say that former President Jonathan created the conditions for APC/Buhari's victory in 2015. It can be food for thought as to whether Buhari has created or will create conditions for Atiku in 2019.

The 2015 presidential election was keenly contested. A few days around Christmas in the last week of December 2016, I watched Dame Patience Jonathan, former First Lady of Nigeria, on television appearing on a programme in Enugu State. She was complaining about the population of the North: northerners were not contributing to the growth of Nigeria as much as they were increasing the population through uncontrolled marriages and births. Her concern was about the possible outcome of the election. At that time, I doubted the possibility of Buhari winning this election, scheduled to take place in February 2015. My worry was not that Jonathan was more acceptable, nor that he had achieved much to warrant re-election, but based on the experience of the past that no incumbent had lost an election in the history of Nigeria. However, on a deeper reflection, I told myself that God can make the impossible possible within the twinkling of the eye.

One week after, on 6 January 2015, as the campaigns commenced and I was watching the first public appearance of the APC opposition candidate, Muhammadu Buhari, I concluded and anxiously made a pronouncement that 'Buhari will be president, God willing'. What was behind this thought was not the rollout of the political manifestos of the major political parties but the way events turned out within a short time, as I had noticed that some former and serving governors had defected to the APC before the political campaigns began. It was then that I was convinced they were really committed to wresting power from Jonathan. But more than that was the signal that some powerful generals, including Obasanjo, Babangida and Danjuma, were likely to openly express their support for the opposition candidate. That was what ultimately happened.

It is impossible to recall completely and accurately all the factors responsible for the outcome of the 2015 presidential election. Nevertheless, we can highlight a few that can serve as lessons learned in our political history and probably reflect as we approach the 2019 elections. Critical among these factors included the bad shape of the economy, the Boko Haram insurgency, 'a united opposition and a crumbling PDP', the fact that it was harder to rig the election and, most importantly, the fact that a change was really needed in the political leadership. Therefore I will examine in this chapter the state of the economy as I recalled in the book[22] I wrote soon after the election, the security situation and how it affected the feelings about a possible second term for former President Jonathan.

---

22. A.Y. Shehu,*Nigeria: The Way Through Corruption to the Wellbeing of a People,* National Open University of Nigeria, Lagos, 2015.

## The Economy

One of the concerns of the citizens in every country is their welfare and wellbeing, and the state of the economy is the parameter for measuring that. Let me recall verbatim my references to authoritative sources to describe the state of the economy.

As at January 2015, Nigeria's foreign reserve was estimated at US$34.38 billion, and Charles Soludo, a former Governor of the Central Bank of Nigeria, wrote in the *Leadership* newspaper (26 January 2015):

> I note that when I assumed office as Governor of CBN, the stock of foreign reserves was $10 billion. The average monthly oil price during my 60 months in office was $59, but foreign reserves reached the all-time peak of $62 billion (and despite paying $12 billion for external debt, and losing over $15 billion during the unprecedented global financial and economic crisis) I left behind $45 billion… My calculation is that if the economy was better managed, our foreign reserves should have been between $102-$118 billion and exchange rate around N112 before the fall in oil prices. As of now, the reserves should be around $90 billion and exchange rate no higher than N125 per dollar'.[23]

Similarly, Dr Oby Ezekwesili, a former Vice President of the World Bank, characterised the poor state of the economy under the PDP:

> Empirical evidence points to poor governance – especially corruption as the biggest obstacle to the development of Nigeria. Understanding the cancerous impact of corruption helps explain how a country with… enviable potentials that are hardly available to more than other one third nations of the world has remained at

23. A the time of this commentary by Soludo, the oil price had plummeted from $118 pb in October 2014 to $45 pb in January 2015, meaning a drastic revenue decline that necessitated some austerity measures in the 2015 budget. But according to Soludo, the economy growth rate soared to an average of 7% between 2003 and 2007 (when the monthly oil price was an average of $38 pb) and the poverty rate was reduced from 70% to 54% in 2004

the bottom of global socioeconomic ladder as a laggard. Economic growth rate and ultimate development of nations are determined by a number of factors that range from sound policies, effective and efficient public and private investments and strong institutions. Economic evidence throughout numerous researches proves that one key variable that determines how fast nations outgrow others is the speed of accumulation of human capital especially through science and technology education. No wonder for these same countries, by 2011- South Korea of fifty million people has a GDP of $1.12trillion, Brazil of one hundred and ninety six million has $2.48 trillion; Malaysia of twenty eight million people has $278.6 billion; Chile of seventeen million people has $248.59 billion; Singapore of five million people has $318.7 billion. Meanwhile with our population of 165 million people we make boasts with a GDP of $488 billion – completely way off the mark that we could have produced if we made better sets of development choices.

More dramatic is that this wide gap between these nations and Nigeria was not always the case as some relevant data at the time of our independence reveal. In 1960 the GDP per capita of all these countries were not starkly different from that of Nigeria – two were below $200, two were a little above $300 and one was slightly above $500 while that of Nigeria was just about $100. For citizens, these differentials are not mere economic data. Meanwhile by 2011, the range for all five grew exponentially with Singapore at nearly $50,000, South Korea at $22,000, Malaysia at $10,000, Brazil at $13,000 and Chile at $14,000. Our own paltry $2,688 income per capita helps drive home the point that we have been left behind many times over by every one of these other countries. How did these nations steer and stir their people to achieve such outstanding economic performance over the last five decades? There is hardly a basis for comparing the larger population of our citizens clustered within the poverty bracket with the majority citizens of Singapore fortunate to have upper middle income standard of living. (Shehu, 2015:7-8).

It was because of the deteriorating economic situation that most

Nigerians felt Jonathan could not make a difference if he was re-elected and they called on the electorate to peacefully vote him out. And they did vote him out. In endorsing candidate Muhammadu Buhari for the election, former President Obasanjo assured Nigerians of Buhari's competence to tackle corruption and insecurity in the country. But he also observed that Buhari's knowledge of the economy and foreign affairs was limited. He then urged Buhari to consider talented Nigerians who might have the skills in those areas for appointment in his government to make up the deficiency. This was also the persuasion of many Nigerians, and on the basis of that they pitched their tents with Buhari. In a nutshell, the economy was growing but the wealth had not spread down to the masses of the people; rather, a few privileged people became excessively rich through rent-seeking and other prebendal practices. But the issue of the economy was less important in voting Jonathan out than insecurity and the prevalence of corruption.

## Insecurity – the Boko Haram Palaver

By far the most important factor that led to the defeat of former President Jonathan in 2015 was perverse insecurity occasioned by the dreaded Boko Haram insurgency. While a lot has been said and written about this, including by former President Jonathan himself,[24] it was the handling of the problem, particularly when it took Jonathan more than nine days after the kidnapping of the Chibok girls to be convinced that they had indeed been kidnapped by the insurgents. This brought into question his capacity to be President and led to his being described as 'clueless'. But what provoked anger the most was his journey to campaign in Kano on the same day the Nyanna bombing took place with its many casualties.

Besides, he constituted different committees, including a

24. Goodluck Jonathan, *My Transition Hour* (Ezekiel Books, Kingwood USA), launched in Abuja on 22 November 2018.

Presidential Dialogue Committee that investigated the remote and immediate causes of the insurgency, and yet nobody was penalised, nor could he stop the killings and the destruction of properties by the insurgents. Worse still, he could not inspire the confidence of the international community to persuade them to give him the necessary support. Rather, he alleged in his book that former US President Obama had openly showed his displeasure towards his (Jonathan's) second term. Under Jonathan, the US Government declined to sell weapons to Nigeria to fight Boko Haram on account of human rights abuses in the military operation against the insurgency. The Nigerian army had made significant efforts and recorded some gains in the fight against Boko Haram, but these successes were not enough to convince Nigerians that the Jonathan administration could effectively tackle the problem.

Most importantly, the corruption that characterised the war against Boko Haram was particularly worrying; no wonder that soon after his departure from government, the new administration exposed the Pandora's box of humungous corruption that was involved in purported arms procurement for the fight against the terrorists. All this is now bygone, but the impact remains memorable and that should be the lesson for further electoral choices in the forthcoming presidential election. But we should ask the question that aside from these issues, did the Jonathan perform creditably enough to warrant re-election? That is hard to measure, especially now that comparative data do not add up properly.

The other security issue that put President Jonathan at a crossroad with the northern elite even before the escalation of the Boko Haram insurgency was the attack on Abuja by some people who claimed to be members of the Movement for the Emancipation of the Niger Delta (MEND). The attack took place on 1 October 2010 while the Heads of State and governments of several African and other countries were seated at Eagle Square for the celebration of Nigeria's 50th Independence Anniversary. This attack was perceived as intended to embarrass Nigeria and create another excuse for Jonathan to contest the election for the presidency in 2011. The Northern political leaders, in a press statement signed by Adamu Chiroma (Madakin Fika), swiftly condemned the attack and alleged that it was merely to give the 'false impression that Nigeria is on the verge of a violent political conflagration ahead of the general elections of 2011. It was also meant to intimidate the international community that Niger Delta criminal gangs have the capacity to influence political outcomes beyond their traditional area of influence.' The northern political leaders called on President Jonathan to resign as 'he has proven that he is incapable of leading the nation justly and fairly and that he is desperate enough to want to hang mass murder around the neck of unnamed Northerners to achieve his second term, we as citizens of this country have totally lost confidence in his leadership and hereby call on him to immediately resign'.

## Corruption was Hydra-Headed

There is no denying that corruption had become so rampant under the Jonathan administration that many electorates felt the country might collapse if that administration was allowed to stay in power. The prevalence of corruption was visibly displayed even during the electioneering campaigns, when money was shared for vote buying. Even religious leaders and traditional rulers lined their pockets. The value of the naira correspondingly depreciated because the bribes were given in foreign currencies, particularly the US dollar, which was sourced from bureaux de change and other open market sources. The impact of corruption on the society was obvious and scary to anybody who cared to see.

Nigeria's corruption rating by Transparency International

(TI) was nearly the worst ever. Foreign businesses were losing confidence, not only because of the deteriorating security situation but more so because of the high level of corruption. Corruption had pervaded Nigerian society and impacted negatively on virtually all aspects of national life, including the fight against the dreaded Boko Haram.

Corruption predates the Jonathan administration, as allegations of theft, mismanagement or non-remittance of proceeds of oil revenues have been levelled against the NNPC, the main revenue powerhouse of the nation, including:

1.  allegations of mismanagement of an $12 billion oil windfall from the Gulf War in the 1990s;

2.  keeping of different account books by the NNPC and failure to audit its accounts;

3.  many allegations of non-remittance of proceeds of crude oil sales and mismanagement of the so-called oil subsidy presented to the President in a memo by Sanusi Lamido Sanusi, then Governor of the CBN, which led to his suspension from office in February 2014.

During the 2015 campaigns, General Buhari, the APC candidate, persuaded Nigerians to vote out the PDP. He described the PDP government as corrupt and said that a corrupt government is worse than armed robbery: 'I believe that a bad and corrupt government is as much danger to national security as armed robbers, kidnappers, and terrorists.'

In a similar vein, Mallam Nasir El-Rufa'i, one of the figureheads of the Buhari campaign organisation, had alleged that a staggering 5 trillion naira – or $31bn was stolen under Jonathan's 30-month stewardship of our nation's affairs. Assuming that Jonathan has been in power since May 2010, that works out to an [incredible] $1bn stolen each month. If you add the average borrowing of another $1bn per month since Jonathan took office, then the true scale of the epic theft becomes clearer.[25]

To assure Nigerians that the fight against corruption would be a major plank of the Buhari administration if elected, Buhari himself chose no other place to make a policy statement on this problem than Chatham House in London, where on February 17, 2015, he argued that:

> Even by official figures, 33.1% of Nigerians live in extreme poverty. That's at almost 60 million people, almost the population of the United Kingdom. There is also the unemployment crisis simmering beneath the surface, ready to explode at the slightest stress, with officially 23.9% of our adult population and almost 60% of our youth unemployed. We also have one of the highest rates of inequalities in the world.
>
> In the face of dwindling revenues, a good place to start the repositioning of Nigeria's economy is to swiftly tackle two ills that have ballooned…: waste and corruption.

This was basically the message for Nigerians to vote out Jonathan, and they did.

### Buhari's Personal Integrity

Buhari's record in public service as former Minister of Petroleum Resources, Military Governor, Head of State and Chairman of the Petroleum Trust Fund (PTF) were 'unblemished', and that was the main issue for the electorate in 2015. The majority of the voting population, especially from the northern parts of the country, believed that Buhari would not steal their commonwealth, so they decided to give him their mandate. But while the issue of personal integrity was crucial, very little thought was given to

25. Shehu, *Nigeria*, p. 15.

his capacity to perform as he did when he was in those positions earlier mentioned some years back, and considering his age. The allegation of insufficient knowledge and health by former governor Fayose of Ekiti State and the propaganda of the spokesperson of the Jonathan Campaign Organisation, Femi Fani-Kayode, did not in any way sway or change the minds of most Nigerians. At one point, former President Obasanjo confessed that he preferred to be in jail under Buhari to save Nigeria from a precipice under Jonathan. I had argued that Buhari's integrity was a great asset for Nigeria.[26] Today, Nigerians are in a position to say whether integrity on its own is enough to salvage Nigeria. This is what I seek to interrogate in subsequent chapters.

## Performance of the PDP Government

Whereas the PDP ruled for sixteen years (1999-2015), and made significant landmarks, especially in the areas of building institutions and creating the necessary legislative framework for the security, anti-corruption, infrastructural and economic development of Nigeria during its initial reign, it was obvious that Nigerians were not satisfied with the performance of the PDP under Jonathan. I would like to believe that it was merely a sort of 'giving a dog a bad name in order to hang it' that Jonathan had to bear the brunt of criticisms for non-performance. Candidly, and without attempting to make a comparison at this stage, I would confess that although the economy was not in good shape, the fundamentals were relatively strong, perhaps because of the high oil price. The major anti-corruption agencies, namely the Economic and Financial Crimes Commission (EFCC) and the Independent Corrupt Practices and Other Related Offences Commission (ICPC), had stable leadership and were focused on their assignments with modest achievements despite the allegations of selective action, which is not peculiar to that era.

26. Ibid.

During the 2015 elections campaigns, the PDP 'laundered' its image in the garb of numerous projects it executed, but its support was at its lowest and the centre could no longer hold. It was obvious that the expectations of Nigerians were many and high, especially when it was really a time for Jonathan to leave the stage and for Buhari to replace him.

Nevertheless, there were a few exceptional tangential achievements under the Jonathan administration, including the improvement on the anti-money laundering and counter financing of terrorism (AML/CFT) framework in Nigeria. It was under his administration that the Terrorism (Prevention) Bill was enacted as a response to the problem of terrorism and insurgency; the Money Laundering (Prohibition) Act was amended in 2011 to meet acceptable international standards and protect the Nigerian economy from misuse/abuse for the purposes of laundering the proceeds of crime.

One of the negative connotations given to former President Jonathan was his being described by the opposition as a 'clueless' president. Femi Aribisala asked 'What Exactly is Clueless about Goodluck Jonathan',[27] and concluded that the use of 'cluelessness' to describe Jonathan was an insult, politically motivated and unfair, as according to him, Jonathan was the most educated President Nigeria ever had (with a PhD degree) and could not have been the most clueless among all former heads of state. He argued that every leader has his own weaknesses, and whatever the opposition can say about the Jonathan administration some important landmarks it achieved cannot be erased by propaganda and these include the fact that within four years the Jonathan administration:

1. Built 125 *Almajiri* schools in 13 states in the North.

27. Tuesday Comment, published in *Thisday* newspaper, 7 October 2014.

2. Established ten new universities, seven of them in the North,[28] and created 34 NCE awarding institutions.

3. Sponsored 7000 lecturers for postgraduate studies at home and abroad; licensed 100 Innovation Enterprise Institutions; and granted 101 Presidential Scholarships for innovation and development.

4. Caused a 10-million student increase in basic education enrolment through Universal Basic Education Commission (UBEC) programme.

5. Executed several road transformations from the regular budget and SURE-P projects and many were listed for verification, etc.

6. Noted the incremental growth in the economy averaging an annual rate of 7% and the debasing of the economy, making it the largest in Africa with GDP of about $503 billion, again, making Nigeria the 23rd largest economy in the world.

7. Noted that Nigeria was 'ranked the number one destination for investments in Africa and as having the highest returns on investment in the world' two years in a row.

8. In the health sector, the high point of Jonathan's administration was the effective way and manner it dealt with the outbreak of the Ebola epidemic.

## Ethnicity, Regional and Religious Politics

The political landscape was influenced principally by the PDP zoning formula, where it was argued that since former President Umaru Yar'Aduadid not spend eight years in office and since

28. Located in Lafia, Nasarawa State, Lokoja, Kogi State; Kashere, Gombe State; Wukari, Taraba State; Dutsen-Ma, Katsina State; and Duste, in Jigawa State. During the campaigns, the opposition APC described the universities as 'mushroom or glorified secondary schools' because they lacked facilities, yet, the APC has not merged this record so far in their first term in office.

Jonathan had been given the chance to be president for six years, it was the turn of the North to produce the next President in 2015. This was the main reason that motivated prominent PDP members, including Atiku Abubakar, Bukola Saraki, Aminu Waziri Tambowal, Rabiu Musa Kwankwaso and Murtala Nyako to decamp from the PDP to the APC. It is interesting to note that as we approach another presidential election in 2019, all of them except Nyako have returned to the PDP and are playing active roles in an attempt to seize back power.

But while the party politics was on, the religious and ethnic dimensions also played important role in defeating Jonathan. In the North especially, while majority Muslims had consistently voted for Buhari, the wind of change galvanized more support for him from a large number of northern Christians in the 2015 election. It would be good if politicians could play politics without religious division or partisan bitterness. Overall, however, the overriding consideration was not any of these but purely the fact that in politics there is no permanent enemy or friend, only permanent interest. Every politician wants recognition and a role to play in any dispensation.

## The Elite Factor

As stated in the previous chapter, democracy is about the elite struggle for power and influence. In every society, the elite have and will continue to play an active role and even change the pattern of democracy. The elite class is highly conscious of its individual and group interests and is ready to go to any extent to join forces to deal with any perceived threat to such interests. They are also cohesive in their approach to issues, and can make unexpected compromises to arrive at a consensus on what they want. But most importantly, their capacity for conspiracy is beyond imagination, and that was how these four 'Cs' influenced the outcome of the 2015 election. I shall examine the prevailing situation and attempt to estimate whether the elite factor has a combination of the elements and whether or not that can influence the outcome of the 2019 elections.

Even among the elite class, however, there are active and passive participants, and there is also some modicum of seniority or hierarchy. In other words, it is a structured class. The single action of the elite class that dealt a blow to the chances of President Jonathan was the Open Letter written to him by former President Obasanjo on the many observable deficiencies in his administration and the advice not to seek re-election. Specifically, Obasanjo recalled to Jonathan the gentlemen's agreement that he (Jonathan) was not going to seek re-election and that the North would be compensated for the death of Yar'Adua. He accused him of several weaknesses and failures but justified why he had to write him publicly in his opening paragraph as follows:

> I am constrained to make this an open letter to you for a number of reasons: One, the current situation and consequent possible outcome dictate that I should, before the door closes on reason and promotion of nation interest, alert you to the danger that may be lurking in the corner. Two,…the four or more letters I have written to you in the past two years or so ha[ve] elicited neither an acknowledgement nor any response. Three, people close to you, if not yourself, have been asking what does Obasanjo want? Four, I could sense a semblance between the situation that we are gradually getting into and the situation we fell into as a nation during the Abacha era. Five, everything must be done to guard, protect and defend our fledgling democracy, nourish it, and prevent bloodshed. Six, we must move away from advertently or inadvertently dividing the country along weak seams of North-South and Christian-Muslim. Seven, nothing should be done to allow the country to degenerate into economic dormancy, stagnation or retrogression. Eight, some of our international friends and development partners are genuinely worried about

signs and signals that are coming out of Nigeria. Nine, Nigeria should be in a position to take advantage of present favourable international interest to invest in Africa – an opportunity that will not be open for too long. Ten, I am concerned about your legacy and your climb-down which you alone can best be the manager of whatever you so decide.

Although Obasanjo does not and did not claim to have the monopoly of wisdom, any imaginative reader can discern the traits of patriotism and nationalism in this letter. Regardless of his reputation of writing open letters to 'non-performing leaders', as he himself is a mortal and cannot be perfect, this letter was the straw that broke the camel's back in their relationship; thereafter he withdrew his support for Jonathan and started looking for an alternative. Many sympathisers of Jonathan chastised Obasanjo for writing the letter, but nobody, not even in the uninspiring reply that Jonathan sent to Obasanjo, has really disputed any of the allegations Obasanjo made. He was quick to pitch his tent with Buhari and only God knows how that helped in changing the landscape in 2015. Far from alluding that Obasanjo can make or mar anybody from becoming a president, what I am simply suggesting here is that God carries out his will through his creatures and it seems Obasanjo was only used among many by God Almighty. We shall see whether history will be repeated when we discuss another letter he wrote to President Buhari early 2019.

### Time for a Change – the APC Message

In 2015, the APC message to the electorate was that enough was enough and they needed a change for the better. The campaign was more organised and coordinated and the message was clear on three key points: securing Nigeria and managing it efficiently; fighting corruption; and revamping the economy, including poverty reduction and employment generation. Indeed, these were the main problems of Nigeria at that time and it was possible for the APC to propagate the message with the help of very many civil society followers and social media.

In what was termed 'Commonsense Revolution', the APC Leader, Bola Ahmed Tinubu, persuasively asked Nigerians to vote out the PDP and replace it with the APC. He said there can be no more fence-sitting because:

> that fence has been torn down by the vast disparity between our current reality and our desired future.... And those who hear the APC message must respond to its call because history is impatient when it has set itself in motion.... Commonsense revolution speaks to the need to elect patriotic leaders that can give hope to our best aspirations as a nation and people... It speaks to how we must elect thinkers and doers to work together to bring about a beautiful revival of the national spirit and the good fortune of the people.... Our APC Government will use its fiscal and monetary space to jump-start the economy... 20 billion dollars – enough to fund government for a year – shall no longer disappear as if by magic!

When it was apparent that the PDP had lost, Jonathan made history by placing an unexpected phone call to his opponent (Buhari) and congratulating him. That single action of conceding defeat was highly commended, as it saved Nigeria all the speculation of a serious political crisis. On my part, and indeed many Nigerians, I thought that was the end of the PDP in Nigerian politics, but whether the resurgence of the PDP would change that narrative we do not yet know; we wait to see whether it will spring a surprise in 2019. If the PDP wins the presidential election, it would prove that losing an election is not a death sentence but part of the democratic process.

## Were the 2015 Elections Carried Out with Integrity?

The outcome of the 2015 presidential election, though it was obvious that the incumbent would lose, became a reality with the modicum of transparency and professionalism demonstrated by the INEC, under Professor Attahiru Jega. Could it have been possible for Jonathan to remove Jega when his loyalty was in doubt? Perhaps yes, but the consequences far outweighed the yes. By that feat, Jega had set a standard for the independence of the electoral body and that has become a model for other African countries. At the personal level, he left the INEC with his integrity intact and is well respected all over the world when it comes to conducting free, fair and credible elections.

## The Role of the International Community

The international community, led by the major western democracies, the USA and the UK in particular, is keenly interested in elections anywhere in the world, as they are the key element of a democratic government. One of the reasons why the 2015 election was free, fair and acceptable was the involvement of the international community, which engaged constructively, impartially and consistently with the Nigerian Government, the electoral body, civil society and other international stakeholders. Without the strong support from the USA, UK and UN in particular, it is possible that the process would have been interfered with and even undermined. Does that mean unwarranted interference in Nigeria's domestic affairs? In my view, no, because they engaged Nigeria under the Universal Declaration and Covenant on Civil and Political Rights, which Nigeria had assented to, and the international community only observes and does not poke its nose into election matters. Will it be the same in 2019?

## Conclusion

Many factors may have contributed to the outcome of the 2015 presidential election, but those mentioned above are considered the most important. The conclusion we can draw from Nigeria's experience with leadership confirms my earlier observation that democracy is an elite struggle for power and influence. Even as I write this book to contribute to knowledge on Nigerian political history, most of the electorate do not have the means and access to read it. Even the elite who have the means and access would only read if the headlines caught their interests and they had the leisure to read. Nevertheless, such knowledge is important in enriching our reservoir of wisdom on how to make choices in our elections.

The 2015 election marked a watershed in the political history of Nigeria, as it was the first time an incumbent president had been defeated and also the first time the president could concede defeat without bloodshed. With what we have experienced in Africa, where leaders sit tight even when support is lowest, what former President Jonathan did, even though it seems he had no better option, was unprecedented and commendable. Consequently, on 29 May 2015, Muhammadu Buhari was sworn in as President and Yemi Osinbajo as Vice President of Nigeria. That is where we are coming from. So, where are we now? Whether the APC managed its victory well is the issue we shall examine in the next chapter.

# CHAPTER 3

# Managing Victory: Buhari's Story

After three serial attempts in 2003, 2007 and 2011, in 2015 General Muhammadu Buhari finally clinched the presidency of the Federal Republic of Nigeria on the platform of the APC. He started his political struggle under the platform of the All Nigeria Peoples' Party (ANPP) under which he had contested the presidential elections in 2003 and 2007. When he was not satisfied with the way and manner politicians were changing parties like clothes and was even disappointed with the running of the party, he decided to create his own party called the Congress of Progressives' Change (CPC), under which he contested the 2011 election. The ANPP had about seven elected governors at the time Buhari joined in 2003. It lost some ground in 2007, yet by 2011 it was still considered a major opposition party that could wrest power from the ruling PDP. Buhari's main support areas were in the northern states, but the CPC could produce only one governor[29] in 2011.

---

29. Governor Tanko Al-Makura was popularly elected under the platform of the CPC to defeat the incumbent Governor, Aliyu Akwe Doma, of the PDP in Nasarawa State in 2011. He won a second term with overwhelming majority under the APC in 2015.

For the first time in the political history of Nigeria, Buhari contested under the APC and defeated the incumbent President Goodluck Jonathan in 2015, thus changing the perception and political narrative, not only in Nigeria but in Africa, that it is possible to defeat an incumbent in a free, fair and credible election. The main thrust of the Manifesto of the APC is to change the lives of Nigerians; Nigerians were happy with that and voted for Buhari and his party. The impetus for Buhari's victory lay in what was described as his 'covenant with Nigerians', which will be discussed in this chapter. Obviously, that victory could be attributed to several factors, principal among which are those factors that were against Jonathan in 2015 which have been discussed in the previous chapter. It is important to recall that among these factors, the trust in Buhari, the high expectation for a rapid change based on a perception of his strength of character and moral integrity, as well as the time for change, were the most crucial in determining the outcome of the election.

The election of President Muhammadu Buhari (PMB) triggered not less than a N903 billion, about 8.42% gain in the Nigeria Stock Exchange. Capitalisation closed at a new high of N11.62 trillion, while the All-Share index rose by 2,635 basis points or 8.30%, the highest among 93 global indices tracked by Bloomberg. Indeed the election was a confidence booster as 65 stocks recorded gainers.[30] Similarly, Nigeria's $500 million of Eurobonds due July 2023 rose for the 11th day, pushing the yield down to the lowest since December 2014 in reaction to President Jonathan's phone call to Buhari to concede defeat, thus reducing the threat of post-election violence.

In addition to electing Buhari, Nigerians also elected about 24 governors on the platform of the APC to strengthen the change agenda at the state level. They also gave the APC/Buhari a majority in both chambers of the NASS to steer the leadership of the country.

30. Including Nestle (N47.00 each); Seplat Petroleum Development Company (N31.50 per share); Dangote Cement (N16.40); Forte Oil (N18.14); and Nigerian Breweries (N14.64).

Obviously, by overwhelmingly electing Buhari and most of the governors and legislators on the platform of the APC, Nigerians had kept to their own covenant with Buhari and with the APC.

Furthermore, it is crucial to mention that never has any leader been endowed with the kind of goodwill that was given to PMB both within and outside the country, to the extent that for the first time in the history of fuel crisis and price increase in Nigeria, he set a record of having increased the pump price of petroleum products from 87 naira per litre to 145 naira per litre, and yet the trade unions who had resisted any slide increases in the past did not embark on any strike action to protest the price increase. On top of that, the several slides in economic indicators, such as the rise in prices of foodstuffs and general inflation from 10.5% under Jonathan to about 18% within one year of the Buhari administration taking office, did not give cause for agitation, all in the spirit of understanding the many challenges the administration inherited and in a bid to give it time to address the problems in a more pragmatic way.

In view of the above scenario, the Speaker of the House of Representatives, Yakubu Dogara, who defected from the APC to PDP in 2018, at an empowerment programme organised by a member of the House, Binta Bello, in Kaltungo, Gombe State, on 18 December 2018 declared that the 2019 presidential election 'will be a referendum on insecurity, killings, and hunger in Nigeria'.

I have given this somewhat lengthy introduction in order to provide the background for a more objective and compassionate assessment of the people's expectations and the way in which President Buhari and the APC have managed the victory given them by Nigerians. In doing so, I should state from the outset that:

(1) Although Buhari's perceived attributes of incorruptibility, honesty and moral integrity have been with him for a long time, these attributes were only appreciated when the elite perceived

these to be in their own interest. They wished to save Nigeria from collapse with the mistakes of Jonathan and to retain their monopoly on power.

(2) Second, the APC Manifesto encapsulated an all-round change in the ways things were being conducted in Nigeria, but the impetus behind its acceptability was the alliance of strange 'bedfellows' who saw the victory of the APC as a step to their being political godfathers in some ways. Hence, most of the promises of the Party were overly ambitious, if not unrealistic.

(3) Third, the massive propaganda, aided by the technological advantage of social media, galvanised support for a change.

(4) Fourth, the APC presumably intended all those promises to be achieved fully or largely within the four-year tenure of their campaign. Was it realistic or was it just a gimmick to seize power?

(5) Fifth, as Soludo observed, 'we must support them to succeed by contributing when we can, and criticizing when we must – tough love!'[31]

(6) Sixth, any objective assessment of the performance of the APC Government, and President Buhari in particular, must take into account several factors that are complex and interlocking, such as every administration has faced or will face in the future.

Against this background, it is not possible to provide a detailed analysis of the APC Manifesto and all the challenges it has had in implementing that in the past three and a half years; I shall therefore focus attention here on an overview of the promises President Buhari and the APC made to Nigerians and struggled hard to secure their confidence and mandate to steer the mantle of leadership

31. Charles Soludo, 'Can a New Buharinomics Save Nigeria?', 3rd Anniversary Lecture of the RealNewsmagazine, published in *Thisday* newspaper, 20 November 2015.

of Nigeria. There were several reasons why Buhari and the APC emerged victorious in the 2015 elections: the high expectations of Nigerians amidst obvious challenges and the efforts made by the APC Government to fulfil its promises, as well as the constraints in doing so, including the lack of cohesion in the party, lack of team spirit and credible policies and competent implementers.

This chapter will focus on Buhari because the President in Nigeria is the ultimate power for most decisions and should be held accountable according to the tenets of democracy. To constructively criticise any government should not be misconstrued as lack of support or goodwill; it is simply for the purposes of posterity and in an attempt to make the future better. The main thrust of this chapter is to provide an accurate and unbiased account of the progress or lack of it so that the reader can discern what choices to make in the selection of future leaders.

## The APC Manifesto and Buhari's Covenant with Nigerians

As stated earlier, it is not possible to provide a detailed analysis of the APC Manifesto here, but its main thrust, which is to change the lives of Nigerians, is my point of departure. The APC Manifesto included several ambitious policies and plans for the country, including the contentious issue of restructuring the country without providing the methodology to achieve that. The Manifesto was translated and interpreted to Nigerians through the campaign slogan of 'Change' which captivated Nigerians as a quick fix alternative to the problems of the country. I shall make sparing references to the statements of the APC leaders with a view to understanding where we are coming from, where we are and possibly what is the future of democracy in Nigeria. Thus, 'a minimum standard for measuring 'change' is the extent to which APC government beats the record of the PDP in measurable terms. As the saying goes, if you can't measure it, you can't improve/change it'.[32]

32. Soludo, 'Can a New Buharinomics Save Nigeria?', p. 3.

In a nutshell, the Manifesto, christened 'an honest contract for Nigeria', aims to provide three key outputs, namely, relief, recovery and reform within four years:

1. **Relief:** the APC promised to provide a decent life for every Nigerian through:
a. Jobs, jobs, jobs; 3 million new jobs a year
b. Healthcare for all
c. Guaranteed free education
d. Urban renewal & housing
e. Tackling poverty; A safety net for every citizen
f. Keeping Nigeria safe
g. Sports and culture: A vibrant Nigeria.

2. **Recovery:** with regard to recovery and the glory of Nigeria, the APC promised the following:
a. Building a 21st-century economy
b. Building modern infrastructure
c. Creating a value added economy
d. Restoring good government
e. Ending reliance on oil and gas
f. Agriculture & land; A green revolution.

3. **Reform:** in the area of reform, the APC promised to Nigerians:
a. A government you can trust
b. Guaranteeing human rights and justice
c. Foreign affairs and trade; a strong Nigeria in a growing Africa
d. A fair deal for women
e. Protecting Nigeria's environment.

These main objectives were sold to Nigerians through a strategy which comprised radio and television adverts, jingles and discussions, media forums and chats, public lectures and debates, columnists, opinions and features writing in newspapers and magazines, and most importantly physical campaigns in all the states of the federation. Let us examine a few of these in order to put the issues in proper perspectives.

## The Campaign Issues

To succeed at the polls, every political party tries to be on top of the topical issues that would convince the people to believe in its policies and programmes and vote for it. The APC took advantage, and rightly, of the failures of the PDP to address the critical issues affecting the wellbeing of the people and premised its campaign on three main issues: (1) securing the country and managing it efficiently; (2) fighting corruption; and (3) efficient management of the economy, including poverty eradication and job creation. I will refer to two documents, 'My Covenant with Nigerians' by General Muhammadu Buhari and 'Commonsense Revolution' by Asiwaju Bola Tunubu, to illustrate how the campaign issues were amplified and communicated to Nigerians by the leaders of the APC.

## 'My Covenant with Nigerians'

A few days to the 25 March 2015 presidential election, and in a determined bid to seize power from the incumbent, the APC/ Buhari Campaign Organisation issued a detailed statement of intent by General Muhammadu Buhari as his contract with Nigerians if elected to the office of President. The 8-page document contained every imaginable pragmatic action a leader could take to address the immediate and long-term problems of Nigeria, in all sectors. I would have reproduced the entire document for efficacy of impact, but due to its length, I decided to paraphrase and summarise the key issues which will be relevant in our subsequent analysis of results and impact in this chapter.

In the preamble, Buhari stated that during his campaign tour he experienced the beauty of Nigeria's diversity, and as he traversed from Port Harcourt to Kano, from Abeokuta to Gusau, he saw first-hand not only the daily sufferings and struggles of Nigerians but also their quest for a change. Consequently, he had to assure the people that he will 'lead with integrity and honour and commit myself totally to everything that is of concern to our people: security, employment, health, education, good governance and others'.

He stated in the document:

> This Covenant is to outline my agenda for Nigeria and provide a bird's eye view of how we intend to bring about change that our country needs and deserves. This Covenant is derived from the manifesto of my party, the All Progressives' Congress (APC). It however, represents my pledge to you all when I become your President'. He went on to make several promises on how he would address corruption, security, access to justice and respect for fundamental human rights, how he would manage the Niger Delta, Nigeria's diversity, health, education, agriculture, economy, power, sports and culture. Since the APC campaign issues were based on a tripod of anti-corruption, security and the economy, I shall highlight a few of the promises in the Covenant with respect to these three. The following points are presented partly with Buhari speaking in the first person.

### On Corruption and Governance

'No matter how vast our resources, if they are not efficiently utilized, they will only benefit a privileged few, leaving the majority in poverty. I believe if Nigeria does not kill corruption, corruption will kill Nigeria.'

I pledge to:

- Publicly declare my assets and liabilities and encourage my political appointees to also publicly declare their assets and liabilities.

- Affirm that our strategy for tackling corruption will not only focus on punishment. Rather, it will also provide incentives for disclosure and transparency.

- Show personal leadership in the war against corruption and also hold all the people who work with me to account.

- Inaugurate the National Council on Procurement as stipulated in the Procurement Act so that the Federal Executive Council, which has been turned to a weekly session of contract bazaar, will concentrate on its principal function of policy making.

- Review and implement audit recommendations by Nigeria Extractive Industries Transparency Initiative (NEITI).

- Work with the National Assembly towards the immediate enactment of a Whistle Blower Act.

- Work with the National Assembly to strengthen ICPC and EFCC by guaranteeing institutional autonomy including financial and prosecutorial independence and security of tenure of officials.

- Make the Financial Intelligence Unit (FIU) an autonomous and operational agency.

- Encourage proactive disclosure of information by government institutions in the spirit of the Freedom of Information Act.

- Ensure all MDAs regularly comply with their accountability responsibilities to Nigerians through the National Assembly.

- Work with the leadership of the National Assembly to cut down the cost of governance.

- Present a national anti-corruption Strategy.

## *Access to Justice and Respect for Fundamental Human Rights*

One of the biggest challenges facing Nigeria is building a country that is fair to all of its citizens; a country in which all individuals feel and know that they are valued members of society with constitutionally guaranteed rights; a country that respects human dignity, promotes human development, fosters human equality and advances human freedom.

I pledge to:

- Lead a government founded on values that promote and protect fundamental human rights and freedoms. I will promote the supremacy of the Constitution and the rule of law, affirm separation of the powers of government and support an independent judiciary.

- Present a detailed strategy for protecting the fundamental rights and freedoms provided for in our Constitution. There will be emphasis on the rights of vulnerable persons including women, children and persons living with disabilities as well as access to justice and prisons reforms.

### *Insurgency and Insecurity*

I have had the opportunity to serve my country in the military up to the highest level, as a Major General and as the Commander-in-Chief of the Armed Forces. In the course of my service, I had defended the territorial integrity of Nigeria. And if called upon to do so again, I shall rise to the occasion. As a father, I feel the pain of the victims of insurgency, kidnapping and violence whether they are the widows and orphans of military, paramilitary or civilians.

I pledge to:

- Ensure that under my watch, no force, external or internal, will occupy even an inch of Nigerian soil. I will give all it takes to ensure that our girls kidnapped from Chibok are rescued and reunited with their families.

- Deliver a Marshal Plan on insurgency, terrorism, ethnic and religious violence, kidnapping, rural banditry and ensure that never again will Nigerian children be slaughtered or kidnapped at will.

- Boost the morale of our fighting forces and the generality of Nigerians by leading from the front as the Commander-in-Chief and not hide in the comfort and security of Aso Rock.

- Give especial attention to the welfare of our armed forces and all other security personnel and their families, including State-guaranteed life insurance for all officers and men as well as protecting the families of our fallen heroes.

- Ensure that acts of heroism and valour in the service to the nation are publicly recognised and celebrated.

- Establish close working relationship with governors of the states affected by insurgency, with leaders of our neighbouring countries and with leaders around the world to cooperate in combating insurgency, oil theft, piracy and criminality.

- Activate regular meetings of the National Police Council to ensure the discharge of its true constitutional roles in a transparent and accountable way.

- Fight for you, and alongside you. We will fight together to defeat terrorism. But I will be honest with you about our challenges and I will bear the responsibilities of my charge. I will not lie to you or exaggerate our triumphs. My administration will be thoroughly transparent in every step of our daily struggle and together we will win the war.

## *Management of the Economy for Shared Prosperity*

All Nigerians deserve to benefit from our collective wealth. We promise not to leave any Nigerian behind in our determination to create, expand and ensure equitable and effective allocation of economic opportunities. No matter the amount of wealth we create, it would be meaningless unless it benefits the majority of our people.

The tone of the document suggests that some of the promises may have been candidate Buhari's intentions, but most appear to have been 'doctored' by his handlers to add flavour in order to whet the electorate's appetite. This was revealed shortly when PMB was asked how he had fulfilled the 122 promises he made. He said he did not make those promises himself.

While significant landmarks have been made in a few of those promises, most remain largely unachieved or unrealistic. I will defer that discussion to a subsequent section in this chapter in order not to digress from the point I intended to make, which is how the APC leaders sold their promises, or as some commentators said, how they 'deceived' Nigerians to embracing change that is yet to be seen. That leads to a second example where soon after the APC was declared winner of the 2015 Presidential election, specifically on 25 March 2015, Asiwaju Bola Ahmed Tinubu, the APC Leader, orchestrated what he termed 'The Common-Sense Revolution' to appeal to the conscience of Nigerians. The tenets of this common-sense revolution were expressed in the following words:

**Common-Sense Revolution** speaks to the need to elect patriotic leaders that can give hope to our best aspirations as a nation and people. It speaks to how we must elect thinkers and doers to work together to bring about a beautiful revival of the national spirit and the good fortune of the people...

There can be no more fence-sitting because that fence has been torn down by the vast disparity between our current reality and our desired future... Those who hear must respond to its call because history is impatient when it has set itself in motion...

Our APC Government will use its fiscal and monetary space to jumpstart the economy... 20 billion dollars – enough to fund government for a year – shall no longer disappear as if by magic!

### Why Buhari and the APC Emerged Victorious
### in the 2015 Elections

Without any reservation, I can say that Buhari and APC won the election by destiny. Nothing explains that better than the fact that he contested three times in a row and lost; he tried to forge alliances which could not propel him to victory; he created his own party, yet he could not win any election; he went through lengthy and frustrating litigation up to the highest court in the land, yet he could not win; I could can go on and on. But when it was time for him to become president of Nigeria, God in his infinite mercies created conditions for him in the following ways:

● President Jonathan made the great mistake of not keeping his promise to his party, especially the northern gladiators, not to seek a second term of office.

● His many errors included the spread of the Boko Haram insurgency, prevalent corruption, deteriorating economy, and most importantly the split in the PDP, which led to the departure of some powerful state governors to the new APC alliance.

- The new alliance was forged between three opposition parties: the Action Congress of Nigeria (ACN) led by Bola Tinubu; the ANPP which did not have any influential leader; and the CPC led by Buhari himself. This platform in no small way provided a formidable opposition that merged the power of incumbency of the PDP.

- The defection of some PDP governors[33] and influential party members, including the former Vice President Atiku Abubakar, former Speaker of the House of Representatives Aminu Waziri Tambowal, Senator Bukola Saraki, to the APC and regardless of their own ambitions. Following the emergence of General Buhari as the APC candidate, they rallied round and supported him throughout the campaigns. All of them have significant influence in their respective states.

- For all practical purposes, public opinion, especially the influential views expressed in writings and public debates, was certainly in favour of a change, and while Jonathan and the PDP were the greatest losers, Buhari and the APC were the greatest beneficiaries. One cannot calculate the volume of newspaper editorials, columns, opinions, television discussions and social media chats, but certainly it was obvious that they were very influential in determining the outcome of the 2015 elections. As Shaka Momodu observed, 'it was the first time the social media had propelled an individual, particularly an ill-prepared, ill-equipped, and a candidate totally lacking the wherewithal to govern a modernizing economy, to power on the strength of half-truths, misinformation and outright fiction in Africa.'[34]

- The open letter written to former President Jonathan by former President Obasanjo signalled the direction of the political elite who control public opinion or influence the choice of a president.

33. Namely, Murtala Nyako of Adamawa state, Rabiu Musa Kwankwaso of Kano, Abdul Fatah Ahmed of Kwara,

34. 'Buhari: The End of Optimism', *Thisday* newspaper back page commentary, 30 December 2016.

● By far, it was the elite consensus that eventually endorsed Buhari as President. Let me briefly explain how the elite consensus works using what Shehu (2015) referred to as the four 'C' theories. In every society, there are certain people who determine the power equation and this should not be strange in Nigeria.

1. The first 'C' refers to the consciousness of the elite to protect their interest at any given moment. In the previous years when Buhari contested in 2003, 2007 and 2011, the elite did not see any way he would have served their or Nigerian interests at that time. But when it was obvious that Nigeria was almost degenerating into a crisis, the dimension of which no one could ascertain, and considering the deterioration of the economy and all aspects of life in the country, the elite felt they needed someone with Buhari's strength of character and integrity to stabilise the country. Whether they were convinced he was competent or not was really not the issue; it was like one finding oneself between the devil and the deep blue sea. Hence the consciousness that if they did not rescue the situation, the country might collapse and their own interests, perhaps including the collective national interests, would be jeopardised. This made Buhari the best candidate at that time. This was explained by former President Obasanjo when General Buhari visited him in Abeokuta in January 2015, during which he expressed open support for Buhari even though he had earlier destroyed his PDP membership card and declared that he was no longer going to be involved in partisan politics. Obasanjo, who never supported Buhari in his three previous attempts, was convinced that Buhari was the best alternative. He acknowledged that Buhari was poor in economic management and advised him to get competent people to assist him. When asked if he had no fear that Buhari would go after him on allegations of corruption during his tenure

in office, he said that given the situation in which we were, he preferred to sacrifice his freedom and go to jail for Nigeria than to exist and be better. How else can one explain this level of elite consciousness?

2. The second 'C' refers to cohesion – meaning that since the elite class is very conscious of its interests and status in society, they forge a common ground that allows them to remain cohesive. This cohesiveness is necessary regardless of their individual interests; the overall elite interest is sacrosanct and often that is explained to the people in the context of national interest. It is not important to state here what makes them cohesive, but the fact that regardless of their individual differences, they have a common ground on their strategic interests.

3. The third 'C' refers to consensus – this means that the elite have the capacity to compromise their lower interests for higher ones perceived and defined only by them and arrive at a consensus on certain issues; in the 2015 presidential election it did not matter who Buhari was or whose interest he would promote most, but keeping their differences aside, even those who could not see eye to eye supported Buhari to be president. Without mentioning names here, the reader can guess the rivalry among the elite class which had manifested at different times on different issues.

4. The fourth 'C' refers to the most important political weapon of the elite, which is their capacity and propensity for conspiracy. This was clearly demonstrated when they abandoned Jonathan and promoted Buhari overtly and covertly. To me, all these Cs are crucial in the power struggle in Nigeria and I shall refer to them again in the subsequent chapter in our analysis of the unfolding situation towards the 2019 elections.

Overall, there are several factors which were in favour of Buhari in the 2015 election but which cannot be discussed here for lack of space. In a sense, most if not all the factors that were against Jonathan turned out to favour Buhari, and to that extent we may say God chose Buhari but used Jonathan who created the conditions for Buhari to win the election. And since no condition is permanent, I shall attempt to explain whether the APC government has managed its victory well to win another election.

## Translating Electoral Victory into Governance

One of the greatest challenges Nigeria, and indeed most developing countries, face in nurturing democracy is how to make a clear distinction between party politics, winning elections and providing good governance. Ideally, once election has been won, the primary concern for the victorious is governance and politics, although as the instrument for securing power, this should be secondary. This assumption leads to the hypothesis as to whether we should first have a strong democracy before having good governance or whether it is possible to achieve good governance in the practice of democracy in Africa today.

Experience all over the continent shows that with a few exceptions, African elections and power politics have been characterised by the 'winner takes all' syndrome, where governments are formed on the basis of exclusivity of the winning political party. This is so because of the appurtenances associated with public office but most especially because of the greed of politicians. Without any attempt to be controversial, I'd prefer consolidating democracy through good governance, though it would seem like a 'chicken and egg' theory since those who should deliver the good governance are produced through certain processes that favour party or individual interests over the national interests; even in each policy or action of the government, the national interest is often said to be the overall consideration.

On the basis of this assumption, therefore, we can attempt to analyse the way and manner PMB and indeed the APC government have (mis)managed their victory so far. To do that objectively, it would be appropriate to identify a few parameters for assessing its performance. First, let's look at the agenda and performance of the government over the last three and a half years.

## Setting the Agenda

For any political party or government to succeed, it must have clarity on its objectives, mission and vision and also have the willpower and capacity to carry out its plans. How has the APC government fared in this regard?

As stated earlier, the key policy framework of the APC is its Manifesto, which has been interpreted through different channels as discussed above. Although during the campaigns most commentators did not focus much on the Manifesto but the credibility of the APC candidate, many were quick to propose soon after the declaration of the APC as the winner, what the agenda of the Buhari administration should be. Without any attempt to mention everything, I shall merely refer to a few to show that even if PMB had no ideas on what should constitute priority for the country, his vision was enriched and widened by public contributions.

The expectations from Nigerians were ambitious and even overwhelming, and this is particularly where PMB deserves sympathy. Nevertheless, it should be recalled that he was equally aware of the daunting challenges, and yet he was adamant in seeking a chance to prove his mettle. In fact, in one of his televised interactions with Nigerians a few days before the election, he was practically begging to be given a chance to prove to Nigerians that under him their lives could be transformed within a short time.

Soon after the elections, various commentators attempted to set the agenda for the Buhari administration through diffident media. Aniebu Nwamu[35] was quick to propose an inaugural speech for the President in which he attempted to highlight the priority issues that were to form the policy thrusts of the administration. These included:

- The President to reassure Nigerians that he would not 'Islamise' Nigeria;

- That he should adopt the slogan 'Do what is right' for his administration, upon which the government's action plan would depend for the next four years;

- On corruption, which is one of the main pillars of the Buhari policies, that he should declare that 'anyone who steals shall have no place on earth to hide'; and that he should declare an amnesty for corrupt persons to return looted assets failure of which shall lead to seizure and prosecution;

- That a tax regime be introduced; and Buhari should assure Nigerians that 'not a kobo will henceforth miss from the NNPC, Nigeria Customs Service, FIRS, NIMASA and others';

- That Buhari should make a policy pronouncement on how he intended to reduce the cost of governance and specifically to 'abolish gratuities and severance allowances for former presidents, governors and legislators';

- 'That jobs will be created when power supply is adequate and stable, when food imports are forsaken, and when our education system is transformed so that schools produce job creators';

- That PMB should make a policy to 'reform our politics so that money would play little role in determining who stands for election, etc'; and

35. Titled 'Covenant With The Nigerian people – Proposed Inaugural Speech', *Leadership* newspaper,24 May 2015.

● Assure the international community that he will rule by the rule of law and that agreements will be respected.

Curiously, Aniebu only succeeded in portraying the narrow mindset of Nigerians towards what is their own interests and not necessarily the national interests as he advertently or inadvertently failed to remember that security and the economy were the other pillars of the tripod of the Buhari agenda.

Writing in the *Leadership* newspaper of 3 April 2015, Adesuwa Tsan[36] stated that 'now that another administration is set to take over, it is pertinent to note that if it fails to do better than the Jonathan-led administration, as the adage goes, 'the broom that was used to beat the first wife is waiting to be used on the new wife'. Meaning, PMB has to tackle these issues headlong if he seeks to retain the goodwill of Nigerians that swept him to victory at the polls.' She then recalled that corruption was the biggest stain on the Jonathan administration and that Buhari should make the fight against corruption his priority because he promised during one of his interviews with CNN's Christiane Amanpour 'that he would fight corruption in Nigeria at every level'.

Tsan also observed that over 67 per cent of Nigerians live below the poverty line, and identified (consistently with the Buhari campaign agenda) the need to fix the economy; in particular to adopt policies and immediate measures to address the falling oil prices, declining value of the naira, introducing meaningful oil sector reforms, including the passage and implementation of the Petroleum Industry Bill (PIB) in to law; and diversifying the economy.

On security, Tsan observed that business activities had suffered unquantifiably; for example, 'in Kano, which has suffered from Boko Haram attacks, business activities dropped by 80 per cent in the past three years'. She then identified the fight against Boko Haram, and in particular the release of the Chibok girls kidnapped by the insurgents, as a priority for the President.

36.'Challenges Ahead of Buhari's Administration'.

Eniola Bello[37] identified five key areas to serve as the vehicles of change and these are:

1. Eliminating fuel queues, and ending subsidy. He noted that subsidy payments, which result in fuel shortages and long queues at filling stations, rose from N250 billion per annum under the presidency of Olusegun Obasanjo to over N300 billion under Umar Yar'Adua, and N1.2 trillion under Goodluck Jonathan. Removing subsidy would be consistent with Buhari's campaign agenda, but more than six months into the administration Nigeria was still having fuel shortages and long queues at filling stations due to delay in reconciling and payment of the N413 billion subsidy claims to marketers.

2. The second priority agenda, according to Eniola, was for Buhari to immediately and drastically address the epileptic power situation as promised during the campaigns. This remains a challenge.

3. Dealing with the Boko Haram headlong and in a professional manner.

4. Eliminating the psychic of business as usual – fighting corruption transparently.

5. Institutionalising due process in the running of government.

Other commentators, including Mathew Page of the US Council on Foreign Relations,[38] attempted to set the agenda for the Buhari administration to (1) 'carefully clean house' – that is, fight corruption thoroughly; (2) 'pare down the parastatals' – that is, down size the bureaucracy and reduce cost; (3) 'tame the white elephants' – meaning to revive the two 'white elephant' projects – namely domestic oil refineries and the steel mills; (4) 'rein in sub national

37. Eniola Bello, 'The Sameness of Change', *Thisday* newspaper, 1 December 2015.
38. '5 things that the President of Nigeria can do to get his country back on track', accessed online through Google search on 2 November 2015.

debt' – that is, to put public finances in order; and (5) 'legislate for the long run' – meaning – 'the best way to protect his legacy is to partner with the National Assembly to enact legislation enshrining key reforms'.

All these proposals were appropriate and timely. While President Buhari touched on virtually all of these directly or indirectly, he set the tone for his administration's policies in his Inaugural Address, perhaps in a different tune and style.

## President Buhari's Inaugural Speech – Setting the Agenda

As provided in the Constitution and as is customary in Nigeria, President Muhammadu Buhari delivered his Inaugural Speech to an 'august audience' and excited the population in the Eagle Square in Abuja, shortly after taking the oath of office on 29 May 2015. While the acceptance speech he delivered on 1 April 2015 laid the foundation of his administration's policy thrusts, the Inaugural Address went beyond that in terms of specific actions to be taken to confront the mountain of problems inherited by his administration.

I paraphrase what he stated in his acceptance speech for the records as follows:

> My team and I shall faithfully serve you. There shall no longer be a ruling party again: APC will be your governing party. We shall faithfully serve you. We shall never rule over the people as if they were subservient to government.
>
> Democracy and the rule of law will be re-established in the land.
>
> We must forget our old battles and past grievances—and learn to forge ahead. I assure you that our government is one that will listen to and embrace all.
>
> There shall be no bias against or favouritism for any Nigerian based on ethnicity, religion, region, gender or social status. I

pledge myself and the government to the rule of law, in which none shall be so above the law that they are not subject to its dictates, and none shall be so below it that they are not availed of its protection

You are all my people and I shall treat everyone of you as my own. I shall work for those who voted for me as well as those who voted against me and even for those who did not vote at all. We all live under one name as one nation: we are all Nigerians.

If I had judged myself incapable of governing, I would never have sought to impose myself on it. I have served in various capacities and have always put in my best.

This will not be a government democratic only in form. It will be a government democratic in substance and in how it interacts with its own people.

But I assure you that Boko Haram will soon know the strength of our collective will and commitment to rid this nation of terror, and bring back peace and normalcy to all the affected areas. We shall spare no effort until we defeat terrorism.

Furthermore, we shall strongly battle another form of evil that is even worse than terrorism—the evil of corruption. Corruption attacks and seeks to destroy our national institutions and character. By misdirecting into selfish hands funds intended for the public purpose, corruption distorts the economy and worsens income inequality. It creates a class of unjustly-enriched people.

But we shall never take you for granted; so, be rest assured that our errors will be those of compassion and commitment not of wilful neglect and indifference.

We shall correct that which does not work and improve that which does. We shall not stop, stand or idle. We shall, if necessary, crawl, walk and run to do the job you have elected us to do.

A critical analysis of this speech suggests that he or his handlers were acutely aware of the major accusations and campaign of calumny orchestrated by the PDP against him during the electioneering campaigns and he made an effort to allay the fears of Nigerians on some of those issues. It is unnecessary to disgrace Buhari in order to ascertain whether he has lived up to his words. It is a matter of perception, but I will try to assemble public opinions and attempt to better understand how the administration has (mis)managed its victory in the subsequent sections of this chapter.

Here are some key issues that constitute the building blocks for an effective policy framework in the speech. First and foremost, he made it clear from the outset that 'I belong to everybody and I belong to nobody'. This singular statement was a strong message of his independence in thought and action and it sent shivers down the spines of those who wanted to take advantage of his person to do anything to promote their own self-interest and personal aggrandisement. Unfortunately, this is not the case, as aggregated public opinion suggests that his administration has been highjacked by a 'cabal' who throw a clog in the wheel of the administration, thereby making progress either very slow or completely retarded. The wife of the President, Aisha Buhari, has had course to publicly express her dismay and disgust at how this small group of people have caged the President and are running the government in the way they like.

When declaring open a Women's Forum on 'Project 4+4' to promote the candidacy of her husband at the National Women Development Centre in Abuja, on 4 December 2018, Mrs Buhari had cause to burst into anger that '15 million Nigerians voted her husband into office with the hope of improving their lives, but the government has been taken over by only two people who have not allowed the president to fulfil his promise to Nigerians. Unfortunately, the men who should act like men and stop those people are the ones licking their shoes to curry patronage and favours.'

It is this perception of not being in control that made Faroog

Kperogi[39] lose confidence in President Buhari as 'not competent to govern any country'. Kperogi recounted the several times he defended Buhari, including how when some people described him as 'clueless', he said Buhari 'wasn't 'clueless' but was suffering from age-induced memory lapses, colloquially called 'senior moments' in America'. When asked what was the way forward, in view of the call by some people that Buhari should resign because he had failed, Kperogi remarked:

> If Buhari resigns, that would be wonderful. It is obvious by now that he is superintending the most unprepared government in Nigeria's history. He has absolutely no business being president. But should Buhari stay on in power in spite of his proven incompetence and cluelessness, we have no option but to wait until his tenure expires. All we can do is put his feet to the fire and hope that he would get a clue and do – or get the right people to help him do – the right thing.

The second important issue in President Buhari's inaugural speech was the assurance of cooperation with the international community in combating transnational organised crime. He stated inter alia: 'I also wish to assure the wider international community of our readiness to cooperate and help to combat threats of cross-border terrorism, sea piracy, refugees and boat people, financial crime, cyber crime, climate change, the spread of communicable diseases and other challenges of the 21st century'.

In setting out his agenda for the country, President Buhari stated that the most immediate was Boko Haram's insurgency:

> Progress has been made in recent weeks by our security forces but victory cannot be achieved by basing the Command and Control Centre in Abuja. The command centre will be relocated to

---

39. Associate Professor at the Kennesaw State University, Georgia, United States, and 'former ardent supporter of President Muhammadu Buhari', in an interview with Bayo Akinloye in *Punch*, 29 January 2017.

Maiduguri and remain until Boko Haram is completely subdued. But we cannot claim to have defeated Boko Haram without rescuing the Chibok girls and all other innocent persons held hostage by insurgents.

This government will do all it can to rescue them alive. Boko Haram is a typical example of small fires causing large fires. An eccentric and unorthodox preacher with a tiny following was given posthumous fame and a following by his extrajudicial murder at the hands of the police. Since then through official bungling, negligence, complacency or collusion Boko Haram became a terrifying force taking tens of thousands of lives and capturing several towns and villages covering swathes of Nigerian sovereign territory.

Boko Haram is a mindless, godless group who are as far away from Islam as one can think of. At the end of the hostilities when the group is subdued the Government intends to commission a sociological study to determine its origins, remote and immediate causes of the movement, its sponsors, the international connexions to ensure that measures are taken to prevent a recurrence of this evil. For now the Armed Forces will be fully charged with prosecuting the fight against Boko Haram. We shall overhaul the rules of engagement to avoid human rights violations in operations. We shall improve operational and legal mechanisms so that disciplinary steps are taken against proven human right violations by the Armed Forces.

Boko Haram is not only the security issue bedevilling our country. The spate of kidnappings, armed robberies, herdsmen/ farmers clashes, cattle rustlings all help to add to the general air of insecurity in our land. We are going to erect and maintain an efficient, disciplined people – friendly and well – compensated security forces within an over – all security architecture.

The inaugural speech delved extensively on security problems and said little or nothing about the economy. It was predicted by Obasanjo that Buhari's weakness would be in the area of managing the economy.

Against this backdrop, all the policy documents referred to above – the APC Manifesto, Tinubu's 'Commonsense Revolution', Buhari's 'Covenant with Nigerians', as well as his acceptance and inaugural speeches – form the basis for evaluating the policy direction and performance of the Buhari government over the years.

It is important to mention that as a result of greater awareness, civil society organisations have over the years become active in monitoring the performance of the government. In its report titled 'Nigeria: The Promise and Practice of Change – Citizens' Perception and assessment of Buhari's Administration in the last one Year', the Centre for Democracy and Development under what it called 'Buharimeter',[40] undertook 'a multi-pronged' assessment of the Buhari administration based on an aggregated promises that were made by PMB and the APC. It revealed that the 'change agenda of President Buhari made two hundred and twenty-two promises to Nigerians'.

My assessment is based on public opinions expressed in different media, including my personal interviews conducted during the course of writing this book. The results of the Buharimeter will be quoted to buttress my own assessments in the different policy areas of the Buhari administration. The issues are too many and in order to minimise the risk of bias and emotions, I will focus on the key policy areas to enable the reader see where real progress has been made; where and how and also what could have been done better.

## Security

Based on the president's personal experience and strength of character, security is the main concern of the Buhari administration.

40. The Buharimeter is an online aggregation of all promises attributed to President Buhari during his campaign. It is a platform that recorded promises achieved; those in progress and those not achieved. It draws from extensive reports in news media and online. The assessment was conducted through a questionnaire administered in all the states of the federation to gauge citizen's perception of the performance of the government.

This is understandable and commendable because of the security challenges, especially the Boko Haram insurgency that has devastated the northern parts of Nigeria. Without repeating the President's pronouncements on how to deal with Boko Haram and other security challenges, the fight against Boko Haram is where PMB has made the highest mark on the governance of Nigeria since assuming office in 2015.

Two years into the Buhari administration, remarkable successes were recorded with regard to fighting Boko Haram. For example, it may be recalled that prior to the inception of this administration, about 14 out 24 local government areas in Borno State were under the control of Boko Haram. Today, we are told that no territory is occupied by the insurgents. The Nigerian Security Tracker, a portal of the US Council on Foreign Relations, reported in its violence mapping report on Nigeria a decline in Boko Haram-related deaths from 767 in May 2015 when the Buhari administration came to power, to 250 deaths in December 2016. It also reported that Boko Haram's capacity had declined and its impact reduced from 22 attacks per month in 2015 to 9 per month in 2016. Within the same period, 21 of the abducted Chibok girls were released in October 2016; with another (Rakiya Abubakar) rescued by Nigerian security/ armed forces. At the end of 2016, Sambisa forest was reportedly 'liberated' and the Boko Haram flag was dismantled.

Our quest for solutions must begin with an honest and objective appraisal of where we are coming from, where we are and where we wish to be with regard to relative security. While commending the efforts of the government and the gallant efforts of the military in fighting this insurgency in spite of the obvious difficulties, one should address the following issues to provide a balanced perspective on security management under the Buhari administration.

First, we must acknowledge that fighting insurgency is not an easy task and no one should assume that it would be over within the shortest anticipated time. At the same time, the expectation that PMB would deal with the problem within a short time is not misplaced, because that was the assurance he and his party gave to Nigerians. When Jonathan explained the difficulties, most people felt he was just incompetent; when he explained that the USA and its allies refused to sell arms to Nigeria, most people said he was corrupt; when he said fighting insurgency takes time and our troops needed more training and equipment to deal with the problem, most people felt he was just 'clueless'. I could go on and on comparing the situation then and now, but in the end the reality is that the challenges are enormous and even the efforts by the Buhari administration appear to be insufficient.

Soon after his swearing in to office, PMB under took official visits to the neighbouring countries, Niger, Chad, Cameroun and Benin, which does not share a border with the Boko Haram space except for Benin's involvement in security management in the Lake Chad Basin. For the first time, PMB made a 2-day visit to nearby Niamey, something no Nigerian leader has done in history. He also extended his diplomatic shuttle to garner the support of world powers, including visits to the UK and USA and being invited specifically to discuss his needs with the G-7 Countries during their Summit in Germany in his less than three months of assumption of office.[41] No leader had so received this kind of goodwill. The important issues to note are these:

1. Although details of government policies and official exchanges are often not made public, it is still curious to ask what were the outcomes of all these diplomatic contacts and negotiations. Has PMB been able to break the jinx on an arms embargo? If so, what amount of arms have been sold or given to Nigeria to

41. In response to public criticisms on the lack of measurable outcomes of these foreign visits by PMB, Babatunde Fashola, Minister of Power, Works and Housing, in an article titled 'PMB's Foreign Trips – My Takeaway' published in *Thisday* on 18 April 2016, tried to placard the benefits of such foreign tours but he did not mention a single measurable outcome in terms of hardware support provided to Nigeria in the fight against terror.

fight the insurgency? How long would it still take to train the military on counter-insurgency? Apart from reports attributed to foreign government officials that they were supporting Nigeria with intelligence, what other support has be given to Nigeria since the APC Government took office? The answers to these questions should form the basis for assessing achievements in the war against terror.

2. President Buhari, on assuming office, fulfilled his promise to move the operational command headquarters of the army to Maiduguri. This was the right decision, and for the first time the Chief of Army Staff demonstrated exemplary and courageous leadership by leading the troops in the war front and some successes were recorded. Over time, however, it would seem that this has not been sustained as recent attacks on the military, in particular by insurgents, seem to have escalated with a lot of casualties. For the first time, the Nigerian Army 157 Task Force Battalion located in Metele, Borno State, was swamped and several soldiers, including their commanding officer (Lt. Col. Sakaba) were killed by Boko Haram fighters.[42] Earlier, Lt. Col. Muhammad Abu Ali, one of the unit commanders of the Nigerian Army whose legendary courage and professionalism led to the reclaim of several territories hitherto held by Boko Haram, was killed in a resurgence of Boko Haram's attacks. The patterns of the attacks are far from proof of incompetence on the part of the military; rather the evidence suggests that the military are ill-equipped, less motivated and less prepared to confront the

---

42. The Nigerian Army refuted the story that hundreds of soldiers were killed in the Metele attacks and stated that only 23 soldiers were killed. However, a surviving soldier told *Punch* (reported on 10 December 2018), that the Theatre Commander exposed the soldiers to the attack because the Insurgents used 15 vehicles they had earlier seized from the army to attack them, leading to 200 soldiers being killed in the attack. He added that the video that was circulated by the army purported to be the Metele attack was false; rather it was that of an earlier attack in Jeli. The soldier attributed the attacks to the wrong location of the base, faulty Armed Personnel Carriers, APCs, which cannot run for 10-15 minutes, old Anti-Aircraft Artillery, and absence of aerial support from the Nigerian Air Force; and that soldiers on the war front were not paid sufficient cash ration allowances and were being owed several months' arrears, etc.

insurgents. Part of the challenge in the Boko Haram war under PMB has been attributed to corruption too. *Defense and Foreign Affairs* revealed in its Special Analysis released on 28 December 2018 and published by the International Strategic Studies Association (ISSA), a Washington-based non-governmental organisation, that it blames corruption in the higher echelons of the military for the faltering war against Boko Haram in Nigeria. As a result, according to the report, the insurgents grow stronger while the government forces get weaker and more beset by morale decline: 'The conflict will almost certainly prove the undoing of the present government of President Muhammadu Buhari at the February 16, 2019 presidential elections.'[43] With government claiming a lot of savings and recovery of stolen funds and foreign assistance, one would think that there are more resources to deal with the problem than ever before; or is there more to it that one can understand?

3. Following significant successes in the war against Boko Haram, the government said Boko Haram had been 'degraded, incapacitated or technically defeated'. This was all in a bid to shore up praise while Nigerians are still being killed by Boko Haram. Would it then be fair to say that the number of killings has reduced and therefore the few lives being lost are inconsequential? The efforts being done by the government must be commended, but the claim of Boko Haram's defeat is a farce and merely political propaganda to shore up electoral sympathy. This is evident when the President said in his inaugural address on 29 May 2015, 'We cannot claim to have defeated Boko Haram without rescuing the Chibok girls and all other innocent persons held hostage by the insurgents'. While the government succeeded in rescuing some of the Chibok girls with the help of the international community, especially the Red Cross, that

43. Reported in *Thisday*, 30 December 2018, pp. 1, 8.

progress suffered a setback with the kidnapping of another set of girls at Government Girls College, Dapchi, in Yobe. All the girls except Leah Sharihu have been rescued alive. The remaining girl in Boko Haram captivity, the remaining Chibok girls and all other persons kidnapped by Boko Haram remain a major concern.

4. The Nigerian Army claimed to have captured Sambisa forest (the operational base of Boko Haram) and organised a shooting exercise there some time in 2017 to convince the public that Boko Haram has been defeated. But the same Boko Haram is still attacking Internally Displaced Persons' (IDP) camps, seizing their food, killing them and also killing soldiers. The plausible explanation could be that the war is not being fought with any strategy. The military have only succeeded in dispersing the terrorists to unknown locations, only to resurface after attacking and seizing weapons from the same military and using the same weapons to fight the military. Common sense should suggest that when you target the enemy and he runs away, that does not mean he has been defeated. What is perhaps lacking is a definitive and sustainable combat strategy with a specific order of battle that would be subjected to periodic review, monitoring and evaluation. Although the military would claim to have a strategy for fighting Boko Haram, that strategy has not worked efficiently and that is why the war has been prolonged and not simply because it is an unconventional war which takes a long time.

5. In a public statement released by former President Obasanjo titled 'Points for Concern and Action' dated 18 January 2019, and specifically on Boko Haram and the security of Nigeria, he cautioned:

The security situation has deteriorated with kidnapping everywhere and Boko Haram more in action, and nobody should deceive Nigerians about this. With the teaming up of Boko Haram and Islamic State's West Africa Province (ISWAP), Boko Haram is stronger today militarily than they have ever been. Boko Haram has also been empowered by the Nigerian government through payment of ransom of millions of dollars which each administration disingenuously always denies. With ISIS being liquidated in Iraq and Syria, Africa is now their port of concentration. Soon, they may take over Libya which, with substantial resources, is almost a totally failed state. When that happens, all African countries north of the Congo River will be unsafe, with serious security problems. The struggle must be for all West African, Central African, North African and most East African States. Nigeria has to play a vanguard role in this struggle as we have much to lose. This administration has reached the end of its wit even in handling all security issues, but particularly Boko Haram issue, partly due to misuse of security apparatus and poor equipment, deployment, coordination and cooperation.

6.  Overall, more than ten years into the fight against Boko Haram, and despite the modest successes recorded, it seems that we are applying Panadol to cure cancer, which may turn out to make the ailment more cancerous and difficult to cure. In a statement released by the Presidency to the media on 'what the Buhari administration has achieved in two years' and published by *Premium Times* on 30 May 2017, the government flaunted the 'establishment of civil authority in the areas affected by the Boko Haram insurgency' as the most important achievement in the war against terror. Just within the week of 5 December 2018, while giving a report on an oversight visit, the Chairman

of the House of Representatives Committee on Humanitarian Services (Sani Mohammed Zoro), in a video that went viral, alleged that what is said about defeating Boko Haram is a far cry from the truth, as Boko Haram even attacked an IDP camp within Maiduguri metropolis during the visit of the Committee to Borno State. He further said that the claim of recovering some local government areas from the terror group is exaggerated, because none of those local government areas has witnessed the return of the inhabitants, except in Bama (the second major city in Borno State after Maiduguri the capital), where the 50 people who returned to the town were still struggling with shortage of everything humanitarian – shelter, food, medical services, etc. Jokingly, Buba Galadima, one of the critics of PMB, replied that those who claim Boko Haram has been defeated should take their mothers to any of the local government areas in Borno State where the insurgents are still in occupation.

To conclude on Boko Haram, a lot has been done by the Buhari administration to deal with the problem. There is no doubt that there is relative peace in most parts of the country, but the expectations of Nigerians with respect to security seem not to have been met, not because of high expectations but because of the responses and the way the government has handled the various security issues. In any case, it was for the enormity of the problems that Nigerians placed their confidence in PMB to 'secure and manage the country efficiently', as he promised during his campaigns.

However, based on the expectations that Buhari's military background, strength of character and goodwill would stop Boko Haram, it seems there is a lot more to be done. Perhaps it is important to add that if the approach was different, namely in terms of adequately equipping the military and motivating them, the story would have been different. The only question which I may not have the answer is whether anything will change in the remaining six months of this administration or when it is given another chance of four years. That is the choice Nigerians have to make based on their assessment of the efforts as discussed above.

Largely as a result of the activities of Boko Haram, Nigeria has been rated four times in a row since 2015 as the third most terrorized country in the world by Global Terrorism Index. But Boko Haram is not the only security challenge that Nigeria is facing. And as the government put a premium on dealing with the insurgency, other equally disturbing security threats have emerged. The Buhari administration's handling of the Niger Delta insurgency has so far been commendable. However, other pseudo-insurgencies, such as the farmers/herdsmen clashes, also have serious repercussions on national security and stability. Although the farmers/herders conflict is not new, the Buhari administration's response to it has given cause for concern as many commentators believe it has not been properly handled. For example, when such skirmishes broke out in Benue and Plateau, government was slow if not lackadaisical in responding, thus giving room for cynicism. It was speculated in some quarters that since Buhari is a Fulani man and since the herders are suspected to be mostly Fulani, he may have kept mute in order not to hurt his own ethnic group. There is no hard evidence to prove this assertion, but anything that gives room for scepticism is bound to generate concern, if not abhorrence. Even though the evidence suggests that the government is overwhelmed by these crises, it would extend the scepticism too far to insinuate that the President tolerates the taking of innocent lives. Nevertheless, it is his inability to end the killings that led people to believe that he has not shown himself to be President for all, as promised in his inaugural address.

In a press release on 30 May 2017, the Presidency enumerated the many military operations[44] across the country as a mark of its achievements in securing the country. Military presence in support of civil action is allowed by the Constitution, but it should not replace it. During the three and half years of the Buhari administration, the involvement of the military in civil security has increased; the military were involved in providing civil security in 32 out of the 36 six states in Nigeria. This is not a mark of stability nor of military capability. In every country, just as is supposed to be the case in Nigeria, the military should be the last line of defence after other civil security forces like the police, civil defence, security and intelligence agencies. The spread of military operations could be a sign of failure to maintain law and order and overall national security.

Based on the experience of the past administration, when millions of naira were siphoned from the treasury under the garb of fighting the insurgency, accountability is one of the concerns regarding military operations. Consequently, in a Freedom of

44. Including the deployment by the NSCDC of 5,000 personnel to the North-East to protect the Internally Displaced Persons' camps and re-occupy the reclaimed towns and villages; Transfer of 2 Nos. AW 101 Helicopter from the Presidential Air Fleet to the Nigerian Air Force, for deployment in support of Operation LAFIYA DOLE in the North East. Also transferred to the NAF: 3 EC-135 and 3 Dauphin helicopters, from the Nigerian National Petroleum Corporation (NNPC); Establishment of a Naval Outpost in the Lake Chad Basin; Establishment of the 8 Task Force Division in Monguno to further strengthen military presence in the North East; Successful Military Operations across the country:

- Operation Harbin Kunama in Dansadau Forest, Zamfara aimed at flushing out armed bandits and cattle rustlers.
- Operation Safe Haven to curtail the incessant clashes between Fulani herdsmen and farmers in the North Central (Plateau, Nasarawa, and Benue states).
- Exercise Crocodile Smile to curtail the menace of militant activities in the Niger Delta
- Exercise Obangame, a multinational operation aimed at securing and protecting the Gulf of Guinea.
- Operation Awatse, a joint operation between the Military and the Police, in South West Nigeria, to flush out militants and pipeline vandals
- Operation Python Dance in the South East to tackle kidnappers and militant elements.

Information Request[45] sent to Tukur Buratai, Chief of Army Staff, three civil society groups, namely the Socio-Economic Rights and Accountability Project (SERAP), Enough is Enough (EiE), and BudgIT alleged that 'several billions of naira allocated to the military to defend the country and protect its people have neither contributed to improving the ability of Nigerian soldiers to fight Boko Haram and other armed groups nor provided the much needed security especially for Nigerians in the North-east of the country'. The CSOs demanded 'information on the 2015, 2016 and 2017 budget implementation reports of the Nigerian Army, including amounts released (financial implications) and expended in the fiscal years for the various operations carried out by the Army'.[46]

The 'Buharimeter' catalogued 22 distinct promises that PMB made on security and gauged the perception of Nigerians on the actions his administration had taken to fulfil those promises. Their 'survey shows that the administration received an average rating: 16.5 and 21.2 per cent of the respondents rate the government's performance in the area of security as 'very good' and 'good', respectively; 19.8 and 16.5 per cent of the respondents assess the government's performance as 'very bad' and 'bad', respectively; while 24 per cent of the respondents consider the government's performance as 'fair'.[47]

45. By virtue of Section 4(a) of the FOI Act, when a person makes a request for information from a public official, institution or agency, the public official, institution or agency to whom the application is directed is under a binding legal obligation to provide the applicant with the information requested for, except as otherwise provided by the Act, within 7 days after the application is received.

46. Specially mentioned are 'Operation Lafiya Dole, Operation Safe Haven, Operation Python Dance, Operation RuwanWuta, Operation Delta Safe, Operation Mesa, Operation Harbin Kunama, Operation Awatse, Operation TseraTeku and Operation Crocodile Smile.' It gladdening to note that the Chief of Army Staff responded to the FOI request, though the content of his reply was not made public.

47. CDD (2016) 'Nigeria: The Promise and Practice of Change – Citizen's Perception and Assessment of Buhari's Administration in the Last One Year', P.10. www.buharimeter.ng accessed 31 May 2016.

Again, these are the issues that should be of concern to the electorate and which may inform their choices in the forthcoming elections. And 'if as they say, the morning shows the day, it is not too early to ask for the evidence of change we voted for. We want to see it. We want to feel it. We want to touch it. We are beginning to get tired of waiting.'[48]

## Anti-Corruption

While the Buhari administration can be rated highest in the area of security, in particular the war against terror, the fight against corruption is acclaimed to be the strongest pillar of the government. Corruption is not peculiar to Nigeria, but it remains one obstacle, if not the greatest, to the development of that country. Corruption is insidious in any society and its impact is so complex that when you begin to address the impact in one area, you quickly realise that other areas have degenerated if not managed well. Before and after assuming office, hardly would President Buhari complete a public statement without recalling how corruption had undermined progress. His popular saying 'if we do not kill corruption, corruption will kill Nigeria' has become a cliché.

Combating corruption was by far the selling point in PMB's governance agenda. A majority of Nigerians believed that if there was anybody who could deal with the problem of corruption, that person could be only second to PMB. But let me not be too emotional here, because the perception was more about his strength of character and moral rectitude than his capacity to really fight corruption. Ultimately, there are accumulated, widespread and respected views that the fight against corruption under Buhari has been characterised by more noise than results – simply stated, too much sizzle with too little steak!

In assessing the anti-corruption policy of the Buhari

48. Bello,'The Sameness of Change', p. 4.

administration, opinions are sharply divided. That is understandable, because every individual has his or her own prejudices, biases or even stereotypes. It is also not unusual because as it may be recalled, we discussed how despite the spate of criticism of Jonathan and the PDP Government in 2015, there were still strong opinions in his favour, which persuasively but unsuccessfully defended the allegations of corruption within his government. It is not surprising that the same is happening now, with divergent views competing to counteract each other. Perhaps the difference lay in the fact that in 2015 we had only one chapter, that of Jonathan and the PDP, to analyse, while in 2019 we have two, including that of Buhari and the APC to compare. I must confess that I have my own prejudices and biases, but in my attempt to analyse what has worked and what has not and what could have been or can be done better, I have tried beyond reasonable doubt to insulate myself from sentiments that cannot be supported by empirical evidence. The rest I leave it to the reader to discern.

Before proceeding in this section to review the Buhari anti-corruption policy, I must reiterate that corruption is sometimes misunderstood, leading to a wrong approach in dealing with it. For example, while former President Jonathan misunderstood the concept of corruption by asserting that stealing is not corruption, PMB seems not to see the definition of corruption beyond stealing or embezzlement of public funds. Both misperceptions could lead to wrong approaches and therefore make the fight against corruption counterproductive or fruitless. Therefore to objectively discuss the anti-corruption efforts, it would be helpful to do so on the basis of clear parameters and that is what I will try to do here.

The Buhari administration did not demonstrate readiness for governance when it assumed office as many policy decisions were delayed or not taken at all. In the anti-corruption area, which most people thought was going to be the area where the government would hit the ground running, it took the government over 20 months to release a Strategy.[49] Even after the approval of the Strategy, the anti-corruption agencies were least prepared for a robust fight and instead adopted the same old methods. In order to be as objective and measurable as possible, I shall attempt to briefly review the anti-corruption efforts of the Buhari administration based on the specific objectives of the National Anti-Corruption Strategy (NACS).

The broad objective of NACS is to remove impediments to accountability in governance institutions, strengthen mechanisms and platforms by which citizens can hold public officers to account and strengthen the capacity of anti-corruption and law enforcement institutions for increased deterrence and enforcement of anti-corruption measures. This will further foster national cohesion through a re-orientation of the value system and increased adherence to ethical standards at all levels of governance and the business environment, while reforming public management and performance systems for improved service delivery.[50]

The NACS has five specific objectives:

1. **To promote an improved legal, policy, and regulatory environment for the fight against corruption.**

This objective is to be achieved in four years and the scope of the NACS is 2017-2020, beyond the first term of the Buhari administration. Some notable actions have been taken though belatedly, including the forwarding of some bills to the NASS. Overall, strengthening the legal framework is essential, but comparatively, the Buhari administration could be rated below average. For example, soon after assumption of office, the Obasanjo

49. When he received a delegation of the FCT community, who paid him a Christmas visit on 25 December 2018, PMB said his administration is slow in fighting corruption because the system is slow. He was quoted as saying 'I am going by this system and I hope we will make it… I will keep on trying to do my best for this county and get back what belongs to the country.'
50. Section 3 of the National Anti-Corruption Strategy.

administration left no one in doubt that it was going to fight corruption head-on and it went further within one year to enact the Independent Corrupt Practices and Other Related Offences (ICPC) Act (2000), despite the challenges it encountered in the NASS. It further enacted the Economic and Financial Crimes Commission (EFCC) Act (2004). In more than three and half years, the Buhari administration could not pass any institutional legislation apart from the Mutual Legal Assistance (MLA) Act passed and signed in 2018, despite the urgent need to amend and improve on a number of pieces of corruption-related legislation. The Buhari administration has wasted much time on blaming the past PDP administration, and yet it is only relying on the institutional structures created by the past administrations to fight corruption. How then can you expect a change or different results when you keep doing the same thing over again?

2. **To encourage and improve the socio-cultural and political environment for transparency, accountability and integrity.**

This is a noble objective, as it seeks to entrench probity through leadership by example. President Buhari has demonstrated that he is what he was known to be in terms of his incorruptibility and integrity. The problem, however, is that his approach may not adequately address a serious problem in a serious manner. For example, he believes his 'body language' can make the corrupt change their habits.[51] Unfortunately, not everybody understands body language, especially those with vested interests. Nevertheless, a number of preventive measures have been put in place, including the following:

**The Presidential Initiative on Continuous Audit (PICA):** This was set to strengthen controls over government finances through a

51. Corruption is a rational choice activity; perpetrators take advantage of situational opportunities and the absence of a credible deterrence.

continuous internal audit process across all Ministries, Departments and Agencies (MDAs), particularly in respect of payroll. Through the activities of PICA, more than 50,000 erroneous payroll entries have been identified, with payroll savings of N198 billion achieved in 2016. This could be true, but there are no measurable criteria to ascertain this. For example, it is not clear how this figure was arrived at. Who are the ghost workers whose names are not disclosed, and why are none of them investigated and punished? It is however possible to justify that most of the MDAs have been enrolled in the Federal Government's Payroll Platform – the 'Integrated Personnel Payroll Information System', which would minimise payroll fraud and other malpractice.

**Budget Reforms:** the government reported a number of preventive measures including the preparation of the budget in line with International Public Sector Accounting Standards. This is work in progress but there is no empirical data to show the impact.

### Enforcement of the Treasury Single Account (TSA)

Treasury Single Account is a unified structure of Government Bank accounts that gives a timely consolidated view of government cash resources, facilitates budget execution, cash planning and management and minimises the cost of borrowing. The TSA structure is centralised (that is, using one account for all budgetary transactions for both receipts and payments) under the purview of the Accountant General of the Federation. Government approved the implementation of TSA with effect from the 2012 fiscal year, but its effective enforcement commenced in September 2015 as one of the anti-corruption measures of the Buhari administration in public finance management.

According to government statements, its implementation has led to significant savings of public finance, which could have been stolen or wasted through various leakages.[52] The purpose of the TSA is to centralise government accounts, and therefore inflows into it should not be considered as savings. Overall, good as the policy is, there are still weaknesses that need to be addressed to make it more effective.

While appreciating the anti-corruption aspect of the TSA, one obvious economic criticism of it is that 'you don't set your house ablaze because there's a rat in the house… We can rid the system of corruption and realize all the benefits of TSA but still not starve the economy of the necessary liquidity… We don't have to return to the past of having every penny of government largely redundant in [a] central bank. For an economy desperately in need of stimulation, pilling up idle cash at the CBN is not sound economics'[53]

## Implementation of the Government Integrated Financial Management Information System (GIFMIS) and Internal Personnel Payroll Information Systems (IPPIS)

GIFMIS is an IT-based system for budget management and accounting that is being implemented by the Federal Government of Nigeria for the improvement of public expenditure. It has also been put in place to manage the processes of accountability and transparency across ministries and agencies. GIFMIS has a symbiotic relationship with IPPIS, to help plan financial resources more efficiently and effectively. Both programmes are under the supervision of the Accountant General of the Federation, who uses the systems to ascertain the number of employees that government has and what their remuneration is. As a matter of fact, both programmes are supposed to track and check the incidence of ghost workers in the system. However, while most government ministries and agencies have been linked to GIFMIS and IPPIS, some are yet

52. As at 10 February 2017, a total sum of N5.244 trillion had flowed into the TSA.
53. Soludo, 'Can a New Buharinomics Save Nigeria?', pp. 6-7.

to do so, including the Ministries of Defence and Education, who are alleged to have refused to be integrated in a grid that regulates the number of employees in their ministries. The former Minister of Finance, Dr Ngozi Okonjo-Iweala, under whose supervision these measures were introduced, was reported to have said that the Federal Ministry of Finance in 2013 eliminated 46,000 ghost workers and saved N119 billion as a result of partial implementation of the IPPIS. She added that the IPPIS and the GIFMIS were huge successes as they have enhanced the efficiency of personnel cost, planning, budgeting, and improving the acquisition, utilisation and conservation of public financial resources.

Despite these strategies deployed by the Nigerian Government to ensure efficient and effective public finance management, the key indicators of a well-functioning management of public finance in the country, such as effective coordination and timely reports, are lacking. Many of the institutions and legal frameworks lack the political will to instil discipline and adhere to laid down rules and regulations. The major policy weaknesses are that at the federal and state levels, the internal control systems are very weak; audit procedures and accountability are ineffective due to political interference.

The APC/Buhari promised to constitute a Public Procurement Council as provided by the Public Procurement Act in order to take responsibility for enforcing due process in contract awards so that the Federal Executive Council (FEC) would concentrate on policy issues. This promise has not been fulfilled as the FEC still approves contracts as obtained during the PDP era.

A major source of mismanagement is the operation of joint accounts by state governments. This provides avenues for abuse, and there have been complaints about how some governors misappropriated public funds through this process. The constitution was amended in 2017, giving autonomy to State Houses of Assembly, the judiciary in the states and Local Government Councils, but this has not been enforced due to the vested interests of the state governors. It is a travesty that the State Assemblies could not even invoke a law to give themselves autonomy and they remain at the mercy of the state governors, who often starve them of funds or give them a pittance.

At the federal level, despite the Fiscal Responsibility Act, the Fiscal Responsibility Commission has not been properly constituted according to the law. Thus, enforcement is still a problem. The issue of a security vote is another concern in public finance management. The notion of a security vote is neither bad nor is it unique to Nigeria. However, the issue has to do with its application and management. In the USA, for example, security agencies are given security votes that are not published in their budgets, but they would normally have to account for it to a special Committee of the Congress, which consists of people who have taken oaths for that purpose. In Nigeria, however, the assumption about a security vote is that it is not accountable and therefore the managers apply it inappropriately as a slush fund to patronise political loyalists.

**The Deployment of BVN for Payroll and Social Investment Programmes** is another corruption prevention measure and government reported that its enforcement has led to the detection of more than 50,000 erroneous or fraudulent payroll entries. Its introduction in the banks and other financial institutions also has a great preventive potential for fraud.

## Enlistment into Open Government Partnership (OGP)

In May 2016, President Buhari attended an International Anti-Corruption Summit organised by the UK Government. At that summit he pledged that Nigeria would join the OGP, an international transparency, accountability and citizen engagement initiative.

However, the needed infrastructure for the full enforcement of the OGP has not been put in place and most of the recommendations made at the summit remain unimplemented.

Other notable achievements in anti-corruption policy include the establishment of an Efficiency Unit which reviews government overhead expenditure and was reported to have resulted in more than N15 billion savings on official travels, sitting allowances and souvenirs.

In addition to the Presidential Advisory Committee against Corruption, the government also established a Presidential Committee on Asset Recovery.

The government claimed that it had phased out the notorious subsidy regimes on petroleum products and fertilisers, yet it conceded that the cost of landing a litre of imported petroleum product is about 180 naira and since petrol is sold to the public at 145 naira per litre, the difference is paid by the NNPC, not as subsidy but as 'government support' (whatever that means). The NEITI principles of improved transparency through disclosure of payments and receipts on the other hand has been criticised in that transparency has not led to accountability nor has it translated to better living standards for the Nigerian people.[54]

## 3. To provide incentives for sustainability of the anti-corruption policy.

Corruption is partly a product of socio-economic conditions, and we cannot effectively tackle it without addressing the conditions that give rise to it, including improving the conditions of service for public officials. While there is a hue and cry about the huge benefits (legitimately or having been legitimised) for elected and appointed

54. NEITI is advocating for more transparency and accountability in the management of public funds. NEITI is charged with the responsibility among other things, for the development of a framework for transparency and accountability in the reporting and disclosure by all Extractive Industry companies of revenue due to or paid to the Federal Government.

officials, the welfare of civil servants is a far cry in terms of meeting the expectations for earning a living wage.

In December 2018 the government approved an increase in the remuneration of the Nigerian Police, but it is not clear if such an increase was extended to the military, paramilitary, intelligence and security agencies, including the anti-corruption agencies. At the time of writing this book, government is still negotiating a 'minimum wage' with the Nigerian workers.

## The Whistleblower Policy

Another government policy recently launched is the Whistleblower Policy, which is aimed at encouraging anyone in possession of information pertaining to the theft or mismanagement of public funds and other assets and their location to report to the Ministry of Finance. Approved on 21 December 2016, the main thrust of the policy is to fight corruption. The aim is to expose financial crimes, enhance transparency and accountability, as well as improve confidence in management of public funds; the key selling points are to recover public funds and improve Nigeria's Open Government Ranking.

Individuals are encouraged to provide useful information that entails violation of government financial regulations, as well as procurement procedures, mismanagement or misappropriation of public funds and assets, financial malpractice, fraud and theft of public assets. The policy also encourages rewarding genuine whistleblowers. The reward scheme set minimum and maximum standards of 2.5% and 5% respectively to be deducted from the total recovered amount and given to the whistle blower.

Within six months of the approval of the whistleblower policy, about 2,251 reported cases were under investigation: 95 reported through the website; 1550 through a dedicated phone line; 194

through email; and 412 through text/SMS messages. Within two months, by February 2017, about $151 million and N8 billion of looted funds were reportedly recovered; the biggest amount was $136,676, and $600.51 was recovered from an account in a commercial bank where the money was kept under a false name.[55] $15 million and N7 billion were recovered from one person, N1 billion from another person, and 154 actionable tips on various offences.

In addition, $9.8m and £74,000 cash was recovered in a building owned by the former NNPC GMD (Andrew Yakubu); and another $43m, £27,000 and N23m cash recovered from a flat in Ikoyi purportedly kept by the Director General of the National Intelligence Agency; also some 47 sports utility vehicles/buses allegedly bought for N1.5 billion; and the proceeds of N27 billion insurance premiums of deceased workers of PHCN were recovered. In total, estimated recoveries stood at $160 million, and while in June 2017, N375.8 million was purportedly released for payment of 20 whistleblowers as reward for N11.6 billion recovery.[56]

### 4. To improve the operational capacity of anti-corruption institutions.

In terms of institution building, the two major anti-corruption agencies in Nigeria, the ICPC and EFCC, were created by the Obasanjo Administration. In 2015 when the APC Government came to power, Nigeria was rated better by Transparency International (TI) than in 1999, with a TI score of 2.7 and ranking of 136 out of 175 countries. The NACS seeks to improve the operational capacities of the anti-corruption agencies (ACAs) but failed to specify measurable steps that should be taken to strengthen those

55. I put question marks on these figures because they were not verified.
56. Some whistleblowers complained that they were short-changed, but none confirm receipt publicly.

institutions. Some notable achievements have been recorded as a result of enforcement efforts. For example, within one year (from 29 May 2015 to 29 May 2016), following pressure from the public, the government announced the recovery of assets in cash totalling N78,325,354,631.82; $185,119,584.61; £3,508,355.46; and €11,250.

The government also disclosed that recoveries under Interim Forfeiture (cash and assets) during the same period totalled N126,563,481,095.43; $9,090,243,920.15; £2,484,447,55; and €303,399. 17.

Funds awaiting repatriation from foreign jurisdictions were given as $321,316,726.1; £6,900,000; and €11,826.11 respectively. Non-cash recoveries (including farmlands, plots of land, completed and uncompleted buildings, vehicles and maritime vessels), all being financial and assets recoveries made by various government agencies, totalled 239 within one year. Although there is no accurate statistics on the actual recovery as the Federal Ministry of Finance gave conflicting figures from those given by the anti-corruption agencies, the amount of recovery, whether interim or final forfeiture, would have increased for sure.

However, there are some legal and accountability issues, which the government also acknowledged when it released the above statistics, and the fight against corruption in general:

1. These recoveries, commendable as they are, fall short of expectations. The common man out there on the street would think that the Government has recovered ten times more with the much talked about dealing with corrupt persons since the inception of the Buhari administration.

2. Following the release of records of recoveries in 2016, the Honourable Minister of Information himself acknowledged that contrary to their expectation, the recoveries could not even pay the monthly salary of Federal Government civil and public servants.

3. Some of the recoveries are doubtful because in any criminal recovery of asset, the funds would have been identified as proceeds of crime and seized, and the suspected owner or claimant charged with the offence in a court of law. Only after conviction will a final forfeiture and confiscation order be executed, and the funds returned to the consolidated or any designated account. On the other hand, if the funds were recovered through negotiation – a sort of non-conviction-based approach, with which Nigeria had not yet experimented –it would still be necessary to go to the court and charge the assets or funds. Upon lack of proof of ownership, the government could then claim it as proceeds of illicit enrichment.

4. Even when the legal processes are concluded as explained above, another hurdle is how to determine the origin of misappropriated funds and return them to the victim. In this case, if the funds were taken from appropriated funds of any department of the federal or state government, would it be right to say return and use it for the initial purpose it was intended, or to seek legislative power to appropriate it? My intention here is not to expose the weaknesses in the process and make it more complicated; rather, I am just trying to highlight some of the challenges so that even the expectant public would appreciate the daunting tasks of asset recovery.

5. Again, success in the recovery of stolen funds remains a challenge, if not doubtful, because was it as simple as the government suggests, such funds would have been used without delay to cushion the effects of the shortage of funds for the implementation of the budget.

6. From the foreign perspective, it is not as simple as saying 'please return our stolen funds', because even in the best relations

with other countries there are legal processes guiding asset recovery as contained in articles 51-59 of the UN Convention Against Corruption. Because Nigeria did not have mutual legal assistance law with respect to proceeds of corruption, it had to negotiate the terms of recovery and return of stolen assets with the governments of Switzerland and the UK.[57] One issue that remains unresolved in the fight against corruption and the laundering of the proceeds is the role of financial institutions worldwide, who accept and conceal the proceeds of corruption despite their commitment to implement a robust AML/CFT system. Some financial institutions in Switzerland, Luxemburg, Hong Kong, Liechtenstein, the UK, USA and other jurisdictions have been accused of handling the proceeds of corrupt enrichment for some Nigerian officials in the past. Although international efforts are being made to sanction defaulting banks, there is still more to be done in that regard, especially in the implementation of acceptable international AML/CFT standards.

7.   With respect to recoveries from foreign jurisdictions, it appears that the recovery efforts of Nigeria have been limited to the Abacha loot. Does it mean that it was only Abacha and his close associates that stole Nigeria's commonwealth?

8.   The purpose of fighting corruption is to reduce inefficiency and increase resources for development. However, while government has talked a lot about fighting corruption and recovering stolen funds, the complaint about lack of funds to run the government smacks of a charade in prudence and transparency.

Indeed, fighting corruption effectively depends on strong and credible institutions. However, since the inception of the Buhari administration all the anti-corruption agencies have remained

57. The Mutual Assistance Act was passed in 2018.

without substantive leadership.[58] While the NASS has been criticised for the delay in confirming certain appointments and rejecting others, it has also made the point that the Senate is not a rubber stamp because it has the power to decline any nomination if it is not satisfied that such nominations have met certain criteria, including passing an integrity test.

The Centre for Democracy and Development catalogued 13 different promises allegedly made by PMB during his 2015 campaigns to fight corruption and measured the progress through a survey which revealed that the administration received a positive rating from the respondents.[59] About 20.4, 21.4, and 20.6 per cent of the respondents rate the performance of the programme as 'very good', 'good', and 'fair', respectively. Other respondents (21.8 and 13.4 per cent) rated the performance of the government's anti-corruption programme as 'very poor' and 'poor', respectively.

The Buhari administration has come under serious attack on its approach to the fight against corruption. Let me just summarise a few public opinions before stating my personal assessment of this. Giving five reasons 'why Buhari is failing', a policy commentator, Malcolm Fabiyi,[60] observed that Buhari is running a 'half-hearted anti-corruption war' with fewer convictions recorded and persistent complaints about the judiciary, yet 'he has not sent a single bill to the National Assembly to modify Nigeria's laws so that the walls of protection that the current laws offer to the corrupt can be brought down'.

Shaka Momodu, in a back page comment in *Thisday* newspaper of 30 December 2016, queried the fight against corruption under

58. The nomination and confirmation of Ibrahim Magu as Chairman of the EFCC was rejected by the Senate two times in a row, and by law, he cannot be represented to the same Senate for confirmation on the same position. The nominations of the Chairman and members of the Code of Conduct Bureau suffered serious set and were only approved after a long delay; while those of the ICPC were still under consideration as at December 2018.

59. Centre for Democracy and Development, 'NIGERIA: The Promise and Practice of Change – Citizens' Perception and Assessment of Buhari's Administration in the Last One Year, 2016.

60. 'Five reasons Buhari is failing', *Premium Times*, 11 August 2016.

Buhari, alleging that 'it is curious that nearly two years after it rode to power promising a re-audit, nothing has been heard about the alleged missing $20 billion as claimed by Sanusi'.

When asked to comment on the Buhari's war against corruption, Farooq Kperogi, in an interview with *Punch* published on 29 January 2017, opined that 'Buhari's anti-corruption fight is the most invidiously selective, the least transparent, the most brazenly unjust, and the silliest joke in Nigeria's entire history. Here is a man who doesn't give his corrupt political opponents the benefit of the doubt… but tells astonishingly bald-faced and easily falsifiable lies to defend, deflect, minimize and excuse the corruption of his close aides and political associates… he erected a false pedestal and stood on it. But his government is shaping up to be one of the most audaciously corrupt governments in Nigeria's history… Buhari's war on corruption is already lost before it has started.'

## Are we getting it right?

Because of these and many other considerations which I cannot address here for lack of space, many Nigerians, indeed foreigners with interests in Nigeria, still believe that the much talked about anti-corruption crusade of the Buhari administration falls short of their expectations and some have observed that:

● The fight against corruption remains uncoordinated, despite the belated launch of a National Strategy. The previous government is being blamed for the widespread corruption, yet the style of dealing with the problem has not departed from the past. How do you expect a different result when you are doing the same thing in the same way? It is true that we need a retentive memory of the past to assess the present and predict the future, but we cannot construct our future on a skewed narrative of the past, especially when such narrative is negative and unhelpful.

- It is a witch-hunt against members of the opposition party as most of the people arrested were from the main opposition party (the PDP) who ruled the country for 16 years from 1999 to 2015. I disagree, because investigation is a reactive process and would focus on those who have committed offences, and since most of the people arrested were those in government and their accomplices in the private sector, it follows naturally that they would of course be held accountable.

- The fight has generated 'more sizzle than steak' because until recently there has been no conviction in the high-profile cases involving Politically Exposed Persons, most of which have remained inconclusive. In his maiden Media Chat in January 2016, President Buhari put the blame on the judiciary, and that was repeated when he declared a workshop on anti-corruption for judicial officers in June and subsequently in his broadcast to mark the 56th Independence Anniversary of Nigeria on 1 October 2016. This is not a new problem as the former Chairman of the ICPC, Justice Emmanuel Ayoola, had complained of starvation of funds to his 10-year-old Commission and frustration in prosecution due to delays, etc. He expressed concern not only at the 'slowness' in court of the process but also at 'occasional strange decisions'. He said that because of the heavy calendar/number of cases, 'no matter how hard the Supreme Court works, you cannot get the decision within three years'. He advocated for our institutions to become 'healthy in terms of their integrity and procedure'.[61]

- We must try to resist the temptation of creating a barrier with the judiciary as if it is not part of the government. Regardless of the principle of separation of powers, the judiciary is one arm of the government and the President is the Commander in Chief and head of the government. The question is, what new

61. *Sunday Trust*, 1 August 2010, p.55. Quoted in Bukar Usman, 'Combating Corruption in Nigeria', accessed through the internet at www.bukarusman.com/publications on 3 October 2016.

investments have been made since the Buhari administration came to power in furtherance of the fight against corruption?[62] Ultimately, I would say that it is true that our judicial system is not immune to corruption and it has been very frustrating as a result of delays. I have had to elucidate in my book *Strategies and Techniques of Prosecuting Economic and Financial Crimes* (2012) that a successful prosecution is a function of good investigation, and the final outcome of any adjudication depends largely on both.

## To achieve presidential commitment to asset recovery, transparency and accountability

A strong political will is the springboard for an effective fight against corruption. A strong political will is crucial, because it will not only lead to enacting laws but to increased resources and to the independence of the enforcement institutions to do their work without interference. So far, President Buhari has demonstrated a commitment more by way of his body language, but there is room for improvement in terms of fighting corruption transparently and within the rule of law.

While the integrity of the President is the greatest asset in this regard, integrity alone cannot solve the problem of corruption. Because of the perceived failure to deal with corruption fairly and transparently, many commentators have accused the President of being selective. That is not new, as every past government that attempted to fight corruption had been accused of selecting only its enemies. Fighting corruption is a work in progress and a step forward that a government should deal with whomsoever it believes

---

62. Investments in terms of injecting new ideas increase in salaries, welfare of staff and operational costs, as well as building physical infrastructure. The ICPC since its establishment has remained in an old insufficient building, while the EFCC has a new building that was initiated by the previous government.

has committed acts of corruption during its tenure, leaving its own 'protected' sympathisers for another government to come and deal with. If that can be done consistently over a 20-year period, the circle would be complete and hopefully the fight against corruption would have been institutionalised. Nevertheless, we cannot gloss over some serious allegations that certain people within the inner cycle of the Buhari administration were accused of wrongdoing and no action was taken against them, creating the cynicism that there are two separate laws in the land.

For example, a top-ranking official in the Presidency was accused of collecting about $5 million from MTN, a South African mobile telecommunication company in Nigeria. Whether a formal report was made against him to the law enforcement agencies to warrant investigation is not known. Nevertheless, it was expected that the Presidency should have made a statement exonerating him from the allegation after investigation, but that was not the case. What gave credence to the allegation was that the woman official of the MTN who purportedly facilitated the wrongdoing was relieved of her post; and the South African Government was also reported to have recalled its High Commissioner to Nigeria who also was alleged to have been involved in the corruption.

Another accusation of selective treatment levelled against the Buhari administration is that the government has failed to prosecute Babachir David Lawal, the Secretary to the Government of the Federation (SGF), who was relieved of his post after an allegation of corruption in the handling of relief materials for IDPs. In fact, when President Buhari was to be invested as the African Union (AU) Anti-Corruption Champion in late 2017, Babachir was arrested and kept in a guesthouse to avoid public criticism and was released after the AU Summit. Senator Shehu Sani, Chairman of the Committee that investigated the allegation against Lawal and a staunch supporter of President Buhari, described the handling of the Lawal's case as a charade, saying that 'when it comes to fighting corruption in NASS and the general public, the Presidency uses insecticides, but when it comes to fighting corruption in the Presidency it uses deodorant'.

Just as Lawal's case was being investigated, another scandal broke out with the discovery of a huge amount of money in a private apartment in Ikoyi, Lagos, of which the former Director General (DG) of the National Intelligence Agency (NIA), was identified as the culprit. The matter was investigated; the DG was relieved of his post but it took the enforcement agency about 16 months to charge both Babachir Lawal and Ayodele Oke, the former DG, NIA in court at the end of January 2019. The public criticised the subsequent appointment of Ahmed Rufa'i Abubakar, who was the Secretary of the Committee that investigated the allegation against Oke, as DG NIA, asserting it was done to cover up what may have happened.

Again, just as President Buhari observed that corruption is worse than armed robbery, there are other forms of corruption that are more destructive than stealing or embezzlement of public funds. For example, in several media comments, Buhari has been accused of having a skewed definition of corruption by appointing certain close family members, applying religious or ethnic sentiments in appointments against merit, fairness and justice. I do not need to go into the details of that, but I do suggest that nepotism, whether perceived or real, could be tantamount to corruption and should be avoided if one is preaching equity and fair play.[63] It seems 'the 'undue' premium the president places on 'personal loyalty' causes him to ignore, excuse, and even defend the corruption of his close associates'.[64]

---

63. The President has the prerogative to choose who would work for him and by choosing any-one, he has not committed any wrong except if as it is provided in the law of the land, that appointments should reflect federal character, which is another form of injustice in itself and who has the final say as to whether federal character is in the best interest of Nigeria?

64. Faroog Kperogi, 'Electoral Law: 2019 Will be a Contest of rigging', Whatsapp post, 8 December 2018.

In one of its editorials in August 2016, *Punch* observed: 'Muhammadu Buhari appears bent on political self-immolation. While he received massive support from across the country to become president, he is by his appointments, presenting himself as a parochial, sectional leader'.[65]

Aside from PMB's skewed definition of corruption, there is the issue of due process and double standards in the fight against corruption. One example is that some ministers in the Buhari Administration have been accused of corrupt enrichment, but no action was taken to investigate those allegations, let alone prosecute them. The Chief of Army Staff, Lt. Gen. Tukur Buratai, was accused of owning property in Dubai, contrary to the code of ethics and conduct for public office holders. Action was delayed, and when it was eventually taken, due process was followed and the case was referred to the Army Council. How they dealt with the matter is not known. On the other hand, when some judges were suspected, not accused, of corruption, their houses were raided at night not by the agency mandated to fight corruption but a different agency, which smacks of ulterior motives. They were not accused or reported to the National Judicial Council, which has the constitutional power to investigate and discipline judges. Furthermore, a petition was concocted by someone believed to be a close political ally of PMB and that petition was acted upon within three days by the Code of Conduct Bureau, which has been inactive for several years.

The Chief Justice of Nigeria, Walter Onnoghen, was immediately charged before the Code of Conduct Tribunal for failing to declare his domiciliary accounts in his asset declaration form. The amounts suspected in those accounts were nothing compared to one property outside Nigeria, yet that was celebrated

65. See also Akin Osuntokun, 'Obasanjo, Buhari and Nation Building', *Thisday*,19 August 2016.

as the fight against corruption.[66]

On 25 January 2019, President Buhari suspended the Chief Justice of Nigeria, Honourable Justice Walter Onnoghen, saying he was obeying an Exparte Order by the Code of Conduct Tribunal. Honourable Justice Ibrahim Tanko Mohammed, being the most senior after Justice Onnoghen was sworn in as Acting Chief Justice of Nigeria. The suspicious Order, which was issued on 23 January 2019, was widely criticised and the President's action was condemned as a violation of the Constitution[67]. The suspension was described as undemocratic and an attempt to turn Nigeria into a 'fascist' state. In some countries where democracy is fledgling, including Bangladesh for example, the Chief Justice was sacked by the President to allow the President to manipulate the democratic process and remain in power. While the fight against corruption is a noble course, it must be noted that how to make a change is as important as the change you want to make. The timing of the suspension of the CJN close to the election, no matter how well intended, can be misconstrued as intimidating the judicial arm of the government. The speed with which it was executed smacks of some political interests beyond the fight against corruption. It took the Code of Conduct Bureau less than three working days to act on a petition written by someone described as a former ally of President Buhari and charged the Chief justice to the Code of Conduct Tribunal, while there have been several other reported cases that have not been investigated let alone prosecuted.

These are just a few examples of question marks on the fight

66. This matter is still in court and discussing it would tantamount to sub-judice. Nevertheless, suffice it to say that there is a judgment of the Court of Appeal in the case of Nganjiwa v. FRN which says a judge accused on of misconduct must first be investigated by the NJC.

67. Section 292 of the Constitution provides that the CJN can only be removed from office by the President acting on an address supported by two-thirds majority of the Senate; while the Code of Conduct for Judicial Officials stipulates that the National Judicial Council (NJC) shall be responsible for the discipline of all judicial officers, including the CJN, but the matter was only reported to the NJC after the CJN had been suspended and Honourable Justice Ibrahim Tanko Mohammed was invited and sworn in by the President a CJN in Acting capacity.

against corruption. Based on these and other examples, several commentators have even questioned Buhari's understanding of corruption and his approach in fighting it. For example, Farooq Kperogi, in an interview with *Punch* referred to earlier in this chapter, retorted harshly:

> It's a perfect, poignant metaphor to encapsulate the scorn-worthy lies, deceit, double standards and crying unjustness of the Buhari administration's so-called anti-corruption fight. In Buhari's Nigeria, there are two judicial standards for fighting corruption. The first standard is that the President's opponents are always guilty until proven innocent – and they can never be proven innocent. They are always already condemned by the mere fact of being the President's opponents.[68] The second standard is that the President's corrupt aides and associates are always innocent – until they are 'cleared' by the President, who has now reduced himself to the pathetic position of the Clearer-in-Chief of the executhief Corruption.

On Buhari's integrity as an asset for anti-corruption, Kperogi declared: 'Perhaps Buhari never had any integrity to start with. It was our desperation for a hero that caused us to dress him in borrowed robes... what man of integrity perpetually surrounds himself with corrupt people and, worse still, defends their corruption?' In essence, Buhari's integrity alone cannot take Nigeria to the Promised Land. What is needed is transparent action against any person accused or found to have commitment an act of corruption within the rule of law.

---

68. The Archbishop Emeritus of the Catholic Archdiocese of Lagos, Anthony Olubunmi Okogie, was reported to have commented in this direction that 'What they say is given lurid headlines in the media, and it seems to all that some of the defendants cum accused persons are being tried in the press with information conveniently slipping into the hands of the press, presumably from the security agencies, even before such people have been charged to court'; *Vanguard*, 25 January 2016.

## Economy

A third pillar in the agenda of the Buhari/APC Administration is to revive the economy and manage it efficiently. Again, this was motivated by the obvious reality of economic decline under the Jonathan/PDP Administration. But it took the President about six months to constitute a cabinet, which after all, 'did not fly in the eyes' of most Nigerians. Also, as a result of inaction or inertia, no formal decision was taken on time with regard to the fuel subsidy, which was one of many issues on which the APC criticised the previous government and that led to the accumulation of outstanding payments to oil marketers. The negotiation and settlement of the outstanding payment took so long that the President had to present a supplementary budget, the release of which at once triggered the collapse in the value of the naira from N225=$1 to over N500=$1 in early 2016 and increased inflation from 11% to 18%, thus creating the condition for a recession soon after.

After security, the economy is the most important thing to the growth, development and stability of a country. Unfortunately, it is President Buhari's greatest weakness. Although a president does not necessarily need to be versed in economics before he can manage the economy, as a leader, some ingenuity is required even if it is in the form of what might be described as 'native intelligence' (the ability to talent-spot the right people to do what you want). About seven months into the APC administration, and due to some inactions or wrong actions, the economy slid into the 'worst' recession in thirty years.

To fully understand the economy under the APC, it is crucial to recall briefly that the PDP handed over a $550 billion economy (the largest in Africa and 26th in the world), with 7.5% unemployment rate (considered better than the European union, France, Sweden, Belgium, etc.); stock reserves of $30 billion[69]; GDP growth rate averaging 6% over the last 12 years. The PDP administration secured debt relief, thereby relieving Nigeria from the stranglehold

69. The capitalisation of the Nigerian Stock Exchange grew from less than N1 trillion to N12 trillion at handover date.

of the IMF/World Bank policy conditionality. The average oil price in May 1999, when President Obasanjo took, over, was $15.24, while the stock of reserves was about $5 billion.[70] All these suggest that despite the alleged destruction of the economy and falling oil price, the APC started on a relatively stronger and better base than the PDP did in 1999. The challenge therefore for the APC is to show how it has done better.

## Understanding Recession

In early 2016, Nigeria experienced its first full-year recession in 30 years. Global oil prices crashed simultaneously with vandalism and militant attacks on oil facilities in the Niger Delta region, resulting in severe contraction of GDP from oil. The impact of low foreign earnings shrank non-oil sector as well. President Buhari blamed it largely on the mismanagement of the past government, its failure to save despite high oil prices and the declining oil prices. But if we start the interrogation from here, the PDP argued that some of the prominent people in the APC Government who were governors during the last administration had resisted the attempt to save from the excess crude accruals. Ngozi Okonjo-Iweala, who was Minister of Finance and Coordinating Minister for the Economy during the Jonathan Administration, alleged in her book that people like Adams Oshomhole, the APC national Chairman, and Rotimi Amaechi, Minister of Transport, who were governors of Edo and Rivers States, had resisted the idea of saving. It is true that President Buhari inherited a lot of rot in the system, a mess which he fought hard to inherit, but the non-performance of the economy under his watch cannot be entirely attributed to that. Several reasons have been adduced for the slide of the economy into recession and the perceived non-performance of the government in the area of the economy. 'Nigeria's economic hardship from 2015 onward,

70. Soludo, 'Can a New Buharinomics Save Nigeria?', p. 4.

including the recession of 2016, can be seen as something of a self-inflicted wound.'[71]

The first mistake was that PMB did not respond appropriately and quickly to the signs of the recession. In 2008 Barack Obama inherited what some people believe to be the worst recession the USA had witnessed in the past 40 years. He responded passionately and quickly by rolling out the largest stimulus programme ever implemented by any country and hired the best hands he could find to assist him deal with the urgent problem. This should have served as a lesson to PMB. Seven years later before Obama left office, more than 15 million jobs had been created or regained and the US economy had bounced back as the leading economy in the world.

The failure to diversify the economy over the years, leading to the nation's dependence[72] on crude oil as the main source of revenue, is indeed a remote cause of the recession, but the immediate causes of the problem lay in the leadership and policy failures of President Muhammadu Buhari and his government, as well as in the reduction of revenue caused by sharp drop in oil production due to insurgency and sabotage in the Niger Delta.[73]

It may be recalled that when it was obvious that the economy was going to slide into recession, President Buhari ignored the looming economic danger and focused 'unwisely' on the fight against corruption. Indeed, some proposals were made to the President to consider two major alternatives: devaluing the currency or borrowing to save the situation. In his populist attempt to protect the value of the naira, PMB said that devaluation was not an option as experience of the past taught him that devaluation never brought

71. Ngozi Okonjo-Iweala, *Fighting Corruption is Dangerous: The Story Behind the Headlines,* MIT Press, Cambridge, Mass., 2018, p. 62.

72. In the 1960s, when Nigeria was a major producer of cash crops like cocoa, palm oil, and rubber, agricultural exports generated about 75% of its foreign-exchange earnings.

73. 'How Buhari Helped Nigeria into Recession and How he can take Us out of it', *Premium Times* Editorial, 27 September 2016.

the touted benefits of more investment, etc., to the economy. Ultimately, that delay in taking a decision made the value of the naira crash, exacerbated by declining oil prices, and consequently foreign reserves. Some experts believe that if the naira had been allowed to find its equilibrium levels, it would have stabilised between N250 and N260 to the dollar and this drastic decline would have been avoided. It should be noted that the currency market is determined by demand and supply and not by any fiat. 'When it was widely publicized on two different occasions within three months that presidency directs central bank to…, it got many players in the economy seriously worried. When the market knows or believes that the central bank is merely an extension of the presidency and takes daily 'directives' from there, the Bank loses credibility and its monetary policy committee meetings become meaningless.'[74] Similarly, the fundamental driver of economic activities is human behaviour. The economic data used to measure the health of the economy are mere expressions of it. When the patterns of behaviour indicate a positive feedback, investors and other actors in the economy respond in an optimistic frame of mind.[75]

It may be recalled that the APC promised in its manifesto to ensure the independence and autonomy of the Central Bank of Nigeria (CBN). But in practice, by making public statements consistently that Nigeria would not adjust its exchange rate for the naira, it became difficult for the CBN to defy the President, which ordinarily should be independent in determining the exchange rate.

Consequently, the shortage of forex from the interbank and Bureau de Change (BDC) escalated demand on the parallel market, rising to as high as N500 Naira per USD in February 2017, thus creating rent-seeking and round-tripping opportunities and severe distortions in the economy. As a comparator, in 1973 when Nigeria had the oil boom and Indonesia was an agrarian economy, Indonesia

74. Soludo, 'Can a New Buharinomics Save Nigeria?',p. 7.

75. Anya, Anya,'The Economy and You: Tales of the Unexpected',*Thisday,*10 July 2016, p. 2.

adopted a strategy to avoid having an overvalued exchange rate while Nigeria fixed its own. Indonesia used its weak currency to protect its industries from imports and that encouraged domestic production. 'After two decades, Indonesia's export of manufactures accounted for more than 25% of its exports, while Nigeria's was still less than 1% as was the case at the beginning.'[76]

Even with the overtures of favourable credit lines from the World Bank/International Monetary Fund (IMF), the President was not convinced that taking foreign loans was a better way to address the problem. At the end, when he agreed to take the loans, it was already too late to save the situation, as the processes for negotiating the terms and conditions of the loans took some time and the market forces were not waiting for him. This is a clear example of lack of vision and purposeful leadership. As the *Premium Times* observed in its editorial of 27 September 2016, 'the extreme inertia that has become the key definitional attribute of the Buhari administration has stultified both decision-making and policy implementation', leading to undesirable consequences.

But the President is not the only one to blame. The policy mistakes, inconsistencies and unpredictability of the CBN also contributed to the recession. While the CBN had earlier assured that the exchange rate would no longer be fixed, as a result of the sharp depreciation of the exchange rate following the liberalisation of the naira in June 2016, the bank maintained the interbank rate at N305 per USD. The question is, why would you fix the price of something so low when in reality you do not have that thing?

One of the anticipated benefits of liberalising the FX market or fixing the exchange rate was to attract more forex inflow. However, economic theories have proved that monetary policy takes a long time to attract good investment because investors have many options in other jurisdictions. Investors evaluate the environment and ask questions, including by interrogating the fiscal policy

76. Soludo, 'Can a New Buharinomics Save Nigeria?', p. 11.

and determining whether contracts are respected and court orders obeyed. What is the guarantee in terms of security and infrastructure? And if we think in terms of industrialisation, we must equally note that monetary policy is just one decision and it cannot boost local industry, though fiscal policies and incentives do so to a large extent.

The CBN must not be intimidated by the power of the presidency, or else it does not deserve the independence given it by law. It must therefore take responsibility for creating the thriving foreign exchange black market, the scarcity of forex (artificial or real), and the escalating inflation. That is not in any way to exonerate the Federal Ministry of Finance, which is responsible for the fiscal policy. The consequence of all these is loss of confidence by Nigerian domestic and foreign investors. In view of the foregoing, and as the *Premium Times* rightly observed, 'President Buhari's government and economic team, as presently constituted, are not optimally equipped for the fundamental tasks ahead. He must seek new actors that are fit for the purpose.'

Nigeria is ranked 'as the poverty capital of the world' with 86.9 million Nigerians now living in extreme poverty.[77] Even without any empirical data, it is possible to imagine that the level of poverty has increased together with declining purchasing power for all classes of Nigerian society. Despite the claims of prudent management and recovery of assets, the country remains poor. One commentator[78] described the situation in two years of the Buhari administration in the Yoruba language: *iwajuko se lo, ehinko se padasi*', translated as having reached 'a point of abject despair where going forward is stalled and going back is foreclosed'.

The pump price of petroleum products was increased from N87 to

77. During a television interview on 16 January 2019, the Vice President, Yemi Osinbajo, observed that the poverty figure was much higher than 100 million when the APC administration came to power and that the current figure is a remarkable success of the government's poverty reduction programmes.

78. Tunde Fagbenle, 'Bakare's 'revolution' call in a state of anomie', a commentary published in *Thisday* newspaper, 10 April 2016.

N145 per litre on assumption of office of the Buhari Administration, and there was no corresponding increase in income for civil servants and independent people. The much-expected improvement in power supply is far off, as electricity supply remains epileptic across the country.[79] Inflation is galloping. A bag of rice that was sold for N9,500 in 2015 is now N18,000 if not more.[80]Tunde Bakare, in his 2016 annual sermon titled 'Looking into the Future with the Eyes of Faith', narrated the story of a Nigerian woman, Mama Bukky, living in Oko-Oba, one of the suburbs of Lagos, who bought five small tomatoes at a cost of N100 the previous week, only to buy the same size and number at N200 the following week. Her husband Baba Bukky, whose electrical extension box had been damaged by the epileptic power supply, had to purchase a new one at N1000 to replace the damaged one, which he bought two months ago for N500. Schools are increasing fees in order to cope with inflation and the high cost of running generators and other maintenance. Millions have lost jobs according to official statistics from the National Bureau of Statistics (NBS), contrary to what the government spokespersons would want Nigerians to believe. In December 2018, the NBS in its third quarter report revealed that unemployment rate grew from 18.8 per cent to 23.1 per cent between 2017 and 2018, adding that the number of people classified as unemployed grew from 17.6 million in the last quarter of 2017 to 20.9 million in the third quarter of 2018. About 1.8 million graduates from Nigerian universities and other higher institutions enter the labour market each year.

79. The APC government claims to have increased electricity generation from 4000 megawatts in 2015 to 7000 megawatts in 2018, but the impact has not been felt. Experts argue that if that was the case, most of the country would be experiencing more than 20 hours of stable power.

80. Government, however, claimed that inflation declined from a peak of 18.72% in January 2017 to 11.28% in November 2018 according to the budget speech presented to the NASS by PMB.

On the journey so far, Abba Mahmood[81] observed 'there is persistent scarcity of electricity, there is constant scarcity of money; the only thing that is abundant is the rate of poverty and misery!' Another commentator observed: 'in two years of Nigeria under President Buhari, the price of everything has gone up and... the only thing that is cheaper in Nigeria today is the value of President Buhari's campaign promises'.[82]

Official statistics from the NBS suggest that in the third quarter of 2018, aggregate GDP stood at N33,368,049.14 million compared to N29,377,674.03 million in 2017 in nominal terms, representing a positive year on year nominal growth rate of 13.58 per cent. Capital importation into Nigeria by the end of 2018 shows an increase of 56.7% compared to 2016 figures. Yet Shaka Momodu[83] summed up the situation as follows: 'Today, millions are crawling on their stomachs for food. Even the most optimistic of Buhari's supporters now wear long faces, many have become badly emaciated on account of hunger... They gave their endorsement to a man whose only quest to lead was driven by clannish considerations and contempt for progressive ideas but deceptively packaged as change... unemployment figures have hit the roof and inflation is at an all-time high of 18.49 per cent.'

Thus, the APC Change Agenda has been jokingly changed from *chanji* to *shenji* and what was perceived 'as the rallying cry for progressive development has now become associated with retrogression and suffering'.[84]

81. Abba Mahmood,'On the Journey So Far', *Leadership*, 19 May 2016.

82. Reno Omokri, 'President Buhari: Two Years and Forty Thousand Email Addresses Later', published in *Leadership*, 27 May 2017.

83.Columnist in *Thisday*, in his Back Page comment titled 'The End of Optimism', dated 30 December 2016.

84. Tunde Bakare, 'Looking into the Future with the Eyes of Faith', 2016 Annual Church Address, Lagos, Nigeria. p.5.

Ambassador Babagana Kingibe,[85] a former running mate to Chief Abiola in the 1993 presidential election that was acclaimed the freest and most credible, and believed to be an inner adviser to PMB, tried to explain the concept of change in order to dissuade Nigerians from inordinate expectation said:

> The very notion of change in the context of the current national mantra implies the idea of dissatisfaction with what is, and the need to improve upon it or discard it …
>
> But change meant different things to different people. For some, change takes the form of a fantasy in which a new government would right all the wrongs of the past on its first day in office. If the expected magic does not happen, the leader ends up being accused of 'going slow'. For others, change means throwing out a set of Government Ministers and enthroning new ones, preferably themselves or others affiliated to them. There are those who are satisfied with a change of personnel in strategic public service positions even if the failed policies and failing politics, the patronage-driven and corruption-ridden governance practices of the past were retained. Yet, there are those for whom change meant reversing the old policies and immediately introducing new ones, even before an exhaustive assessment is undertaken to determine what was working and what was not.
>
> The most invidious resistance to change, however, will come from strong vested interests who fear that in a new Nigeria where no one is left behind, they stand to lose all. The challenge before us all, but especially before those charged with the task of managing this change, is how we overcome these sources of resistance.
>
> Socrates observed 'The secret of change is to focus your energy not on fighting the old but on building the new.'… Looking ahead, to sustain change and overcome resistance,

85    Babagana Kingibe, 'Nigeria: Why change and how?'*Daily Trust*, 31 October 2015.

Government must communicate very clearly – to Nigerians
and the world at large – their core principles, strategies,
policies, plans and programmes for change.

Despite a surplus trade balance of N681.27 billion in 2018,
representing a significant increase from a deficit of N290.1 billion
in 2016 and reflecting a rebound in crude oil exports, increased
non-oil exports and reduction in the importation of food and other
items that can be produced locally,[86] the World Bank observed that a
combination of the rising costs of power and transport, increases in
petrol prices, the depreciated naira and the growth in money supply
resulted in average inflation of 15.6 per cent in 2016. With respect
to balance of payments, 'the value of goods and services exported
continued to decline in 2016 (USD38.3 billion compared to USD 49
billion in 2015 and USD 97.5 billion in 2014)'.[87] Despite the claim
of reducing unemployment through the government's conditional
cash transfers and N-Power programmes, figures from the NBS as
at June 2016 put the number of jobless Nigerians at 20.3 million. It
has been observed that while we struggle to wean Nigeria off the
oil rent, we should not replace it with another entitlement culture.[88]
Once a welfare system is started, it is difficult to reverse it, and this
is where the challenge is with regard to the economic empowerment
programmes of the government lies; and as the saying goes, you
don't have a second chance to create a first impression.

86. The third quarter report of the NBS actually indicated that Nigeria's trade balance nosedived
by 67.6% quarter-on-quarter; and total imports rising by 73.8%, while exports rose by only 7.8%.
Even though the government, through the CBN imposed import restrictions on rice and introduced a borrowing programme to stimulate local production, *Premium Times* 20 December 2018)
quoted data from Index Mundi and the US Department of Agriculture which indicated that rice
importation increased from 2.1 million tonnes in 2015 to an estimated 2.5 million tonnes in 2016;
2.6 in 2017, and 3.0 million tonnes in 2018 respectively.

87. The World Bank, 'NIGERIA: Bi-Annual Economic Update – Fragile economy', No. 1,
Washington, D.C. April 2017.

88. Soludo, 'Can a New Buharinomics Save Nigeria?', p. 20.

If Nigerians have to make a choice in the forthcoming elections and if the economy is a parameter for doing so, they need to ask themselves the fundamental question as to whether their conditions are better under the APC government than before. If not, are there brighter chances of the situation getting better in the near future? Or would they want to go back to the old days of alleged corruption of the PDP? These are indeed urgent questions, the answers to which cannot be given here until after a comparative assessment of the policy orientation of the two major political parties in the forthcoming elections. Nevertheless, using the campaign policy documents of both the APC and PDP for the 2019 elections, I will attempt a SWOT analysis in the next chapter.

It is in the perception of poor economic management that Nigerians are experiencing excruciating pain and feelings of hopelessness, and it is this situation that has led to some people believing that 'before long, there would be need for us to compare and contrast notes. It is being done through this book with the best of intentions and in the overall interest of Nigeria'.[89]

The comparison must however have minimum standards. For example, the exchange rate of Naira depreciated from N225=$1 in 2015 to N360=$1 as at December 2018. The government provides, presumably drawing from the foreign reserve an average of $210 to $250 million weekly totalling an average of $900 million to $1 billion every month to protect the naira, yet the value has not been stabilised. In November 2018, the CBN released $1.2 billion in that regard.[90] What magic can be done to shore up the value of the naira in the next four years? Exchange rate may not be the magic wand

89. Moremi Ojudu,'An Open Letter to President Muhammadu Buhari', published by Sahara Reporters, 5 December 2016.

90. Experience has shown that some countries, including Japan and Switzerland, who at one point experimented fixed rate or tried to impose artificial influence over the exchange rates of their countries' currencies failed. According to David Edevbie ('Stabilizing the Naira', *Thisday*, 25 March 2016), 'Russia spent $76 billion and €5 bn trying to stabilize the rouble in 2014 and was largely unsuccessful'.

to cure the ills in the economy but getting it wrong can cause major distortions in the macro economy. Nigeria is not the only country that has faced this quagmire. In March 2016, Egypt devalued its currency (the Egyptian Pound) by 13% against the US dollar. Other countries that did the same in response to the severe economic pressure included Russia, Venezuela, Kazakhstan and Azerbaijan.

Unfortunately, there is no guarantee that if the present government is succeeded by another, there is any measure that can be applied to ameliorate this. And this is a hard choice for the electorate.

It is true that oil prices have fallen over the years, but the world economy experienced the Great Financial Collapse in 2008/2009, and despite the collapse of oil prices from $147 to $41 per barrel, the Nigerian economy still absorbed the shocks and the economy grew by over 6%. Compared with the experiences of other countries, the differences in outcomes and impact relate to the different policy regimes and management strategies. From the prognoses on the future of oil, it seems the APC administration has the opportunity to lay the foundation for a post-oil economy, which is what it claims in its promises to Nigerians.

The government claimed that among its major achievements is the increase in the foreign reserve from $30 billion in 2015 to $47 billion as at September 2018, which went down to $41+ billion in November due to the withdrawals to support the forex market. To understand the real growth in foreign reserve, we should look into our debt profile too. It may be recalled that the federal government foreign debt rose from around $10.7 billion in 2015 to about $22.7 billion at November 2018. Hasn't the so-called gain in foreign reserve been debased by the increased debt portfolio, which was occasioned by the Federal Government's borrowings in the last two years?

There have been allegations that a few people, known as 'the cabal', are feeding fat on the forex market through the CBN patronage. What has been done or can be done to stop that and how soon?

Discussion on the policy priorities of the Buhari/APC Administration cannot be complete and exhaustive. 'The challenge of elections is for the incumbents to defend their record; and opposition, to show a vision superior to that record.' In this regard, 'the records of the incumbents in Nigeria have so far been offered in the breach. Where they have been put up they have come as glittering generalities, or intentions presented as accomplishments'.[91]

Having assessed the performance of the APC Government under the tripod of security, anti-corruption and economic reforms, and before discussing the challenges of managing public expectations, I will briefly touch on two critical areas that are fundamental to the well-being of the nation – education and health.

## Education

Education is the livewire of society, because it is the engine that drives development. But not all kinds of education are equally relevant. In the 21st century, priority should be in the area of science and technology, including vocational education that would meet the challenges of globalisation and technological advancement. Any society that neglects education does so at its peril. Unfortunately, over the years, education has not received the required attention in Nigeria. The APC identified education as a key to development and promised to address its decay. Unfortunately, the change that was promised to Nigerians has remained the same as before. Countless strike actions have characterised the education system; yet no meaningful and sustainable measures have been taken to improve the quality and standards of education.

91. Pat Utomi,'The Issues The Campaign Forgot', *Leadership,* 23 March 2015.

Today, Nigeria has the highest number of its citizens going to school outside the country and it loses billions of naira on that. The budgetary allocation in 2018 was not up to the amount allocated to the APC school feeding programme. Despite the huge amounts allocated to support education through the Tertiary Education Tax Fund and the Universal Basic Education Commission programmes, the challenges remain daunting. It seems that if the haemorrhage in the system is not curtailed, Nigeria will mortgage its future.

## Healthcare

Healthcare is another critical area that affects the lives of the citizens. Despite the array of health institutions and the resources purportedly invested in them, the challenges in the health sector remain overwhelming. During the 2015 electioneering campaigns, Buhari/APC promised an efficient health care system that would not necessitate Nigerians seeking health care outside this country. Today, it is estimated that Nigeria loses not less than $1 billion per annum to medical tourism. 'Nigeria has one of the highest maternal mortality rates in the world. At an estimated 814 deaths per 100,000 live births, it is almost four times the global average of 216 per 100,000 live births and significantly higher than the Sub-Saharan African average of 547 per 100,000. This means that in Nigeria 158 women die each day – nearly one woman every nine minutes – from conditions associated with childbirth'.[92] President Buhari, who promised to reform the sector, was the first to show the decay in the healthcare system by travelling to the UK for medical attention. Every important person in Nigeria, and those who can afford it, seek medical care outside the country due to the lack of confidence in the health care system.

92. Okonjo-Iweala, *Fighting Corruption is Dangerous: The Story Behind the Headlines*, MIT Press, Cambridge, Mass., p. 108.

## Managing Expectations

Managing expectations is one of greatest challenges of leadership. An assessment of the performance of the APC Government under President Buhari cannot be said to be below average because the comparative data for arriving at such conclusion may be questioned. It can best be described as below expectations, and I will explain why presently. You never have a second chance to make a first impression, and PMB's 100 days in office did not impress most Nigerians. In the history of Nigeria, every successive government, including the military regimes, was able to manage their legitimacy problems and made the most desirous impacts in their first one or two years. The 100 days expectation has become a tradition not only in Nigeria, but in other countries as well. Since Franklin Delano Roosevelt made his landmark achievements within 100 days, it became acceptable that 'a government that cannot perform in 100 days may as well reconcile with impotence for the rest of its days in office'. Roosevelt's experience is relevant in assessing expectations on the government. He is reputed to have worked hard against time and offered Americans a New Deal: 'He rescued the banking and financial system from collapse and created the Tennessee Valley Authority (which put federal resources at the disposal of weak and vulnerable states); He passed 15 pieces of major legislation, and by the time his first 100 days were over, he had secured a place in the people's hearts and minds which eventually earned him historic fourth term'.[93]

Barack Obama also showed that the first 100 days is the best opportunity to create a good first impression. He inherited from the Bush administration a legacy similar to what PMB inherited in Nigeria. But Obama was able to rescue America from its economic crisis by freezing salaries of White House staffers earning above $100,000, saving up to $443,000 a year. He also signed a $830

93. Azubuike Ishiekwene (2015) 'What is Possible In 100 Days', *Leadership*, 17 April 2015.

billion stimulus bill and clamped down on lobbyists at the Capitol. He rolled out a roadmap for American troop withdrawal from Afghanistan and Iraq. Most importantly, within Obama's 100 days he announced his plan to make America self-sufficient in energy, a plan which today has helped America reduce dependence on imported oil and 'cured the incapacity to think beyond oil'.

David Cameron in the UK and Narendra Modi of India provide similar examples. Prime Minister Cameron made hard choices, including a freeze on ministerial pay that saved the UK about £3 million yearly, cut in perks and cancellation of unnecessary projects. Modi in India, on the other hand, was able to bring back illegal money that was stashed outside by rich Indians in tax havens and put in place strong preventive measures to stem the tide. He was able to enforce drastic measures and reduced bureaucratic red tape; he 'reformed the judiciary and made the financial system more inclusive and focused the 2014 budget on infrastructure'.[94] In essence, there are examples of performance to justify the public's expectations on PMB to perform.

In the early days of the APC administration, Kingibe admonished thus: 'The President and his team of change agents will do well to profit from the warning of Nicolo Machiavelli that 'there is nothing more difficult to plan, more doubtful of success, nor more dangerous to manage than a new system. For, the initiator has the enmity of all who would profit by the preservation of the old institution, and merely lukewarm defenders in those who gain by the new ones.'[95] To retain current public confidence and trust, Government's core principles and strategies for change, if I may suggest, should prioritise consolidating national unity, the rule of law, and the renewal of public service institutions.

However, it is easier to say that the government has performed below the expectations that were raised by the same APC during its

94. Ibid, p.2.
95. Kingibe, 'Nigeria: Why change and how?', p. 6.

campaigns in 2015. While this conclusion remains controversial, there are certain indicators that should guide a Strength, Weaknesses, Opportunities and Threats (SWOT) analysis of the government's performance. To do that, the hypothesis could be developed around why do some people feel that the APC administration has failed to meet their expectations?

## An alliance of convenience, not for governance

Perhaps the beginning of interrogation into the failure of the APC administration should be from the kind of alliance that brought it to power. It is no wonder that instead of focusing on governance, the major gladiators in the alliance upon assuming office started fighting among themselves by calculating who should be what or who is likely to become the next president. This in a nutshell is the plausible explanation of the trial of the Senate President, Bukola Saraki, who emerged President of the Senate 'without' the support of the party. The emergence of Saraki as Senate President, even if it was not the choice of the party, should have been managed in a better way to maintain cohesion in the party and yet tackle corruption effectively. Ultimately, Saraki went through a lengthy trial but was discharged by the Supreme Court on the charges of corruption brought against him, making the trial a vindictive and fruitless exercise. The crisis within the APC even before the defection of the Senate President to his former party, the PDP, made a harmonious working relationship between the executive and legislative arms difficult, yet there was no effective leadership to resolve the power tussle.

Consequently, very little could be achieved in terms of legislation and securing Senate approval on some important policy decisions. Aside from that, the issue of who would carry the presidential ticket of the APC in the 2019 election also polarised the party. Even before the party could come out with a formal position to adopt President

Buhari, since as a sitting President he has the first right to decline or accept, Atiku Abubakar, an influential member of the party and supporter of Buhari in the 2015, defected back to his old party, the PDP. This mutual suspicion among the party top echelons finally led to the departure of the Senate President, Bukola Saraki, Speaker of the House of Representatives, Yakubu Dogara, Senator Rabi'u Musa Kwankwaso and other Senators to the opposition PDP. The governor of Sokoto, Aminu Waziri Tambowal, and that of Benue, Samuel Orthom, also defected to the PDP. They have now formed another alliance against Buhari and the APC.

## Lack of cohesion in the APC

While the failure of the alliance has partially explained the lack of cohesion in the ruling APC, the lack of cohesion in the party goes beyond the defections. Without going into the details of the party's problems, even though it is normal to have intra-party skirmishes, the former Chairman, Chief Odigie Oyegun, could not have the moral courage to exercise effective leadership over the party as its leader, and Asiwaju Bola Tinubu was reported to be indisposed to his leadership. It was as a result of this misunderstanding that the President appointed Tinubu to lead the mediation and reconciliation in the party, which resulted in the election of Adams Oshomhole to replace Odigie Oyegun as party Chairman. Mr Oshomhole is speculated to be a 'Tinubu boy' and has his full support.[96] Since his assumption of office as chairman, however, and following the party's primary elections conducted to produce candidates for elective positions, the party has been going through series of confidence-building programmes as some people who could not secure the party tickets to run for elective posts have either threatened to or actually dumped the party. Of course, such crises are also a problem

96. Mr. Oshomhole was governor of Edo State for 8 years under the platform of the ACN, which Asiwaju Bola Tinubu was the Leader.

in other parties. In summary, this is one of the reasons why the APC Government is perceived not to be performing. But the main reason for the 'non-performance' is largely seen as President Buhari's lack of effective leadership to settle squabbles within the party, though that is not his statutory responsibility.

## Lack of coordination among government agencies

Never before has Nigeria witnessed the kind of lackadaisical approach to governance as under the Buhari/APC administration. Apart from the slow pace in decision making, there is the problem of coordination between ministries and departments of government. There are several examples: the executive-legislature-judiciary face-offs; the lack of coordination between the EFCC and other security/intelligence agencies, for instance the friction that was created in the EFCC's attempts to arrest the former DGs of the Department of State Services (DSS) and the NIA. But more worrying is the lack of synergy between the EFCC and the Office of the Attorney General and Minister of Justice. Why all these? Does it mean that government officials see their roles in a competitive rather than complementary prism? There is no way law enforcement can be effective without the inputs and support of the chief law officer of the land. In spite of these obvious inter-agency rivalries, no body, not even the President who appointed all the officers, could bring them to work harmoniously together in the interest of the country.

## Lack of synergy with the NASS

The beauty of democracy is not only the freedom of choice, but also the separation of powers between the different arms of the government. The Constitution of the Federal Republic of Nigeria recognises this essential element and has provided specific functions for each arm to work not in silos but in tandem with the others. Section 4 of the 1999 Constitution provides the powers of the NASS to include:

4.  *(1) The legislative powers of the Federal Republic of Nigeria shall be vested in a National Assembly for the Federation, which shall consist of a Senate and a House of Representatives.*

*(2) The National Assembly shall have power to make laws for the peace, order and good government of the Federation or any part thereof with respect to any matter included in the Exclusive Legislative List set out in Part I of the Second Schedule to this Constitution.*

*(3) The power of the National Assembly to make laws for the peace, order and good government of the Federation with respect to any matter included in the Exclusive Legislative List shall, save as otherwise provided in this Constitution, be to the exclusion of the Houses of Assembly of States.*

*(4) In addition and without prejudice to the powers conferred by subsection (2) of this section, the National Assembly shall have power to make laws with respect to the following matters, that is to say:-*

*(a) any matter in the Concurrent Legislative List set out in the first column of Part II of the Second Schedule to this Constitution to the extent prescribed in the second column opposite thereto;*

*and*

*(b) any other matter with respect to which it is empowered to make laws in accordance with the provisions of this Constitution.*

This means the NASS is critical to the success of any government. While all arms are independent and interference in the affairs of another is unacceptable, measures to promote good understanding and harmonious working relationships are encouraged. One would not advocate for any interference, but experience has shown that the President, as the Chief Executive of the country, cannot but be interested in what happens in the other arms to ensure the smooth running of government. Unfortunately, from the outset, PMB declared that he was not interested in who emerged as the leader of the other two arms of the NASS (the Senate and the House of Representatives), adding that he would work with whomever the legislators elected as their leaders. Thus, the first mistake for the APC was that while the elected Senators were in the Senate Chamber to elect their leaders as provided by law, the APC leadership convened a meeting with PMB at the International Conference Centre, Abuja, a meeting to which PMB did not turn up after all; and while some elected APC Senators were at that venue, those who followed the rule of parliamentary practice were in the Chamber where elections into various senate leadership positions were conducted with Senator Bukola Saraki elected President of the 8th Senate of the Federal Republic of Nigeria; and Senator Ike Ekweremadu of the opposition PDP emerged as Deputy Senate President, the first time in the political history of Nigeria that an opposition member has occupied that position.

The outcome of this election was not acceptable to the APC leadership, as it was speculated that Asiwaju Bola Tinubu (the APC Leader) preferred Senator Ahmed Lawal to be the Senate President and not Senator Saraki.[97] This, in brief, is the genesis of the friction between the NASS and the APC leadership, which affected the relationship between the NASS and the executive arm of government. The consequences of this are too numerous to document here. Suffice it to say that as a result of this misunderstanding, most of PMB's requests for confirmation of appointments were either delayed or declined, budget passage suffered undue delays, and accusations of corruption, lack of transparency, due diligence and efficiency etc. were common exchanges between the NASS and the Executive. Ultimately, all efforts made by the APC to change the

97. It was later revealed that Tinubu wanted to punish Saraki for opposing his candidacy for the post of Vice President, as he (Sarki) had counselled against fielding a 'Muslim-Muslim' ticket for the Presidential election in 2015. Thus, Tinubu perceived Saraki as a potential rival or competitor both of them Muslims and being of the Yoruba extraction. The subsequent trial of Senator Saraki at the Code of Conduct Tribunal was again speculated as a continuation of this internal fight within the APC.

leadership of the Senate failed.

This unhealthy relationship finally led to the Senate President and the Speaker of the House of Representatives decamping to the opposition PDP, yet remaining in their positions of leadership – again for the first time in the political history of Nigeria.

When Obasanjo was president (1999-2007) he used to invite some members of the NASS to accompany him on any official visit overseas, which gave them the opportunity to see and hear what the Nigerian Government was negotiating with other countries and which made domestication of international instruments and approval of some presidential requests easier. In other words, this makes for a better executive-legislature relationship. Although such practice is not provided for by law, another error of judgment that PMB made was not to involve members of the NASS in his foreign tours[98] and that created a barrier between him and the NASS. While the heads of all arms of the government are independent, it is only the President who has the whole country as his constituency and he should ensure that he takes steps to smooth relationships between the three arms and office holders.

## Why Buhari has failed or is failing

Five reasons were identified mid-way into the first term of President Buhari in office which explains the perception of his failure to meet expectations.

## 1. No sense of urgency

Malcolm Fabiyi[99] observed that Buhari has not exhibited any sense of urgency in dealing with state matters. 'Six months into his administration, Buhari was yet to name his government. When the

98. Even there were a few Parliamentarians that appeared during the President's visits to some countries and functions outside Nigeria; it was not as formal as in the past.
99. 'Five reasons why Buhari is failing', published by *Premium Times*, 11 August2016.

names emerged, it was one that he could have come up with on day one. No one knows how hard Mr. Buhari tried to find capable Nigerians to join him in steering the ship of state. Yet somehow, of the 170 million Nigerians that are alive, some of whom are doing big things in Nigeria and beyond, it was the present batch of overused, recycled names and faces that Mr. Buhari brought forward.'

This lack of a sense of urgency led to the neglect of some agencies and parastatals which long remained, or still remain, without substantive heads. The agencies and parastatal organisations are the engine room for running an effective government. But it was as if Buhari's main goal was merely to secure the presidency since he showed no or little interest in reorganising the parastatals. Even as his tenure is drawing to an end, some agencies are still headed by persons in acting capacity or appointees of the previous government, whose policies the APC criticised.

Fabiyi further asserted that 'Mr. Buhari is slow and steady. However, while a slow and steady hand might be needed for a paediatrician who delivers babies, fast and firm hands are required for a surgeon working in the emergency wing of a hospital'. He continued that Buhari's lack of urgency extends beyond the selection of his cabinet to his slow responses to the clashes between herdsmen and farmers killing thousands of people; and that the power sector is comatose, yet no workable plan for addressing the problem. And for a nation that is trying to encourage foreign direct investment, it should not take over one year to appoint ambassadors.

Against this backdrop, Dele Momodou declared, 'Nigerians wanted to witness a sporadic change in their lives and not listen to a plethora of excuses for failure. If truth be told, the APC frittered away its humungous goodwill and lost a lot of its uncommon equity when it got carried away over the assumption of its invincibility. APC behaved like it had all the time in the world and failed to take cognisance of the traditional impatience of Nigerians'.[100]

100. Pendulum by Dele Momodou, 'The Season for True Change', *Thisday* Newspaper, 31 December 2016.

## 2. Hiring for loyalty

A second reason advanced by Fabiyi for why Buhari is failing is that he values loyalty over all other things in his appointments. He said that could be due to Buhari's experience with betrayal during his tenure as military head of state in 1984-85. Although the President reserves the prerogatives to appoint anybody to any position he wishes without explaining why and how, the principles of fairness, equity, justice, transparency and inclusiveness would warrant some balance. For the first time in the history of Nigeria, PMB's lopsided appointments in key positions, especially in defence, security and law enforcement, are obvious.[101] Nevertheless, hiring for loyalty can never give the best options for hiring over merit, which would normally consider attitude and aptitude as the main ingredients. Against this background, Dele Momodou concluded that 'There may truly be a powerful mafia that has grabbed the jugular of Nigeria while the President has been practically hypnotised by them. Whatever it is, only the President can confirm if he thinks the current mafia is what he needs to deliver on his attractive promises to Nigerians made on the soap box.'[102]

101. Since inception in 2015, PMB has concentrated the following positions in the North with His Chief of staff, which though not a position recognized under the constitution has become more powerful than that of the Vice President as the occupier of that office is acclaimed to perform the delegated functions of the President; the Secretary to the Government of the Federation (SGF); the National Security Adviser (NSA), the Chief of Army Staff; the Chief of Air staff; the Comptroller General of Customs; the Chairman/Chief Executive of the NDLEA; and the Comptroller General of Prisons Service; the Managing Director of the NNPC, DG of NEMA,, Chairman of the EFCC and the Permanent Secretary in the State House, are all from the North East; while for the first time, the positions of the Director General of the DSS, NIA and the Chief of Defence Intelligence (CDI); Chairman of the Civil Service Commission (CSC), the MD of the Nigerian ports Authority, National Health insurance Scheme, all high-profile positions, are from PMB's geopolitical zone, the North West. The Inspector General of Police and the Commandant of the Nigeria Security and Civil Defence Corps (NSCDC) are both from one state, Niger in the North Central zone.

102. Dele Momodou, 'Time to Re-Write the APC Manifesto', *Thisday*, 5 March 2016, p.3.

## 3. No strong team to develop and implement coherent policies

The importance of a strong team, whether economic or however it is called, in driving government policies and making an impact on governance cannot be overemphasised. Although the APC/Buhari administration has consistently argued that it has an economic team, the impact is not felt in terms of policy outcomes. The team was criticised for being predominantly lawyers and accountants without a single economist.[103] The reflection on the need to have a strong economic team is reminiscent of the Obasanjo administration when there was a strategy which the public could criticise and even fight, and there was a strong team whose members were believers in the strategy and who regularly took up their critics; there was also a healthy and productive debate on the policy direction of the government and the overall development of the country.[104]

---

103. Until later when an Economist was appointed as the DG Budget Office.

104. Jibrin Ibrahim observed in 2016 that 'In 2003, President Olusegun Obasanjo established an economic reform group that become known as the 'Dream Team', composed of a crop of technocrats who had proved their mettle professionally. The team was led by Ngozi Okonjo-Iweala, the Minister for Finance recruited from the World Bank, the institution so many of us love to hate. Professor Charles Soludo, Governor of the Central Bank and Professor Ode Ojowu, Chief Economic Adviser to the President. Other members were Nasir El Rufai, Minister of the Federal Capital Territory and ObyEzekwesile, Head of the Due Process Office in the Presidency. This core team was complemented by other academics and technocrats such as Professor Julius Ihonvbere in charge of the policy monitoring team in the Presidency, C. Chikwelu, the Minister of Information, Bode Augusto, the Director-General of the Budget Office, Ad Obe who led on returning the public service to service provisioning, Dr. Goke Adegorowe leading on the Bureau for Public Service Reform and Dr Mansur Mukhtar handling the Debt Management Office. We knew who was doing.The team drew up an economic reform agenda - the National Economic Empowerment and Development Strategy (NEEDS) and engaged civil society and the wider public on it. They were constantly in the media arguing that they had a comprehensive economic reform programme aimed at laying the foundations for economic growth and employment creation based on four basic elements. They were a reinvigorated effort in combating corruption and promoting transparency and accountability; promoting macro-economic stability through the acceleration of privatisation and liberalisation of the economy; public service reform, including reform of public expenditure, budgeting and the civil service and strengthening basic service delivery through improved governance and institutional strengthening. Some of us did not like the package and fought it. We argued that the anti-corruption element was a lie. We pushed the case that the liberalisation programme was a disguised form of the promotion of crony capitalism in which those in power were personalising public assets. We contested the plan to make massive cuts in the public service employment and attacked it as cruel and unworkable'.

## 4. Policy vacuum

According to Fabiyi, 'Not a single coherent and consistent policy framework that is aimed at correcting many of the ills that Buhari has complained about has been put in place. Nothing has been done to make it easier for Nigerian businessmen to manufacture [a] toothpick in Nigeria than for them to import it. There are no plans for providing them with the energy they need to cut the wood, shave and package it.'

While the scenario painted by Fabiyi has been largely the case since 2016, two years later some notable achievements have been recorded, including the Presidential Fertilizer Initiative, which involves partnership with the government of Morocco for the supply of phosphate, and which has resulted in the revitalisation of 11 blending plants across the country; the Ease of Doing Business Reform; support for micro small and medium enterprises; the issuance of some Executive Orders on improving efficiency; and the implementation of the Social Investment Programme, including conditional cash transfers and school feeding programme, all of which I could not assess objectively for lack of reliable data.

## 5. Half-Hearted Anti-Corruption War

Despite efforts in the anti-corruption area as discussed earlier in this chapter, there is a groundswell of cynicism regarding the transparency, comprehensiveness and fruitfulness of the anti-corruption efforts of the Buhari administration. Some people feel that on account of these shortcomings, the administration has failed and several examples have been cited. In my view, however, it is a matter of perception and managing expectations.

## 6. Economy – Fire Fighting Approach, No Strategy

Indeed at the time of Fabiyi's assessment in 2017, the ambitious set of structural reforms in the Economic Recovery and Growth Plan (ERGP) of the Buhari administration, which is the main economic policy framework of the Buhari administration, had not been released.[105] Nevertheless, some of the observations made above under the economy suggest that the sort of 'command and control' approach adopted in management of the economy cannot work for a modern economy. According to the World Bank, the credibility of the ERGP will depend on evidence of concrete progress in implementing the reform programme.

### Lessons learned from Buhari's Leadership Performance

In his book *Why I Fail* one of my former staff members (Comrade Laiba), who requested me to write a foreword, agreed with the saying that 'experience is the best teacher' and added that a wise man would say 'it is better if it is not your own experience', yet he wrote the book for others to learn from his experience. Another writer who merely described himself as 'a leader, a management consultant and author, identified '15 striking lessons to learn from Buhari's leadership performance', which I summarise as follows:

1. Have a plan before you set out to lead. A plan is a roadmap to every achievement. The APC and PMB never had a plan, they only had promises. The question is, is PMB willing and ready to accept good plans? If he was, then the proposals sent to him by Nasir El-Rufa'i, one of the influential members of PMB's entourage, soon after the election of PMB and some months

105. The ERGP was released only in March 2017, almost two years into the first term of the administration.

ABDULLAHI Y. SHEHU

after his assumption of office, were for all practical purposes meaningful, specific, measurable and impact-oriented.[106]

106. Concerned about the slow pace or lack of performance, El-Rufai'I, in his memo titled 'Immediate and Medium term Imperatives for president Muhammadu Buhari, dated 22 September 2016, he provided useful pieces of advice on how to move the government forward on all aspects, state of the economy, infrastructure, governance issues, etc, and made insightful suggestions with a 'Draft Decision and Implementation Matrix'. He also attached two other memos: the first, titled 'A Check-List of Hot-button issues that would confront the President on assumption Office', dated April 2015, in which he specifically drew attention to the following critical issues:

1. Risk of Fuel supply bottlenecks due to non-payment of 'subsidies' and subsidy regime itself.

2. Shutdown of the crude oil export terminals due to disputes about levies (and bribes)

3. Position on the $2bn budget support loan from the World Bank and AfDB being rushed by Minister of Finance

4. Merging of duplicating agencies to save costs as recommended in the Oronsaye Report.

5. Rushed nomination of executive director and President of Africa Development Bank by the Minister of Finance and the Presidency.

6. Security sector review and development of rapid response counter-insurgency strategy, particularly urgent depoliticisation of the SSS and polluted branches of the armed forces.

7. Treasury Status – Extent of Salary & Pension Arrears, Crises in state finances, etc. at least 24 states are unable to pay salaries without bridging loans. There is a need to look very closely and early into the operations of the Federation Account. Insolvent states can only add to our inherited significant security and political challenges

8. Immediate Budget Review – Supplementary Budget to refocus tone and direction including the proposed review of VAT and luxury taxes.

9. Agricultural Inputs Prioritization for the 2015 cropping season to avoid a famine in 2015-2016. Maize prices have collapsed due to imports, while warehouses are filled with imported 'duty-free' rice much below our farmers' production costs.

10. Quick Wins and Strategies – Electricity, Insurgency, Road Repairs, Abuja Renewal, etc.

11. A careful look at the exchange rate particularly the sustainability of the current resurgence of the Naira and the stock market and avoiding being blamed for any future exchange rate adjustment.

12. An early consideration of currency policy and operations, including recent redenomination, redesign and rationalization of notes and coins in light of the alleged massive seigniorage of the CBN in the last few months to finance elections and bail out the recently privatised Electricity Distribution companies. The second annex was another memo from Owelle Rochas Okorocha, in his capacity as Chairman of the Progressives' Governors' Forum, on 'Reconstitution of federal government Boards', dated April 6, 2015, respectively.

149

2. Be honest with why you want to be a leader. The writer observed that PMB did not leave according to his declared philosophy of 'I belong to everybody and I belong to nobody'.

3. Promise little, deliver more, or promise more and deliver little.

4. You cannot build a reputation on what you are going to do. Most of the APC promises were on what they will do, not what has been done in the past.

5. The past cannot always determine the future. PMB acknowledged that he was able to make a change under military rule but had challenges under democracy.

6. Never be partial. To succeed in leadership, you may need to step on the toes of those close to you as you did of those far from you.

7. He that must come to equity must come with clean hands.

8. 'You cannot make people rich or happy by sharing 10 thousand naira with them, not even a hundred thousand naira can do that, when indeed the road you took to that place you shared the money are probably in bad shape.'

9. Stop blaming your past. Blame makes people lame.

10. Integrity is everything, but it must be wholistic not only in one area.

11. Take decisions on time; overall, decision taking is leadership.

12. Listen to others, especially wise counsel.

13. Don't surround yourself with only yes, yes people.

14. Use professionals, not propagandists.

15. Accept mistakes sincerely and don't cover them up with more excuses.

## Conclusion

So far, the three and half years of the APC have resulted in mixed feelings among Nigerians. While it would be unfair to say that it has failed totally or has performed below average, it would be better to say that the Buhari/APC Administration has performed below expectations because what propelled it to power were the high expectations it raised at the election.

In reviewing the various sectors, in particular the key campaign issues of the APC – security, anti-corruption and economy – some notable progress was made, though not up to the expected standards. The reason why we say the performance is below standard is not because the efforts made are not appreciated, but because there is tremendous goodwill and the opportunity to perform better. For example, we appreciate the government's focus on anti-corruption, but we are more concerned about the outputs from that. If the government claims to have recovered huge amounts (in billions of naira and foreign currencies); has stopped leakages; saved monies that would have otherwise been stolen if the APC anti-corruption agenda was not there; increased revenue generation through taxes and others,[107] etc, then we expect that the government should be able to invest in infrastructure, education, health and other sectors, pay a living wage, reduce poverty, and improve the overall living conditions of the citizens within four years as it promised.

It is rather unfortunate that since President Buhari assumed office the song has been blaming the past PDP Government for

107. The Federal Inland Revenue Service (FIRS) alone reported the second highest revenue generation of N5.3trillion in December 2018. The highest revenue in the history of the FIRS was N5.7 trillion in 2012 when oil prices hovered between $100 and $114 pb. If we take into account other revenues generated by other 'cash cows'" in the economy – the NNPC, the Nigerian Customs Service (NCS) and the Nigeria Ports Authority (NPA) who reported revenues in trillions, it would be clear that the amounts generated would be more than the total revenue of Nigeria, yet, there is complaint of lack of funds to run government. It should be noted however, that all collectable revenues go into the consolidated revenue account, which is then shared between the three tiers of government with the federal government having up to 50% or more.

mismanagement, corruption, 'squandermania' – you name it! President Buhari/the APC have failed to understand the diversity and complexities of Nigeria and the fact that serious problems require drastic and urgent solutions. Having personal integrity is not enough to run an effective government. You need to manage the expectations of all segments of the society and you need to recruit competent people and give them the opportunity and empowerment to develop Specific, Measurable, Achievable, Realistic and Time-bound (SMART) strategies for the transformation of the country.

Nigeria's problems and the challenges in dealing with its many developmental problems are multidimensional and complicated. Just as one seeks to address one or two problems, two or more have developed elsewhere, and you need a president who can devote at least 18 hours per day to attend to the demanding office of the president. Obasanjo, who has experienced that three times, revealed that 'without impaired health and strain of age, running the affairs of Nigeria is a 25/7 affair, not 24/7'.

What we have seen in the discussion on the APC Administration so far is that it has created a second chapter in the assessment of democratic transformation in Nigeria. The 2019 election is expected to provide a third chapter – either a repeat of the APC four-year tenure or a return to the old days of the PDP. The choice is for the Nigerian electorate. I qualify it to be the electorate because many of the elite, who influence opinions through their intellectual power or wealth, hardly have permanent voters' cards to be able to vote. The choice is therefore, as usual, going to be made by the majority, the not well informed but politically conscious masses of the people.

# CHAPTER 4

# 2019 Presidential Election: Between the 'Next Level' and 'Let's Get Nigeria Working Again'

When the 2015 presidential election was conducted, it was only the record of the PDP in government that was opened to criticism. With the APC being in government for the past three and a half years, a second chapter has been opened for comparison and alternative choice by the electorate. The INEC has registered over 90 political parties, out of which 73 have signified their intention to field candidates for the presidential election. While all candidates have equal rights and chances by law, the reality is that the 2019 presidential election will be a contest between the two major parties (APC and PDP), the reason being that the two parties have the widest spread in both national and state assemblies and have both held power at the centre. Furthermore, the zoning of the post of president by both parties to the North has produced two contending candidates from the same ethnic group (Fulani), the same religion (Islam) and the same region (the North). Both are within the same age bracket (Atiku is 72 while Buhari is 76).[108] Would these natural arrangements affect the outcome of the election? If so, how? and if not, why?

The role of the PDP and APC in managing victory and governance has been discussed in Chapters 2 and 3 to provide a background for understanding the possible scenario that may unfold in 2019. To this end, we shall discuss in this chapter the characteristics of the two parties and determine what it is in a name that would make the difference. The manifestos of the two parties are similar in many ways, and so are the campaign issues. While the APC has produced PMB as its flag bearer, the PDP has Atiku Abubakar as its candidate. Each of them has his unique strengths and weaknesses, but a glimpse into their campaign programmes (tagged 'Next Level' for PMB and 'Let's Get Nigeria Working Again' for Atiku) would provide a basis for comparison and choice. In other words, I shall revisit the key campaign issues with a view to supporting both to succeed and criticising where we must in order to provide a balanced perspective. I shall do that with the yearnings of the electorate (especially the poor) in mind; the conspiracy of the elite and what the options are for the electorate.

### APC and PDP: what is in a name?

The general orientation of the APC and PDP does not provide a clear ideological distinction between them. Both parties seem to have been packaged for convenience and mainly for winning an election. It may be recalled that the PDP emerged out of the formation of Group 38 'prominent' politicians who formed a pressure group to resist any extension of military rule when General Abacha wanted

108. All these are mundane issues that ordinarily should not be the key determinants, but they are sentiments which the electorate consider in making their choices.

to transform into a civilian president in 1998. Almost all those who were in that group became the founding members of the PDP.[109]

The alliance of 'strange bedfellows' lasted for a short time when some of the founders of the party started decamping to other parties for recognition or to secure political positions. Today, about 60% of the politicians in Nigeria have been members of the PDP at one point or another.

On the other hand, the APC emerged as another alliance of different political bedfellows to seize power from the PDP in 2014. The APC was formed through an alliance of the ACN led by Bola Tinubu, the ANPP and the CPC led by Muhammadu Buhari. Of course, as stated in Chapter 2, the failures of the PDP made the APC a 'merger' party and it grew in strength and extent over a short period, only to start to disintegrate towards another round of elections. All this suggests that for the politicians in Nigeria, there is no permanent friend, only permanent interests, and there is no permanent ideology or principle in politics. Consequently, apart from PMB, the Leader of the APC (Bola Tinubu), Bisi Akande (former Chairman of the ACN), Adams Oshomhole and Lawal Shua'ibu(National Chairman and Deputy of the APC), most of the gladiators in the APC migrated from the PDP, and despite the claim of change or departure from the old ways of doing things, the change has left things largely the same.[110] The APC is blaming the PDP for destroying Nigeria for 16 years, yet its Campaign Council consists of (1) Rotimi Amaechi (DG) who spent 15 years in the PDP, 8 years as Speaker of the Rivers State House of Assembly and 7 years governor; (2) Senator

109. Including Dr Alex Ekweme, former Vice President in the Second Republic, Chief Solomon Lar, Audu Ogbe, Barnabas Gemade, (who later became Chairmen of the party), Mallam Admu Chiroma, Chief Jim Nwobodo, just to mention a few.

110. According to some observers, since its establishment in 1998, the PDP has had 13 Chairmen. Two (Chiefs Alex Ekwueme and Solomon Lar) have passed on. Out of 10 past Chairmen, 7 are now members of the APC leaving only 3 in the PDP. Someone asked the question that 'if70% of the PDP we knew is now APC, isn't it clear that the country is still being led by the same people who have decided to adopt another name? The logical conclusion is that 'there is no PDP, there is no APC; there are only politicians'.

George Akume (Vice Chairman, North) who was PDP Governor for 8 years in Benue State; (3) Senator Ken Nnamani (Vice Chairman, South) who was Senate President under PDP; (4) Senator Godswill Akpabio (South-South Zonal Director), former Secretary to State Government and Governor of Akwa Ibom for 8 years and Senate Minority Leader for 3 years under the PDP; (5) Senator Aliyu Magatakarda Wamako (North-West Zonal Director) who was PDP Governor for 8 years; (6) Olusola Oke (South-West Zonal Director) who was PDP National Legal Adviser for 9 years; etc. None of these persons have spent less than 13 years in the PDP, which translates to 81% of the years of destruction. Simply put, 'in one breath, you say PDP destroyed Nigeria for 16 years. In another breath; you need these same destroyers to help you 'change'[111] Nigeria.' So, where should the electorate see the difference to make radical change? This naturally leads us to examine the campaign programmes of the two parties and their candidates.

## Buhari/APC's 'Next Level'

'Next Level' is an abridged version of the APC Manifesto for the 2019 election. It is captioned 'Good for the Common Man', suggesting the poor man's orientation in the APC's governance programmes. An overview of the 'Next Level' policy document states that 'we have worked hard to fulfil our promises – and while the road may have been difficult, over the last three and a half years, we have laid the foundations for a strong, stable and prosperous country for the majority of our people.' It went further to say that 'foundation work is not often visible, neither is it glamorous – it is vital to achieving the kind of country we desire …' It outlines some of the achievements of the APC Government in agriculture, power, security, anti-corruption and asset recovery, poverty reduction and jobs creation.

111. Yusuf Dankofa in Whatsapp chat,12 January 2019.

Specifically, the policy thrust is based on five key priorities for the 2019 election.[112]

## 1. Jobs

While some significant achievements were recorded under the social investment programmes of the APC Government, the re-election manifesto is aiming at bigger and more ambitious job creation programmes, and although not a detailed implementation plan, the next level plan for this objective is clustered around five strategies:

1.  If elected for a second term, N-Power will engage 1 million graduates and skill 10 million under a voucher system in partnership with the private sector.

2.  Agriculture will be used as the vehicle for creating jobs, including through the ongoing 'Anchor Borrowers' Programme to support input and jobs to one million farmers; Livestock Transformation Plan aimed at creating 1.5 million jobs along diary, beef, hide and skin; and Agriculture Mechanisation Policy with tractors and processors to create some 5 million jobs.

3.  The APC Government will provide a $500 million funding for technology and creative industry to create 500 thousand jobs and train 200,000 youth for outsourcing market in technology, services and entertainment.

4.  At least 6 regional Industrial Parks and 109 Special Production and Processing Centres (SPPCs) to scale up Tractors and Processors Plan in each Senatorial District.

5.  Under the next level plan, about 300,000 extra jobs for vendors and farmers to be created by increasing the number of children

112. See Hassan Adebayo, 'Next Level': Buhari's five key campaign promises for 2019', *Premium Times* online, 22 November 2018.

fed under the school feeding programme from 9.2 million to 15 million.

## 2. Infrastructure

The second priority component of the 'Next Level' APC Policy is to improve infrastructure in four areas, namely, roads, rail, power and the technology (the Internet).

In the area of roads, the APC has promised to complete the Second Niger Bridge and reconstruct several other roads across the country.

On railways, the APC/Buhari plan is to complete the Lagos-Ibadan-Kano Rail, the eastern Rail (Port-Harcourt-Maiduguri) through Aba and all the south-eastern state capitals, Makurdi, Jos, Bauchi, and Gombe; and the Coastal rail (Lagos-Calabar).

In the power sector, the 'Next Level' plan is to 'energise' universities and up to 300 markets across the country to have uninterrupted power through renewable energy sources such as solar. It promises 'a minimum of 1,000 MW New Generation incremental Power capacity per annum on the Grid; Distribution to get to 7,000 MW under Distribution Expansion programme'.

## 3. Business, Entrepreneurship Development

The 'Next Level' plan promises to improve on its current policy of enabling the business environment by promoting business and entrepreneurship under the 'people moni scheme' 'market moni' and 'farmer moni' schemes, targeting 10 million Nigerians from the current 2.3 million. The APC promises to establish 'people moni bank' and entrepreneurship bank', which will be technology-enabled and offer credit, capacity building and business plan to support these schemes and young entrepreneurs.

To ease business, the APC Government will 'legislate and enforce deadlines for issuance of government licences and permits' and 'simplify investments, customs, and immigration, trade and production procedures'.

## 4. Human Capital Enhancement Services – Healthcare, Education…

The APC/Buhari promise, if elected for a second term, is to 'retrain all teachers to deliver digital literacy'. In this regard, 10,000 schools will be remodelled and equipped each year. Under health, they promise insurance for all using 'co-payments to share the cost between individuals, the private sector and government', while 'the poorest 40 per cent will be exempted from such co-payments'.

## 5. Political Inclusion

The 'Next Level' plan promises 35% affirmative action for women in federal appointments and increases the number of youth in board appointments, etc.

Giving signal for the commencement of his campaign for the 2019 election in Abuja when a delegation of the FCT community paid him a Christmas visit in the State House on 25 December 2018, PMB announced that his/the APC's campaign focus will be the same as in 2015, namely on security, anti-corruption and the economy. He said these are still the main problems that the government should address in order to improve the living conditions of the people. He further reiterated his commitment to recovering public funds and other assets stolen in the past.

Although the initial reaction to the 'Next Level' was that it was plagiarised, in my view the APC has nothing better than this to offer and if implemented to the letter, it can 'salvage' Nigeria. For sure, the major problems of Nigeria remain the issues of security, corruption, poverty, unemployment and a weak and oil-dependent economy. To prove that there will be a significant difference in the implementation of its policies, the APC has the greatest challenge to convince Nigerians on its record of achievements and its preparedness for better management of the economy, especially when given a second chance to carry out the 'Next Level' change.

'Next Level' is not new, but it seems to be an ambitious programme. It aims at a higher level of performance without providing sufficient ground and justification for the past failures. For example, it aims at creating 10 million jobs without providing specific data on the number of jobs created in the past three and half years to contradict the data on unemployment and job losses in the previous chapter. Also, it aims at supporting 12 million Nigerians through the National Social Investment Programme without providing data on the current level of achievement under the programme. These are just a few examples. Although the implementation strategies are expected to be articulated succinctly somewhere for the public to see, that is yet to be seen, and as in 2015, the debate is going to be a sort of 'fireworks' during the electioneering campaigns as it was during the previous election.

In the course of my research, I stumbled on an online article by Mukhtari Wali, which could not be referenced properly. It is titled 'Before we look at the NEXT LEVEL plans by the APC, can we take a look at the 2014 APC Manifesto and see what has been achieved?' The write-up summarised and extracted 41 promises in two policy documents released by the APC during the 2015 election: 'Securing Nigeria's Future' and 'Roadmap to a New Nigeria', which were signed by the APC presidential candidate, General Muhammadu Buhari. He noted that most of the promises, including those that do not require funds to be implemented, were 'yet to even be initiated' as at December 2018. The extract is presented here verbatim for clarity and precision.

## *Securing Nigeria's Future*

1.  *Initiate action to amend the Nigerian Constitution with a view to devolving powers, duties, and responsibilities to states in order to entrench true Federalism and the Federal spirit[113]. (This simply means that the APC actually promised to restructure Nigeria and entrench true federalism if voted into power). Page 6.*

2.  *Amend the Constitution to remove immunity from prosecution for elected officers in criminal cases. Page 6.*

3.  *Require full disclosure in media outlets, of all government contracts over N100m prior to award and during implementation at regular intervals. Page 6.*

4.  *Amend the Constitution to require Local Governments to publish their meeting minutes, service performance data, and items of spending over N10M. Page 6.*

5.  *Consult and amend the Constitution to enable States and Local Governments to create city, Local Government and State Policing systems. Page 7.*

6.  *Bring permanent peace and solutions to the insurgency issues in the North-East; the Niger Delta; and other conflict prone states and areas such as Plateau, Benue, Bauchi, Borno, Abia, Taraba, Yobe, and Kaduna. Page 8.*

7.  *Initiate policies to ensure that Nigerians are free to live and work in any part of the country by removing state of origin, tribe, ethnic and religious affiliations from documentation requirements in our identification of citizens and replace these with State of Residence and fashion out the appropriate minimal qualification for obtaining such a state of residency, nation-wide. Page 8.*

---

113. This was achieved with the signing into law an Act giving autonomy and independence to the state Houses of Assembly; States Judiciary; and the Local Government Councils, though this law is yet to be enforced.

8. *Make our economy one of the fastest growing emerging economies in the world with a real GDP growth averaging at least 10-12% annually. Page 9.*

9. *Create 5 million new jobs by 2019. Page 9.*

10. *Put in place a N300bn Regional Growth Fund with an average of N50bn in each geo political region… to encourage private sector enterprise and to support places currently reliant only on the public sector, to migrate to a private sector reality. Page 10.*

11. *Amend the Constitution and the Land Use Act. Page 10.*

12. *Create an additional middle class of at least 4 million new home owners by 2019. Page 10.*

13. *Create a Social Welfare Program of at least Five Thousand Naira (N5000) that will cater for the 25 million poorest and most vulnerable citizens upon the demonstration of children's enrolment in school and evidence of immunisation to help promote family stability. Page 10.*

14. *Provide allowances to the discharged but unemployed Youth Corps members for Twelve (12) months while in the skills and entrepreneurial development programmes. Page 10.*

15. *Construct a 5,000km of Superhighway including service trunks and (b) building of up to 6,800km of modern railway completed by 2019; Page 11.*

16. *Embark on PPP schemes that will ensure every one of the 36 states has one functional airport. Page 11*

17. *Speedily pass the much delayed Petroleum Industry Bill (PIB) and ensure that local content issues are fully addressed. Page 12*

18. *Make Nigeria the world's leading exporter of LNG through the creation of strategic partnerships. Page 12.*

19. *Targeting up to 20% of our annual budget for Education. Page 13.*

20. *Provide One Meal a day for all Primary school pupils. That will create jobs in Agriculture, Catering, and Delivery Services. Page 14.*

21. *Establish at least six new universities of Science and Technology with satellite campuses in various states. Page 14.*

22. *Establish technical colleges and vocational centres in each state of the federation. Page 14.*

23. *Increase the quality of all federal government owned hospitals to world class standard by 2019. Page 15.*

24. *Provide free antenatal care for pregnant women; free health care for babies and children up to school going age and for the aged; and free treatment for those afflicted with infectious diseases such as tuberculosis and HIV/AIDS. Page 15.*

25. *Create an Insurance Policy for our Journalists as the nation faces hard times and our Journalists face more dangers. Page 15*

26. *Establish Zonal world class sports academies and training institutes and ensure that Nigeria occupies a place of pride in global sports and athletics; Page 16.*

27. *Assist Nollywood to fully develop into world class movie industry that can compete effectively with Hollywood and Bollywood in due course. Page 16.*

28. *Guarantee that women are adequately represented in government appointments and provide greater opportunities in education, job creation, and economic empowerment. Page 16*

*29. Use the Party structures to promote the concept of reserving a minimum number of seats in the States and National Assembly, for women. Page 16.*

*30. Create shelter belts in states bordering the Sahara Desert to mitigate and reverse the effects of the expanding desert. Page 17.*

### *On the second document titled 'Roadmap to a New Nigeria':*

*31. Create 20,000 jobs per state immediately for those with a minimum qualification of secondary school leaving certificate and who participate in technology and vocational training. Page 4*

*32. Place the burden of proving innocence in corruption cases on persons with inexplicable wealth. Page 7.*

*33. Pursue legislation expanding forfeiture and seizure of assets laws and procedure with respect to inexplicable wealth, regardless of whether there is a conviction for criminal conduct or not. Page 7.*

*34. Provide free tertiary education to students pursuing Science and Technology, Engineering and Math (STEM). Page 9.*

*35. Provide free tertiary education to education majors and stipends prior to their employment as teachers. Page 9.*

*36. Create incentives and dedicate special attention to the education of girls. Page 9*

*37. Ensure every child attending primary school is properly nourished and ready to learn by providing a Free Meal a Day. Page 9.*

*38. Achieve the construction of one million low-cost houses within four years for the poor. Page 11*

39. *Stop all travel abroad at government expense for the purpose of medical treatment. Page 13.*

40. *Provide incentives for Nigerian doctors and health practitioners working abroad to return home, to strengthen the health care industry in Nigeria and provide quality care to those who need it. Page 14.*

41. *Make sure people at a local level benefit from mining and mineral wealth by vesting all mineral rights in land to states. Page 17.*

What the electorate should look for in the 'Next Level' should be answers to the above and some of the issues discussed in the previous chapter with regard to fulfilling the promises of the APC to Nigerians. Briefly recapped, these include:

1. How satisfied are they with the current security situation, including the handling of major threats from Boko Haram, Niger Delta, the Herders/Farmers clashes, kidnapping for ransom, armed robbery and banditry?

2. In the area of anti-corruption, the APC should be open to some critical issues with regard to its strategy and approaches to the prevention and control of corruption, including the allegations of a political vendetta, poor investigation and prosecution of culpable cases, accountability for and management of recovered assets and strengthening of anti-corruption institutions.

3. With regard to the economy, Nigerians are left with the choice of analysing the data provided by the government on its achievements in all its economic empowerment programmes, including job creation, food security, etc., and determining whether or not living conditions are better now than before, since the PDP that lost power to the APC did so on account of poor management of the economy, especially corruption.

4.  The APC claims, just as the PDP did in 2015, to have invested billions of naira into infrastructural development across the country. However, since infrastructure is a visible and measurable indicator, it is left for the electorate to see for themselves and determine whether they can still place their trust in the APC. There is need to be cautious in doing so, as experience has shown that parties exaggerate their achievements when seeking re-election; some of the projects the PDP claimed to have executed prior to 2015 were found to be partially or not executed. The fact that money was released for any project does not mean that the project was actually executed. The money could as well have gone through the same drainpipe of corruption. The APC is not immune to such allegation, as was observed in the case of Bauchi-Gombe road project, for which the APC Government awarded the contract in 2016 and as at the end of 2018, only 7 km of the 150 km road had been resurfaced, and yet the President in his budget speech to the NASS in December 2018 counted that as one of the major projects executed by the APC Government.

5.  In the critical area of power, which is the 'engine room' of the economy, the APC Government claims to have achieved much with less resources and increased power generation from 4,000 megawatts in 2015 to 7,000 as at 2018 with relative improvement in distribution. It is important to point out that experience has shown that the most difficult part of the power supply chain in Nigeria is not in generation but in transmission and distribution. Nigerians may commend the APC for this modest achievement, but as the expectation was high based on the promises of the APC to turn around the electricity chain within six months of assuming office, can the present level be considered satisfactory? Let me be clear that Nigerians should not expect the entire chain to be fixed within four years, but

if the APC should be held to its promise, and the electorate is right to do so, then the present level should be a matter of debate during the electioneering campaigns.

6. Without going into the details of the campaign issues in all areas, the state of our educational system, health, food and transportation, as well as labour unrest, are all issues that should agitate the minds of Nigerians as the elections approach. While the APC Government has shifted the blame for most of our predicaments to the PDP, obviously due to the long period of 16 years that the PDP held power, a comparative paradigm is to assess the progress or otherwise under the 4-year tenure of the APC in measurable terms, discern whether that was how the PDP performed in its first 4 years and determine whether the APC has any new 'magic wand' to reverse the negative indices of high inflation, foreign exchange rates, unemployment and poverty.

In a nutshell, therefore, the APC has had the opportunity to serve Nigerians and has seen how difficult it is to translate campaign promises into governance dividends. For all practical purposes and from available statistics, the APC started on a stronger foundation than the PDP did in 1999.[114]And with the failures discussed in Chapter 3, Nigerians may ask whether their conditions are better now than before, and whether there is a clear strategy within the 'Next Level' to propel them to where they expect to be and by what means.

Other questions to ask based on the issues raised in the previous chapter are: is there a clear strategy, capacity, vision and resources to deal with the Boko Haram phenomenon at the 'Next Level' and how different are the strategy and capacity from the current level? How will the APC reverse the exchange rate of N360 to $1 to the level where they met at N225 to $1? How can the government

114. When the prices of oil were between $15 and 20 pb, high debt burden, and other socio-economic challenges.

sustain the practice of drawing millions of dollars from foreign reserves to support the value of the naira in the foreign exchange market? In what ways can the APC reverse the skyrocketing prices of food items and restore manufacturing and other industries that have been closed down? Will the 'command and control' approach to economic management ameliorate the economic problems within the 'Next Level'? Will there be a more technically and professionally-equipped team to run the affairs of government? Has the current level fulfilled their expectations, and what will be the future of Nigeria within the paradigm of the 'Next Level'?

All these are urgent issues that form the campaign issues and parameters for alternative choices in the coming elections. Therefore the discussion cannot end with the 'Next Level'. We should now proceed to examine the new chapter in what may be called the Atiku/PDP 'Let's Get Nigeria Working Again'.

## 'Let's Get Nigeria Working Again' – the Atiku/PDP Policy Document

Presumably drawn from the PDP Manifesto, the Atiku Policy Document is predicated on the 'observed' failures of the Buhari/ APC Government, including 'under performance by the state; structural fault lines; and unity under threat'. While other aspects of the unity of Nigeria are implied, the obvious threat identified in the document is the dreadful and perennial Boko Haram insurgency. The Atiku campaign policy document covers virtually all aspects of national development from the economy to security, anti-corruption, infrastructure, youth, sports and women development, culture, arts and environment, governance and international relations. Without going into a detailed analysis of the policy document, the salient aspects are highlighted for purposes of comparison with the APC/ Buhari 'Next Level' policy document. The important question to ask in analysing this document is, was Nigeria working before, that the PDP wants Nigerians to get back to that status quo?

## Mission

The stated mission of the 'Let's Get Nigeria Working Again' Atiku campaign document is 'to provide appropriate political leadership for the unity, security and prosperity of the country'.[115]

## Assumptions

The main assumptions in the policy document are many, and these include:

- Growth is slow and uninspiring.
- The economy remains undiversified.
- Economy is uncompetitive.
- Foreign investments in decline.
- The precarious fiscal position.
- The fragile financial system.
- Poor exchange rate management.

Regional disparities, i.e. inequalities among the federating units.

Consequent upon the above major assumptions, the Atiku's Economic Agenda is predicated on the following parameters, among others:

---

115. Leadership is a process whereby an individual influences a group of individuals to achieve a common goal. Leadership is not an act or set of acts, it is a process; is not just to influence, yet it involves influencing others through leadership. The influence is mutual between a leader and followers; and goes beyond goals. Its principles are selflessness, honesty, accountability/ transparency, justice and respect for others. There are three types or characteristics of leadership: 1. Leadership of influence and hope; 2 leadership of impact and timing; and leadership of legacy and reproduction.

- Human capital development.
- Promoting economic diversification.
- Reducing infrastructural deficits.
- Reforming public institutions.
- Developing a competitive and open economic system, aiming at $900 billion GDP by 2025.
- Promoting agri-business through land reform, commodities exchanges, De-risking access to finance, modernisation and mechanisation.
- Promoting the manufacturing sector through sustained increase in output from 9% to 30% of the GDP by 2025; and to work closely with the Manufacturers Association of Nigeria (MAN) to attain the objectives of the policy.

## Priorities

Virtually everything seems to be important in the policy document, but for practical purposes the following are the main priority campaign issues:

### 1. Job creation and entrepreneurship development
This policy thrust aims at the creation of 3 million self-employed and wage-paying employment opportunities annually.

### 2. Poverty alleviation and economic empowerment
If elected in 2019, the Atiku/PDP Government promises to lift 50 million people out of poverty through skill acquisition opportunities by 2025. Atiku promises to 'provide skill acquisition opportunities and enterprise development for job and wealth creation, rather than direct cash distribution and improve citizens' access to basic infrastructure services – water, sanitation, power, education and health care'.

## 3. Infrastructure

The document seeks to 'provide skill acquisition opportunities and enterprise development for job and wealth creation, rather than direct cash distribution and improve citizens' access to basic infrastructure services – water, sanitation, power, education and health care'. It promises to achieve this through a 'broader scope of Infra-Credit to complement the operation of the IDF by de-risking investments in infrastructure to build investor confidence in taking risk and investing capital'. Infrastructural development is perhaps the most ambitious pillar of the policy document, which seeks to intervene through a 'Public Private Sector Partnerships (PPP) for the development of the transport infrastructure' in the following areas:

a. Roads – to develop 5,000km of roads by 2025 through PPPs and community interventions; as well as 'develop and rehabilitate the connecting road networks across the geopoliticalzones'.

b. On power, the objective is to 'review the industry legal and regulatory framework to ensure market viability; ensure coordination of investments in the Power Sector in Generation, Transmission and Distribution; and ensure effective regulatory environment to deliver contract-based electricity market compliant with market rules; as well as intensify rural electrification projects to ensure electricity access to over 80 million Nigerians currently without access to grid electricity'. The actions to achieve these objectives according to the plan include:

• Allowing NERC to perform its regulatory functions without interference and guarantee its independence.

• Reviewing the Aggregated Technical, Commercial and Collection (ATC&C) losses existing in the power networks and extract firm commitments for a revised ATC&C Loss reduction target from the Distribution companies.

- Creating an environment that would enable distribution companies recover full costs for power supplied to their consumers.

- Introducing creative solutions towards addressing the huge debt overhang and liquidity challenge in the power industry.

- Ensuring enforceability of industry contracts.

- Upgrading the transmission grid.

- Adopting short-term emergency measures.

c.  On technological infrastructure, the Atiku plan aims to 'promote the role of technology in governance; build digital literacy; promote private sector technological innovation and enterprise; and promote technological hubs across the country and link them with existing Industrial Development Centres (IDCs)'.

    With respect to implementation, Atiku promises to

- 'implement a four-year plan for the digitization of major government operations such as procurement to achieve transparency and reduce leakages;

- strengthen the use of business intelligence software to analyse public service productivity;

- improve the technology start-up ecosystem by providing financing and infrastructure; review, with timelines, partnership agreements with experienced foreign incubators and accelerators to improve the penetration of technological advancements in the country; and

- enforce and protect intellectual property rights, which form a crucial component in technological innovation'.

d. On refining and petrochemical infrastructure, Atiku promises to:

- 'Enhance local capacity to process larger quantities of our crude for domestic consumption;

- Build the enabling infrastructure to add value to the economy via the development of petrochemical facilities;

- Create 1 million new jobs within 10 years via petrochemicals/ petrochemical-based activities; and

- Privatise existing refineries and create opportunity for new ones.'

- All these will be pursued through a multi-pronged approach, by which the Atiku government, if elected will:

- 'Prioritize investment in nameplate capacity and ensure that Nigeria starts to refine 50% of its current crude oil output of 2 million bpd by 2025.

- Privatize all four outstanding government-owned refineries to competent off-takers with mandates to produce agreed levels of refined output.

- Issue new licences for greenfield investment in crude oil refining and allied activities.

- Introduce market friendly fiscal and pricing policy'.

**4. On human capital development**, Atiku promises inter alia:

- On education, to 'reposition the Nigerian educational system to deliver more efficiently, effectively and sustainably'.

- In the health sector, to 'promote health care delivery system that is comprehensive, efficient and can deliver effective and qualitative services to the citizens'.

- On youth and women development, Atiku promises to 'Break all barriers that prevent women from reaching their best potential whether in adolescence or adulthood; promote equal access to job and education opportunities between men and women.'

- Pursue financial inclusion; create an environment that provides employment and fulfilment to our youth and women population through education, mentorship, vocational training, and technology and entrepreneurship initiatives; and set standards that discourage the unfair exploitation and persecution of women in our society'.

**5. On governance, t**he Atiku plan is anchored on accountability, transparency, participation and predictability.

## 6. Restructuring

Restructuring is very much one of the main thrusts of the Atiku campaign issues. Accordingly, Atiku did not mince words in reminding Nigerians that:

- 'Restructuring is not a new or strange phenomenon.' Nigerians have clamoured for the restructuring of the economy towards a more diversified structure.

- Restructuring challenges the leadership to demonstrate capacity to create wealth for every layer of governance.

- Restructuring is not just about the devolution of powers to the States, it is about transforming the role of the federal government.

- Restructuring is not limited to constitutional tweaks; it is about deliberate, purposeful and sweeping cultural revolution.

- Nigerian states are poor not because they are not receiving a fair share of oil money, but because they are not receiving a fair shot at true federalism'.(p. 54)

Consequently, he promised to:

- Decongest the exclusive and the concurrent list in the constitution.

- The Central Government would also retain the role of providing the required direction for the economy, defence and national security, internal law and order, currency, international affairs and foreign policy, customs, citizenship and immigration, firearms, and related matters.

- Issues bordering on minerals and mines, internal security including police, law and order, railways, communications, transport, environment, land matters, etc, would be devolved to the concurrent list.

- Local Governments shall become an independent tier of government

- Federating units will be supported in economic management.

- Nigeria's common resources will be shared equitably in accordance with a new revenue allocation formula to be negotiated across the board'. (p. 54)


## 7. Anti-Corruption and Rule of Law

The main thrust of the Atiku plan is to 'emphasize prevention of corruption rather than detection and subsequent sanction… and focus on building institutions that will be strong enough not to be manipulated by personalities and also build a culture of accountability, effectiveness, efficiency and transparency, judicious use of public resources, with zero tolerance for nepotism and other forms of corruption'. Consequently Atiku promises to take eight major steps to fight corruption:

- Champion institutional reforms of anti-corruption agencies and strengthening them for more effectiveness

- Launch a comprehensive National Anti-Corruption Strategy that is based on the rule of law, separation of powers, neutrality and non-partisanship

- Strengthen policies and measures for detecting corruption through a strong technology infrastructure that supports the end-to-end operations of government businesses for transparency, accountability, efficiency and effectiveness

- Ensure that judgments on corruption cases are fully followed through and enforced by the appropriate law enforcement agencies

- Review the reward system for public and civil services

- Strengthen anti-corruption public enlightenment

- Enhance whistle blowing and witness protection policies

- Promote rule of law. (p. 55)

## 8. National Security

'The policy thrust of an Atiku government will be based on good governance, visionary leadership and politics of inclusiveness that will reduce citizens' frustration and alienation and eliminate the compulsion to take up arms against the society or fellow countrymen. Our priority will be to restore the citizen's confidence in Nigeria as one indivisible, indissoluble, ethnically diverse but strong country to protect them and secure socio-economic benefits'. He therefore promises the following ten specific actions:

- 'Re-activate meaningful registration at birth as a way to reduce crime and protect Nigerians.

- Conduct the next national population census as the basis for further development planning.

- Dealing with insurgency using alternative approaches to conflict resolution, such as Diplomacy; Intelligence; Improved Border Control; Traditional Institutions; and Good Neighbourliness:

- Restructure and Decentralize Security Institutions.

- Promote Regional Security Cooperation.

- Resolve Militancy Issue in the Niger Delta.

- Improve Civil-Military Relations.

- Strengthen the National Security Council.

- Handle the North East Development Issues.

- Deal with Terrorism, Kidnapping and Other Crimes'. (p. 57)

## 9. International Relations

Atiku promises to focus foreign policy thrust on the promotion of economic diplomacy, ensuring that it affects Nigerians' lives in the most positive way, while being conscious of the economic and employment potential of every activity. About 13 specific promises or steps will be taken to actualise this goal:

- Retool Nigeria's foreign policy instruments.

- 'Re-activating the Presidential Advisory Council on Foreign Affairs.

- Convening of an All-Nigerian Conference on Foreign Policy to promote national consensus on our national interest to guide foreign policy.

- Providing for a smooth and effective running of Nigeria's diplomatic missions.

- Implement the Diaspora Commission Act 2017.

- Strive to attain the level of economic success that should qualify Nigeria to join the group of major decision-makers on the direction of the global economy.

- Promote multilateral trade.

- Maximise gains of participating in ECOWAS.

- Enhance Nigeria's visibility in the AU.

- Enhance Nigeria's international visibility and improving its image.

- Securing Nigeria's leadership in world affairs.

- Curb the threat of illicit small arms and light weapons.

- Get Nigerians in the Diaspora involved in nation building'. (p. 59)


## 10. Sources of Funding

Fulfilling electoral promises is often constrained by lack of sufficient resources. In apparent realisation of this, Atiku promises to explore the following sources to fund his priority programmes if elected President:

1) **Infrastructure** will be funded from project bonds, to finance expansive national railways and new major strategic roads

across Nigeria; and non-interest capital market products like Sukuk will be issued.

2) **Diversifying the economy:** 'enable the capital market to facilitate capital raising across industries and by all tiers of government for sustainable national development and transformation of critical sectors such as infrastructure, agriculture, solid minerals, ICT and education.'

3) **Building a savings culture** through a National Savings Strategy that aims to provide fiscal incentives for each additional naira of savings.

4) **Budget deficit financing:** Atiku promises to adopt a budgeting process to:

a) Ensure early presentation of budget estimates to the National Assembly (at the latest in July of each year).

b) Improve Executive-Legislature relations and interactions to ensure budgets are passed before the commencement of the fiscal year.

c) Innovatively leverage capital markets to raise the funds needed for more effective budget implementation through a combination of domestic and foreign capital-raising.

5) **Democratising prosperity** by 'providing incentives for enterprises in the real sector such as telecom, power, agriculture, solid mineral, oil and gas and SMEs to seek listing and funding from the capital market'.

Former Vice President Atiku Abubakar has been struggling to be president of Nigeria for over 26 years since he contested the primary election of the defunct Social Democratic Party (SDP) and lost to Moshood Abiola in 1993. Most of his struggles ended at the primary elections, until 2007, when he decamped from the PDP and secured the presidential ticket of the ACN. Now, having won the presidential ticket of the PDP for the 2019 election, this will be his second shot at the coveted position of President. Mr Abubakar has been a perennial defector from the PDP to the APC and back to the PDP and has justified that as his democratic freedom to seek for any platform to actualise his ambition.

The fulfilment of these promises is predicated among others on Atiku's experience, especially his business management skills, knowledge of the critical issues affecting the country having been involved at various levels in running the government under the PDP, and most importantly, his commitment to 'get Nigeria working again'.

Just as the CSOs dissected the APC Manifesto and the Buhari's Covenant with Nigerians in 2015 and identified 222 promises, upon release of the Atiku Campaign Policy Document on 18 November 2018, Sahara Reporters extracted 45 promises made by Atiku and documented them for posterity's sake.[116] All the 45 extracted promises have been subsumed in our analysis above.

Both the Buhari/APC promises in 2015 and 2018 and the Atiku/PDP promises in 2018 are not new and seem to share some similarities or characteristics. First, even though Atiku's promises were categorised into 45 against Buhari's 222 in 2015, both are too many and ambitious in several ways, and there is no guarantee that any of the parties can fulfil all the promises they have made, especially when we take into account the state of the economy in 2015 and 2018.

Second, they both attempt to cover all aspects of national development: security, corruption, economy, infrastructure, rule of law and social justice, women, youth, sports and culture. This is understandable, because no party would like to be accused of

116. *Sahara Reporters* is an online newspaper that is known for its critical analysis of issues in Nigeria. The extract was accessed at: www.saharareporters.com/politics by Google chrome on 27 December 2018.

neglecting any sector, and no government can afford to do so. So it is understandable that some key issues have been identified as priorities, and those should form the focus of assessing (potential) performance.

Third, both documents attempted to provide, or provided, a road map of what each of the parties intend to do to get to their destinations, i.e. to improve the living conditions of Nigerians. To be candid, how to make a change is as important as the change you want to make. Therefore, another similarity in the two documents is the fact that there is no clear strategy on how to do what they said they will do. This is why it was observed earlier that the APC did not have a plan in 2015 but a series of promises, whose implementation was challenged after the party had won office.

Perhaps the only difference would be in the *dramatis personae*, and this can be assessed based on their real or perceived antecedents. But before we proceed to briefly compare the possibilities of either of the two candidates winning the 2019 election, it is important to note that there are other equally competent, tested, committed and patriotic candidates, some more agile, including Professor Jerry Gana, Dr Obi Ezekwesili and Professor Kinsley Moghalu, just to mention a few who are contesting the presidency in 2019; our analysis did not include them, not out of disrespect but because of zoning, national spread, and others that I mentioned at the beginning of this chapter. Therefore, since we narrow down our analysis to PMB and Atiku, we may venture into a prognosis of their perceived strengths and weaknesses or chances of winning.

## Predicting the Outcome of the 2019 Presidential Election

Predicting the outcome of an election is like a chase game. It is even more subjective when the parameters of such a prediction are not scientific or acceptable to all. In that regard, prediction becomes really subjective and could be a figment of the imagination. However, using public assessments, comments and perceptions, we may attempt some guesses.

## Why Atiku may lose or win

To say that one may lose or win sounds like a conundrum. But obviously that is the state of politics as the 2019 election approaches. Atiku has his strengths and weaknesses, and each assessment depends on the perception of the assessor. Some commentators have speculated that a number of mostly immediate events following the conduct of the parties' primaries in October have shaped or dampened the chances of Atiku and I shall try to highlight them below.

## 1. The Dubai Plan was a flop

Soon after his declaration as the flag bearer of the PDP, Atiku departed with his team of strategists to develop the 'Atiku Campaign Policy Document' discussed above in Dubai, the United Arab Emirates. Whatever motive could be behind that, some commentators believe that was the first misstep Atiku took in trying to actualise his ambition to become president. They argued that his preference for Dubai to develop a plan for Nigeria smacks of a lack of patriotic feeling for his country. They further argued that some expect power to return to the South in 2023, only for Atiku to come out with a six-year plan implying he would like to stay beyond one term if elected. Apart from a critique that the plan has nothing exciting, unique or exceptional, the figures in it are also exaggerated.

However, in my view, developing a plan outside the shores of this country should not be an important consideration in the choice of Nigerians, since retreats are held in any location for security, logistics or convenience, and none of those could affect the quality of the outcome of such retreat. Without attempting to hold a brief for the Atiku organisation, it was learnt that the purpose of holding the meetings in Dubai were for those reasons, including the fact that as a businessman Atiku already has structures in Dubai which facilitated the development of his strategy. It is also obvious that he decided to retreat to a neutral location in order to avoid security surveillance and possible interruptions in the course of meetings with his campaign team. Thus, this cannot be a major factor in determining his chances in the election.

## 2. His choice of running mate

Immediately after winning the primary election to become the candidate of the PDP, after holding a few initial consultations and shortly before his departure to Dubai, Atiku surprised many people with the announcement of Peter Obi as his running mate. The first reaction came from the governors of the South-East region, who are critical of Atiku's success in their states and who, even though they did not reject their son Obi, declared that they were not consulted by Atiku in choosing who should represent the region or Igbos if the choice was made to pacify them. The ripples of that choice have not settled yet as Peter Obi is being criticised as a non-core PDP person, having served as governor of Anambra State for two terms under the All Peoples' Grand Alliance (APGA), not the PDP. Consequently, some South East governors and other potential candidates who had expected that they would be considered are said to be unenthusiastic in the campaign.

Apart from the South-East governors' concern or grievance that Obi was chosen over their heads, another problem is coming from the North, where Peter Obi is perceived as 'an ethic bigot with an anti-Hausa/Fulani track record, and that in itself is working in Buhari's favour'.[117]

Atiku was faced with a difficult decision in choosing his running mate. He had an option of choosing from the South-West to counter-balance the APC choice of a Vice President and running mate already from that zone. But how feasible could that have been in assuring the South-West to abandon their own man, who is already in office, for someone who aspires to be there? Besides, who could have been a potential candidate that would merge the financial and political muscle of Bola Tinubu in that region? Politics is arithmetic. Ultimately, the choice of South-East running mate was meant to retain the support of the South-East and South-South regions for Atiku. Whether that decision was sound remains to be proven by the outcome of the polls.

### 3. 2023 Presidency calculation

Related to the above is the 2023 presidency calculation, where Atiku is said to be disadvantaged because the whole South is expecting that after the next four years power should shift to the region according to the unwritten zoning agreement in both the APC and PDP. Some fear that if Atiku wins, that might give him another chance for a second term, but electing Buhari could bring back the presidency to the South within a shorter time.

However, the South-West is using this factor to canvass for support, with the assurance that after a second Buhari term power will shift automatically to that region since the Vice President originates from there; on the other hand, the Igbos in the South-East are being persuaded to believe that APC will not hand over power to them, neither will it hand over to the South-South, so their best bet is to vote for Atiku with an Igbo running mate who will hopefully take over even if that will take up to eight years. How this will play

117    Jibrin Ibrahim, 'Predicting the Outcome', *Daily Trust*, 31 December 2018.

out in their choices at the polls will provide a lesson for subsequent political balancing.

## 4. Atiku's inability to split the Northern votes

Another permutation regarding Atiku's chances or otherwise is his ability to secure up to 50% of the Northern votes. Despite the poor performance of PMB, many people believe that he remains very strong and popular, especially among the 'poor population' in the North. Besides, he comes from the North-West, the region with the highest number of voters in the country. As some people believe that the 2019 election will be a referendum over the campaign issues of both candidates, the outcome will certainly be a great lesson in the personal attributes of the candidates in political choices. That leads to the next issue, which is Atiku's alleged corrupt background.

## 5. Atiku's personal reputation

Atiku is perceived by many as a 'corrupt' person, largely because his former boss President Obasanjo had portrayed him as corrupt and had vowed not to support him for any political office. However, Atiku has made it clear that he is not a saint, but if anybody has any scintilla of evidence of corruption against him, that person should report him to law enforcement for investigation or to the court for a necessary decision. So far, no one has done so, and the allegation against him remains a mere allegation meant to scuttle his political career. Furthermore, for Obasanjo, who had vowed not to forgive Atiku, turning around to endorse him for the 2019 election speaks volumes about the allegations, which meant that Obasanjo just wanted to get back at Atiku for opposing his third term bid. More so, the allegations of corruption that were levelled against Atiku were investigated by the EFCC since 2007 and no *prima facie* case was established against him. With regard to the allegation of his wrongdoing with US Congressman Thomas Jefferson, although the Senator was jailed for corruption in the USA, neither the US government nor any other competent authority has invited Atiku for interrogation or requested his extradition.

In response to Obasanjo's allegations of corruption against Atiku, 'the Atiku Media Men' in a book titled *Atiku Media* described Obasanjo's allegations as 'petty and vindictive' and declared that:

> ...the EFCC claimed in its report that its investigations were pursuant to a request for assistance that it received from the U.S government (a 'request' that came after all the investigations of the EFCC had been carried out). Atiku went to court and on 28 November 2006, Justice Inumidun Akande of the Lagos High Court ruled that the EFCC report and the administrative panel report and the consequent gazette of the purported indictment do not exist in law and in fact. Justice Akande stated, in her landmark decision that: 'The preparation of and submission of the report in Exhibit 2 by the 2nd respondent to the President, instead of filing a charge or information at the High Court against the applicant and other persons, it erroneously indicted therein, amounting to usurpation by the Executive arm of government of the power of the High Court or the Judiciary which has power to try and convict or indict any person found to have committed any offence under the Act. The report in Exhibit 2, in as much as it is not a charge before the High Count and the President to whom it was submitted was not the High Court as prescribed under the Act is ultra vires and shall be set aside in this ruling.[118]

On the other hand, some commentators asked why the APC government did not refuse financial and other support from Atiku during the 2015 election and did not investigate him on assuming office with the promise to fight corruption 'no matter whose ox is gored', only for them to start flogging the issue after Atiku

118. Atiku Media Team, p. 52.

had emerged as a candidate of the opposition. Would they have overstated the corruption allegation as they are doing if Atiku had supported Buhari for a second term? Can they prove that Atiku's wealth is the proceeds of corruption and Bola Tinubu's wealth legitimately owned?

Far from condoning any act of corruption, I am not implying that corruption should not be exposed wherever it is suspected or seen. For if Atiku is corrupt and Buhari failed to investigate and prosecute him while he has all the powers to do so, that would leave some doubts in the minds of some people with regard to the veracity of such allegations. Nevertheless, these are prognoses that would warrant some thoughts from the electorate.

### 6. Atiku's 'mercantilist economic policy'

One factor supposedly against Atiku is that he promised to run 'a mercantilist economy', which included his intention to privatise or sell off the NNPC, the main cash cow for the government; and that he will risk inflation to attract foreign investment (by whatever means). Based on the experiences of privatisation of major public corporations such as NITEL, the contemplated sale of NNPC would certainly send shivers down the spines of the many Nigerians because it would be tantamount to selling the major revenue source of the government, as well as the source of guaranteed petroleum products at affordable rates. Privatisation per se is not bad, but the way it is carried out could destroy confidence in the process. With regard to Atiku's promise to risk inflation, with or without full knowledge of what that means, it is perceived in some quarters as 'indefensibly reckless, unfeeling and an indication that Atiku would be a poodle of racist, anti-people neo-liberal rascals in Washington D.C.'[119]

---

119. Farooq Kperogi, 'Atiku Doesn't Want to be President', Social Media chat circulated via Whatsapp, 8 December 2018. Yet he concluded that Nigeria's greatest tragedy is that Buhari and Atiku are the only validly realistic options for the president.

## 7. Restructuring

Restructuring is one of the main thrusts of Atiku's campaign promises. Restructuring means different things to different people. While some assume that it would amount to the dismemberment or disintegration of the country, others think in terms of greater autonomy for the other tiers of government rather than the centre, yet there are those who believe that adjusting the revenue-sharing formula in favour of resource-producing areas would suffice.

Atiku's restructuring agenda has been summarised earlier in this chapter under his priorities. Some commentators believe that it is one of his weaknesses, which is perceived in some quarters as alienating the North, which has been accused by the South for benefiting more from the current (unbalanced) federal system. Since the issue of restructuring is one of major agitation in Nigeria, it may be a strength for Atiku's campaign. Having learnt from experience, Atiku has demonstrated an acute awareness of the sensitivity of this issue and it is crucial to recall that even before winning the presidential ticket of his party, Atiku wasted no time in showing his open support and preference for restructuring.

In a paper titled 'Restructuring Nigeria for a Greater National Integration and Democratic Stability',[120] Atiku Abubakar provided a detailed conceptualisation of restructuring, including why it has become necessary and how in his view it should be done and how it will impact the North with a view to allaying the fears of the North about restructuring. Atiku premised his restructuring agenda on the ceaseless agitation for it, especially from the South, and he believes that restructuring can still be done without jeopardising the interests of the North. Consequently, he articulated his vision as follows:

120. Presented at the Gen. Usman Katsina Memorial Conference, at the Umaru Musa Yar'Adua Memorial Hall, Murtala Square, Kaduna, on 30 July 2016.

We have over the years responded to these agitations in a variety of ways and with a variety of measures. These include the creation of states from the earlier three (and later four) regions to the current 36 states; a civil war, and other military operations in different parts of the country at different times; federal character principle; changes to revenue allocation formula; National Youth Service Corps; federal take-over or establishment and management of schools, universities, hospitals, and huge federal presence in the economy as an investor. Others include the excessive centralization and concentration of power at the federal level and the weakening of the federating states; and amnesty for 'repentant ex-militants' of the Niger Delta.

Unfortunately these measures have not worked adequately to enhance national integration and the sustenance of our democracy. If anything, our unity has been fragile, our democracy unstable, and our people more aggrieved by their state in the federation. We have always responded with a suspicion of the 'other' in trying to deal with these challenges to our integration and democratic survival. And, quite naturally, our responses/ solutions have also been, at least partly, shaped by sectional interests and sentiments. The problem though is that sometimes what is in the short-term interest of a group may not be so in the long-run. And, more importantly, nation-building requires sacrifices of some sectional interests for the overall interest of the nation and all the segments. Unless we do not think that the nation's unity is worth sacrificing for or that the sacrifices have to be made only by others and not by us!

Personally I believe in one strong and united Nigeria. I believe that we are stronger united, and that together our potentials are enormous. And I believe that Nigeria's unity is worth sacrificing for.

My focus here, however, is to show that the north and Nigeria have not been served well by the status quo and there is need for change. Who among us who went to primary and secondary school in the 1960s had much to do with the federal government? Did the northern regional government wait to collect monthly revenue allocations from Lagos before paying salaries to its civil servants and teachers or fixing its bridges and roads? In May this year the Governor of Niger State publicly stated that his state could no longer pay salaries because of dwindling federal allocations. And he is not alone. A recent report by Economic Intelligence published in a number of Nigerian newspapers showed that 9 out of the 10 States with the lowest internally generated revenue are in the north. And they are among the 15 states that the report said may go bankrupt if federal allocations to states continue to decline because their IGR is less than 10% of their federal allocations. There is something wrong with the structure of this country and we must see it for what it is. Even in the unlikely event that federal allocations are shared equally among all the states, we would still be in trouble if we cannot generate revenues internally.

My brothers and sisters, government revenues are based on taxation. Infrastructure for economic development is built with taxation. Rents on natural resource extraction, including oil rents, are not sustainable sources of revenues for government. And whenever and wherever they are dominant for a nation they tend to distort the economy, discourage productivity and encourage rent-seeking activities and dependency.

I suggest we resolve today to support calls for the restructuring of the Nigerian federation in order to strengthen its unity and stabilize its democracy. I believe that restructuring will eventually happen whether we like or support it or not. The question is whether it will happen around a conference table, in a direction influenced by us and whether we will be an equal partner in the process. Or will it happen in a more unpredictable arena and in a manner over which we have little influence? It should be at a table and we need to be at that table. A nation is an organism; it grows, it evolves, it changes, it adapts. And like other organisms if it does not adapt, it dies.

It is one thing to say that Nigeria must remain a united nation. It is quite another thing to forge that sense of nationhood without which you can never have national integration. And to forge that nationhood requires, at the very least, three critical things:

1) A sense of something beneficial that the nation does for a people that they feel they cannot get elsewhere to the same vital degree.

2) People's perception of fairness and equity in the way and manner they are treated.

3) Arising from these, a sense of pride in the nation and its leadership by most segments of the population. All three are linked to government performance, integrity of the leadership and honesty of purpose, all evident to the citizenry. From these, ideologies that project the nation as special can arise and help to cement the people's commitment to it.

Restructuring has been one of major agitations affecting the political stability of Nigeria. While some think that it means division or even dismemberment of the country into regions, others, including Atiku, think that restructuring is possible without dismembering Nigeria; rather he thinks it will help to strengthen unity and democratic stability. It may be recalled that the APC promised to restructure Nigeria during its 2015 campaigns, but apart from enacting laws for the independence of the judiciary, state assemblies and local government councils,[121] no other major step has been taken towards restructuring, perhaps due to the sensitivity of the issue. The agitation for restructuring has come mostly from the South, where it has been portrayed as a slight on the North because it is believed the North benefits more from the current structure.

The issue of restructuring will therefore be a double-edged sword and it may favour or disfavour Atiku. It remains to be seen if the South-West, which has been at the forefront of restructuring, will vote for Atiku and discount the other considerations discussed

---

121. Those laws are yet to be enforced all over the country due to vested interests by State Governors.

earlier or choose to go for those other appurtenances and forgo restructuring. As it is, there has not been any mention of restructuring in the campaigns of the APC so far and no strong voice from the South-West has criticised PMB on restructuring apart from the opposition PDP.

At the same time, there has been no major criticism of Atiku from the North on account of his stance on restructuring, apart from pockets of criticism from APC supporters. On the other hand, since Atiku articulated his campaign policies, the 'Afenifere' (the Yoruba ethnic group) and the 'Idi-ngbo' (the Igbo ethnic group) have expressed support for him on account of that and may likely vote for him in anticipation of his fulfilment of that promise. The 2019 election will surely be a test for the restructuring agenda.

## 8. Buhari's inroads in areas he lost in 2015

One other factor presumably counting against Atiku is Buhari's perceived inroads into areas he lost in the 2015 election, mostly in the South-East and South-South, which implies more votes coming to him from Atiku's strongholds. Again, whether the Igbos who had accused PMB of sidelining them in his administration would now see a better side of him and pitch their tents with him remains to be seen.

However, reacting to PMB's refusal to assent to the Electoral Amendment Act (2018) Farooq Kperogi, in a Whatsapp chat, observed that 'the game is over for Buhari. He and his minders know it. Atiku will win at least 45 percent of the Muslim north and more than 45 percent of the southwest... Atiku will win more than 70 percent each of the Christian north, the southeast, and the southern ethnic minority bloc.'[122]

---

122. Farooq Kperogi, 'Electoral Law: 2019 Will be a Contest of rigging',Whatsapp post, 8 December 2018.

## 9. Declining excitement in the Atiku camp

In addition to the choice of running mate, there is the perceived declining excitement on the part of most of Atiku's supporters, who had expected to reap from the money they expected he would release for the campaigns, which does not seem to be flowing. Why this disappointment is a plus for his opponent (PMB) is because Buhari's supporters know that he has no money and even if he had, he would not spray money around for the campaign. Yet they support him because of their trust for him as an 'incorruptible' person. This also remains speculation.

Nevertheless, Atiku still has a vast network of friends and associates who are in modest circumstances and may be willing to provide financial assistance to him. In addition, the PDP machinery still has the capacity to generate a lot of support for him, but one is not sure they are committed to the course to do so as some of the gladiators who contested the primary election with Atiku are reported to have developed cold feet in the campaign. A small number of them feel that the Atiku campaign is dominated by the runaway PDP members, thus siding with those who stayed in the party when the chips were down.

## 10. Atiku/the PDP lack the federal might and incumbency power that the APC has

Incumbents seldom lose elections in Africa, but the 2015 election in Nigeria was a trendsetter. In many elections in Nigeria in the past, the powers of incumbency have been purportedly used by the PDP to secure victory. In many cases, the federal might and incumbency factors were applied when 'opposition members were either restricted in hotels, loyalty curried, results re-written, unused votes counted for the winner, opposition party agents refused access, vote buying, thugs having free reign, etc were common occurrence'.[123] Obasanjo has raised the alarm and cautioned:

> We should remember that there had been reports of INEC sponsored rigging in the past, and also with INEC officials through collation and with officials being put in party coordinators' dresses and working for the political party favoured by INEC and also putting the dresses of other parties on INEC-favoured parties and police uniforms on INEC-favoured parties to rig all the elections for the favoured party.Like all of us, INEC knows all thise and it should devise means to make sure they do not happen. But will they?[124]

PMB has consistently assured Nigerians that the 2019 election will be free, fair and credible. Whether or not the APC will misuse the state apparatus to rig the election in its favour, as is alleged, remains to be seen, but one thing that is certain is that the PDP will not enjoy the privilege of the state apparatus for the first time since 1999. But if the INEC is truly independent, what is PMB's business with assuring Nigerians that the election will not be tainted?

I have characterised how the elite conspired to influence who becomes president and how Dr Jonathan was a victim of that conspiracy in 2015. The elite factor is a reality in Nigerian politics. Although most of the elite or educated people do not even vote in an election, the influence of the powerful ones can determine the outcome of election, as it did in 2015. Let me recall briefly how PMB struggled for 12 years without being successful until we had a semblance of the elite support in his favour before he could win in 2015. It is obvious that PMB has a massive support of the ordinary

123. The writing is already on the wall with a police siege on Senator Dino Melaye's residence on 28 December 2018 and reported arrest of some opposition party members. There is already a hue and cry on the impartiality of law enforcement agencies, especially the police, in the 2019 election. The rift between the Inspector General of Police (IGP) Ibrahim Idris and the Senate leadership has further worsened their relationship over time.

124. Olusegun Obasanjo,'Points for Concern and Action', Abeokuta, 20 January 2019, p. 5.

people, but he does not seem to have the support of the elite class, who have complained of his lack of inclusiveness, patronage and non-performance.

A social media chat predicted that Atiku would win the PDP primaries. It alleged in a thread captioned 'the Generals Have Spoken' that the outcome of the primaries in Port Harcourt on 6 October 2018 became obvious when a retired top-ranking Army General and former Security Chief surfaced at the venue around midnight as voting was about to commence and after holding a few strategic consultations, which were believed to be conveying the decision of the generals, it became clear by 3 a.m. that Atiku was considered the preferred candidate. The reasons for that are not hard to see: (1) he has the longest experience in political struggle for the presidency and he might have learned some lessons that put him in a place equal to PMB; (2) Atiku is perceived to have sufficient resources of his own to invest in his campaign; and (3) his capacity for organisation and rigorous campaign may put him above PMB, whose alleged failing health may not favour him.

It is no wonder therefore that in his acceptance speech as candidate of the PDP, Atiku publicly acknowledged Chief Obasanjo as his mentor and former boss, which was a clear attempt to massage Obasanjo's ego, and true to it, Obasanjo, who had earlier told Nigerians that Atiku was not good material for the Presidency and that God wouldn't forgive him (Obasanjo) if he supported Atiku, suddenly changed his mind and not only pardoned Atiku but endorsed him as an option in a 'bad situation'. Regardless of what anybody would say about Obasanjo, and despite his own weaknesses, he has demonstrated uncommon patriotism and leadership with regard to the Nigeria project and he would do everything possible to ensure that he is involved in the process of electing a leader for the country[125]. His vast international connection is widely acknowledged, giving his antecedent as the first military head of state to hand over power to a democratically elected government. Even though he had earlier declared that he is no longer active in politics but remains a statesman, he responded to a report about his neutrality in the 2019 election by saying 'only a fool can remain neutral when his country is being destroyed by an incompetent leadership'. All this is not to say that Obasanjo is indispensable or that one cannot win an election without his support or the collective support of the elite class. Only God gives power to whom He pleases. Nevertheless, as God uses his creatures to perfect His plans, the elite choice is a crucial objective factor in the 2019 elections and that seems to be in favour of Atiku.

Attempting a SWOT analysis of the candidates for the election and predicting the outcome cannot be exhaustive. In order to provide a balanced perspective, it is appropriate to review some of speculated reasons why Buhari may lose or win.

## Why Buhari may lose or win

The analysis of Jonathan's failures in Chapter 2 was balanced with Buhari's victory (mis)management in Chapter 3. The Buhari/APC campaign issues in 2019 are the same as in 2015, namely security, anti-corruption and the economy, perhaps with slight modifications in a few action areas. Utomi rightly observed that 'oppositions do not win elections, incumbents lose them'. Having been in power for three and half years, the APC/Buhari records provide another chapter for political comparison and can also be used as a yardstick for predicting or guessing factors for losing or winning the 2019

125. Obasanjo's critics often point to his weaknesses rather than addressing the issues in his messages. In most cases, he anticipates much criticisms and he is quick to lay aside the probable issues some people may raise about his actions and reactions. For example, in his recent statement alleging plans to rig the 2019 elections, he said he was not afraid of being investigated as he has been investigated four times by the EFCC and the ICPC; and that the Report of the House of Representatives Committee that investigated him can be referred to by anybody who wishes to do so.

election. It is necessary to recall some of the factors why Buhari has or is perceived to have failed or is failing and which influence his chances. These include:

1.  The breakdown of the alliance of convenience in the APC leading to the departure of some Buhari's political supporters in the 2015 election, including Atiku, Saraki, Tambowal, Kwankwaso and a host of others would likely weaken Buhari's strength in 2019. But Buhari also made some gains with Godswill Akpabio (former Governor of Akwa Ibom state and Senate Minority Leader), Ahmed Adamu Mu'azu (former Governor of Bauchi State for 8 years and a former National Chairman of the PDP), Ibrahim Shekarau (former Governor of Kano State), Musliu Obanikoro (former Minister of state for defence), and a host others who defected from the PDP to the APC. Most of them were alleged to be seeking sanctuary because all of them were under investigation for corruption.

2.  Buhari may have lost some of his 2015 financiers, who may have thought that his winning in 2015 would bring them some financial rewards, which was not realised. However, since much of political campaign financing comes from patronage by government, it is expected that those managing the campaigns of PMB would have accumulated enough resources to upset any financial might of the opposition. Buhari may have also lost the support of the Northern technocratic elite and some prominent national elite, including the powerful generals who determine who, when and where power goes to and may have helped him in securing power in 2015, but who now accuse Buhari of incompetence and non-performance.[126] In a press statement issued by former President Obasanjo in January

126. The Open Letter former President Obasanjo wrote to PMB advising him not to contest the election and giving reasons for doing so seems to be the views of the majority of the elite class. God chose Buhari to be president but God uses His creatures to perfect His plans. It is believed that God used Obasanjo and his co-elite generals to promote PMB to win the 2015 election.

2018, he characterised PMB's failure as follows: 'The lice of poor performance in government – poverty, insecurity, poor economic management, nepotism, gross dereliction of duty, condonation of misdeed – if not outright encouragement of it, lack of progress and hope for the future, lack of national cohesion and poor management of internal political dynamics and widening inequality – are very much with us today. With such lice of general and specific poor performance and crying poverty with us, our fingers will not be dry of 'blood".[127]

Nevertheless, it is believed that Buhari retains a cult-like following in the North and it is unlikely that Atiku can match this. Buhari's massive supporters in his home base North-West and North-East do not believe he has failed; they disregard his alleged non-performance and blame it on others, the Nigerian factors or the system.

3. The lack of cohesion in the APC remains a major setback, especially the outcome of the party's primary election in October following which two governors (IbikunleAmosun of Ogun State and Rochas Okorocha of Imo State) are predicting the loss of their states to other parties, but remain committed to working hard to ensure Buhari is re-elected. While there are aggrieved members in all parties, those in the APC may likely affect the chances of Buhari in their respective spheres of influence. Besides, many of the APC members who worked towards Buhari's victory in 2015 and who could not be carried along or patronised through contracts and appointments may not be enthusiastic in campaigning for Buhari in 2019. As a result of the outcome of the primary elections, the APC might not have candidates for the gubernatorial election in Rivers and Zamfara States. Regardless of the alleged lack of cohesion in the APC, there is a strong consensus on the candidacy of

127. Olusegun Obasanjo, 'The Way Out: A Clarion Call for Coalition for Nigeria Movement', Abeokuta, January 2018.

PMB, and even with the grievances, no member of the party has threatened not to work towards his victory.

4. If objective criteria will contribute to the chances or otherwise of the APC, the lack of synergy within the government may affect Buhari's chances of winning the election. In other words, the power of incumbency is seen in the manner the state machinery, including law enforcement, is (mis)used to promote the interests of the incumbent.

5. Again, while cordial relationship with the other arms of government is not essential for winning or losing elections, the lack of it cannot have positive effect on the outcome. And for an incumbent, it may count as an objective criterion for non-performance. The relationship between the executive and judicial has not been cordial.

6. Yet the farmers/herders conflict seems to have turned much of the North-Central zone against PMB, whom they believed allowed it to fester 'because he is a Fulani man'. This seems to be the case with a vast majority of the Christian community. Obasanjo in his January 2018 Press Statement observed that 'The herdsmen/crop farmers issue is being wittingly or unwittingly allowed to turn sour and messy. It is no credit to the Federal Government that the herdsmen rampage continues with careless abandon and without finding an effective solution to it. And it is a sad symptom of insensitivity and callousness that some Governors, a day after 73 victims were being buried in a mass grave in Benue State without condolence, were jubilantly endorsing President Buhari for a second term! The timing was most unfortunate. The issue of herdsmen/crop farmers dichotomy should not be left on the political platform of blame game; the Federal Government must take the lead in bringing

about a solution that protects life and properties of herdsmen and crop farmers alike and for them to live amicably in the same community'.

7. Other objective indicators for assessing Buhari's performance (already discussed in Chapter 3) include the lack of a sense of urgency in dealing with or taking decisions on state affairs; Buhari's style of hiring for loyalty not merit; the absence of a concrete plan and policy vacuum, leading to poor management of the economy; the half-hearted anti-corruption war and continued blame on the PDP government are all indices of weakness. However, Buhari has his own strengths, which may help him to win.

8. Buhari's personal integrity remains his greatest asset. However, this personal integrity has been questioned because of his 'half-hearted' anti-corruption war. As Patrick Wilmot, a former Sociology teacher at the Ahmadu Bello University, Zaria, in an article titled 'The travails of Caesar's Wife' observed, 'President Buhari is an honest man', but 'in politics, however, honesty is not a sufficient condition for the fulfilment of the hopes and aspirations of the people… Integrity is an admirable quality but cannot put food on the table or a roof over one's head.'

9. Another area of concern has to do with PMB's record of ill-health. In this regard, former President Obasanjo advised him not to seek re-election. He stated 'President Buhari's illness called for sympathy, understanding, prayer and patience from every sane Nigerian. It is part of our culture. Most Nigerians prayed for him while he was away, sick in London, for over a hundred days and he gave his Deputy sufficient leeway to carry on in his absence. We all thanked God for President Buhari coming back reasonably hale and hearty and progressing well

in his recovery. But whatever may be the state of President Buhari's health today, he should neither over-push his luck nor over-tax the patience and tolerance of Nigerians for him, no matter what his self-serving, so-called advisers, who would claim that they love him more than God loves him and that without him, there would be no Nigeria say. President Buhari needs a dignified and honourable dismount from the horse. He needs to have time to reflect, refurbish physically and recoup and after appropriate rest, once again, join the stock of Nigerian leaders whose experience, influence, wisdom and outreach can be deployed on the side line for the good of the country. His place in history is already assured. Without impaired health and strain of age, running the affairs of Nigeria is a 25/7 affair, not 24/7'.

While supporters of each of the two candidates are flaunting different public opinion polls and research findings suggesting that their candidates will win in different parts of the country, foreign predictions about the outcome of the 2019 election are mixed. *The Economist* magazine in its Country Report on Nigeria (October 2018) revealed that 'the Economist Intelligence Unit expects that President Muhammadu Buhari will lose power at the February 2019 elections and that the next government will be led by Atiku Abubakar of the People's Democratic Party, although his administration will be fragile'. The same magazine changed its position in its subsequent edition and 'believes now that President Muhammadu Buhari would win next year's election. They also came out with the view that the opposition coalition may collapse before the general election.'[128] Thus, Ibrahim concluded that 'foreign predictions about the 2019 electoral outcome has become a game with the Economist Intelligence Unit, the research unit of *The Economist*, and a multinational banking and financial services company, HSBC,

128. Jibrin Ibrahim,'Predicting the Outcome', *Daily Trust*, 30 December 2018, p. 7.

coming out with 'a pro-Atiku prediction'.' The Buhari side then had to re-read a report by the US Institute of Peace, claiming they have predicted a Buhari win. The Institute had to come out with a statement captioned: 'Correcting a Media Error: USIP Makes No Prediction on Nigerian Election.' They explained that the institute's 20-page report 'on risk to a peaceful election in Nigeria, predicting victory for Buhari was false'.

The platform is an important consideration in elections. When the PDP lost in 2015, many people, including myself, thought that was the end of the party. Former President Obasanjo in his January 2018 press statement also said that 'What has emerged from the opposition has shown no better promise from their antecedents. As the leader of that Party for eight years as President of Nigeria, I can categorically say there is nothing to write home about in their new team.'

However, while receiving and endorsing Atiku in his Abeokuta residence in October 2018, Obasanjo had also predicted that Atiku would be the next President of Nigeria. Whether that view represents the view of the intelligentsia or the elite class is not certain. The problem with predicting the outcome of elections is that such predictions are based on some 'objective criteria of performance or non-performance, but in reality, the outcomes of election are often determined by the sentiments of the electorate'. It appears that the power brokers that matter in Nigeria are against a Buhari second term because of their conscious perception that he will literally 'kill the nation from which they steal'.

In view of the above, Farooq Kperogi summed up by saying: 'In 2015, Buhari didn't win the election; Jonathan lost it. That's another way of saying the 2015 election was more of a repudiation of Jonathan than it was an endorsement of Buhari. In 2019, it's looking like Buhari won't win again, but the opposition would lose. That's another way of saying the objective factors for the easy defeat of Buhari are already there, but the major opposition to him would bungle it and hand him an undeserved victory'.[129]

Thus, predicting the outcome of elections is merely academic, where commentators play with words and the intelligence of readers and say little or nothing judgemental. For example, after dissecting the 'objective factors and sentiments' that would influence the 2019 election, Ibrahim (2018) concluded in a similar vein that the South-West would be the ultimate arbiter to decide whether to vote for Atiku for his promise of restructuring, which is their pet project, or hand over victory to Buhari who has given them the Vice Presidency and key ministerial posts. He further observed that the media and social media would make overtures weeks before the election: 'President Buhari has a difficult but feasible chance of winning the 2019 elections. It would however require that he is able to quickly mend fences with supporters he has hurt or ignored and is able to mobilize against apathy. Atiku Abubakar also has a difficult but feasible chance of winning the 2019 elections if his campaign structure grows in coherence and is well funded and is above all able to carry the South-West with the promise of restructuring.'[130]

Finally, those who focus on the objective factors believe that PMB can only win the election as a result of incumbency, indicating rigging through the influence of law enforcement and security apparatchiks, and particularly the INEC. The appointment of the INEC Chairman from the North (same with the President) is seen as unusual (not illegal) and it is speculated to be on purpose to utter sentiments in favour of the President.

A counter argument to this is, what gives the impression to Atiku's supporters of being too optimistic of winning despite the 'baggage of corruption allegations' against him? Truly, God Almighty has destined the winner of the election. Our attempt to predict the outcome should not be misconstrued as doing God but playing in His hands as mortals and fallible.

129. Kperogi, 'Electoral Law'.
130. Ibrahim, 'Predicting the Outcome.'

## Conclusion

While about 73 candidates from different political parties have signified their intention to contest the presidential election in Nigeria in 2019, the reality is that it is clearly going to be a contest between the two candidates of the APC (PMB) and that of the PDP (former Vice President Atiku Abubakar).An election is a contest in which every contestant feels eminently qualified and most likely to emerge victorious, until the outcome is announced.

I have attempted to analyse the potential strengths and weaknesses of both candidates with a view to highlighting real campaign issues, not necessarily the candidates, but it turned out that the campaign issues are almost the same and therefore the only difference would be the 'whose and how' promises can take Nigeria to the promised land. Ultimately, the choice lies with the electorate, who are influenced by both the objective factors and sentiments discussed in this chapter. This naturally brings us to the point where we should be concerned about the future of democracy should the choice swing in any direction whatsoever. And this is what we seek to examine in the following chapter.

# CHAPTER 5

# Reflections on Elections and the Future of Democracy and Good Governance in Nigeria

The most creative scholarship, which speaks to the challenges of our present and predicts the future, emerges from sustained reflection on current issues and the state of affairs in society. In the Introduction, I borrowed a line from Abraham Lincoln and gave a concise definition of democracy as 'the government of the people, by the people and for the people'. I also suggested that elections, especially those within specified intervals, constitute an important, if not the most important, element of democracy because they are the distinctive feature of democracy, one that distinguishes it from other forms of government. In the Introduction, I attempted to give an overview of Nigeria's chequered journey to democracy through various political transition programmes, mostly managed by the military. In Nigeria the 2019 election happens to be one of a few landmarks in the transition from one civilian administration to another. It is on the threshold of repeating either the 2003, 2007 and 2011 elections, in which the incumbents were returned elected, or the 2015 political revolution, when an incumbent was defeated. Either way, the elections will have significant consequences on democracy and good governance in Nigeria.

From the analysis in the preceding chapters, the political atmosphere is tense as the political campaigns have commenced in earnest, but it is too early to say whether the campaigns will be issues-based as envisaged. In the 2015 elections, the campaigns became rough, dirty and even nastier towards the end of the campaign periods. Even at the risk of sounding repetitive, the beauty of democracy lies in the variety of alternative choices that the electorate can make about who governs them. But that is not to say that wishes always become winners, as only one person or party can be a winner in an election. Here lies the flip side of the system – not all expectations are met. With the improvement recorded in the 2015 elections in Nigeria, largely due to the introduction of the card reader machine, the 2019 elections are expected to be even better, despite the refusal by President Buhari to assent to the amendments proposed to the electoral law by the NASS.

Every election provides opportunities for learning lessons and this one is no exception. Therefore, since election is a crucial element of democracy and since democracy is the arbiter of good governance, I shall in this chapter reflect on whether any society that seeks to entrench good governance through the processes of democracy has first to establish a strong democratic foundation before attaining good governance and ultimately development; good governance, even in a non-democracy, can satisfy the yearnings of the populace for developmental fulfilment. Although there is no obvious threat to the success of the 2019 elections, nevertheless, as part of the lessons we need to learn, this chapter examines the potential threats to the success of the elections and makes some recommendations for the greater improvement in the electoral system.

# Reflections on Democracy and Good Governance:
## Some Theoretical Issues

In the developing world, and Africa in particular, democracy, despite being practised in some countries that have never experienced military intervention, such as Senegal, is still considered a learning process and most countries describe their experience in democratic governance as 'nascent'. Among the visible rewards of democracy in Nigeria in the past 20 years are the increased legitimacy, not only of the government but also of debates on policy issues such as elections and the yearning for better policy orientation and implementation through political parties' manifestos and programmes.

In his *Nicomachean Ethics*, Aristotle stated: 'since politics uses the rest of the sciences and since, again, it legislates as to what we are to do and what we are to abstain from, the end of this science must include those of the others, so that this end must be the good for man.'[131]

In a democracy, election defines the relationship between the citizens and those who govern them. Thus, John Locke (1632-1704) stated that such a relationship should be in the form of a social contract that is subject to periodic public renewal of confidence;[132] he rightly observed that the authority of government should be based on 'just powers from the consent [i.e. delegation] of the governed'. This, according to him, 'gave rise to variants of the social contract theory, particularly in the 18th and 19thcentury that became the bases of the evolution of systems of government powered by periodic elections. Thus, in the event of the elected authority losing the confidence of the public, the people, under the Lockean social contract system of governance, reserve the right to change it through the ballot box or,

131. For details, see Christian Breede, 'The Challenge of Nation-Building: Insights from Aristotle', The Royal Military College of Canada, 2012.

132. Buakar Usman, 'Leadership, Security and National Development', public lecture delivered at the Faculty of Arts, Ahmadu Bello university, Zaria, Nigeria, 20 January 2015, p.7.

if necessary, by violent means. By this stance, revolution becomes justifiable in the last resort.'

By May 2019, Nigeria would have practised 'uninterrupted democracy' for twenty years, so even a child who was born in 1999 should have completed school or graduated from the university according to the Nigerian educational curriculum. In that sense, the student or 'child' should be grown up, adult enough to be on his/her own with a full sense of judgement and accountability. Can we say that is the case with regard to Nigeria as a fledgling democracy? I will return to that question shortly.

But let us be clear that the purpose of democracy is not only elections. Democracy is not an end in itself, it is rather a means or road map leading to specific goals, those of improving the living standards of the people who practise it, ensuring freedom and justice for all, rule of law and safeguarding and protecting the integrity of institutions and respect for all mankind. In this regard, the essence of democracy is good governance. The basic elements of good governance, including fundamental rights and freedom of speech and choice, rule of law, security and welfare of the citizenry, are arguably the dividends which democracy is expected to deliver. In other words, democracy in name may not be the best form of government; rather the best form of government depends on what is conducive for stability and development. But the roads to all these dividends are not easy, due to the rules governing the conduct of democracy, and here lies the conundrum. Let me attempt to explain it.

In Africa, Western democracy has been embraced in the absence of an alternative for any form of government, but its practice is fraught with many setbacks. One of the problems of democracy is conducting free, fair and credible elections with integrity. In Africa, incumbents, no matter how unpopular, seldom lose elections, and the reasons are not difficult to see: the institutions that should conduct and forestall flawed elections are either weak, compromised or both. It's only when there is a semblance of good governance that the rule of law and strong institutions, rather than individuals, can take root and foster good democracy. Now, the dilemma is, do we have first to establish the strong institutions before contemplating elections and institutionalising democracy, or do we have to allow delinquent politicians who abuse their office to compromise elections, thereby producing bad leaders? I leave this theoretical question for further research.

One experience in Nigeria is criticism of the instrument of democracy, i.e. the Constitution being a product of the military. Some people believe it is deficient in several ways and their interests cannot be served under the current constitution. The Constitution makes strong provision for the welfare and security of the citizens and, for example, the separation of powers between the different arms of the government in order to devoid drifting into dictatorship. The Constitution is forward-looking and provides for possible amendments that would meet the yearnings and expectations of the people. However, amending most parts of the Constitution has been difficult due largely to vested interests; where such amendments have been effected – for example, the 2018 amendments to the Constitution providing for the independence of the judiciary at the state level and the Local Government Councils – such amendments have been jettisoned at state level, thus depriving the expected rewards of democracy.

The rule of law is an essential element of good governance. Unfortunately, in Nigeria, this is sometimes interpreted by government to mean the authority to override individual rights in matters of security; and by civil society and human right activists to mean 'absolute due process' even when there is an obvious threat to the country. Advanced societies provide models on how to manage this challenge but obviously, because of their impunity and vested interests, politicians in Africa are yet to embrace this good practice and that means we have a long way to go before we can entrench good governance and democracy.

Politics is an extension of war by other means, and democracy is the platform for nation building through good governance. Reflectively, nation building itself is about building a political entity; it is about building institutions that reflect or symbolise the entity, in this regard, institutions of good governance; and nation building is also about building a common sense of purpose, which is also symbolised by democracy.

Another conundrum between democracy and good governance is in the fight against corruption. While everybody agrees that corruption is an encumbrance to progress and development in any society, we do not all seem to have a consensus on the definition of corruption, let alone how to deal with it. When politicians make promises to fight corruption, they have often turned out to reflect an animus towards their opponents. Every government has to deal with its opponents, and by the time we have four regimes in a row, corrupt persons should have been dealt with and corruption minimised. Fighting corruption is an important aspect of good governance and a condition for sustainable democracy. But would the politicians forgo their quest for power by dealing with their closest entourage who are accused of corruption in the same way they deal with the opposition? This is a major fault line in the practice of democracy and nation building, and it needs to be addressed by leaders who mean well.

Reflecting on these few points and many others, I will attempt to contextualise the potential threats to the 2019 elections in Nigeria, drawing specific examples from other jurisdictions. Based on our assessment of and prediction of the outcome of the 2019 presidential election, I will start with the four major threats to that election: religion, region, ethnicity and illiteracy.

**Religion:** Until recently, religion was not a major consideration with regard to who becomes the president of Nigeria. Under the military, while there was some balancing between the head of state and his second in command, such balancing was done tacitly, and this served the country without any rancour. But there was one example which also served Nigeria without rancour when Major General Muhammadu Buhari, a Muslim and northerner, was Head of State and Major General Tunde Idiagbon, also a Muslim and northerner, was his second in command. Nigerians did not care about religion but about what they would do to salvage Nigeria from the precipice. In 1993, Nigerians overwhelmingly elected Chief M.K.O. Abiola and Ambassador Babagana Kingibe as President and Vice respectively, and though the election was annulled by the Babangida Administration, that election was a signpost of Nigeria transcending the clutches of ethnicity and religion in our national polity. Had that team been allowed to govern, this country would hopefully have seen a different story with regard to religious sentiment as a choice in elections.

Over time however, due to the greed and selfish aggrandisement of the political elite, since 1979 religion and the other factors have become important considerations in elections.

While it is not a bad thing to respond to the sensitivity of the electorate, the point of departure is that when merit is substituted for religious balance and other cleavages in selecting leaders, it further erodes the sense of oneness and divides the country and its peoples along religious lines. It was for that reason that the APC was wise enough not to field a candidate on a Muslim-Muslim ticket during the 2015 election. It is obvious that religious sentiment went against former President Jonathan in that election. The APC candidate Muhammadu Buhari was portrayed in some quarters, especially by the southern media, as a 'religious bigot', which, rather than damaging his reputation, gave him popularity among the northern predominantly Muslim voters. He seems to retain that cult-like followership to the extent that those who are passionate about him would disregard his mistakes and put the blame on others or attribute them to the will of God. For example, one of the mistakes such voters made in the last election was that they prayed for God to make Buhari President without praying for God to give him the vision, wisdom, courage and the right persons to help him lead the country. When some complained that there is poverty in the land under Buhari, such sentimental supporters would reply that it is God who brought poverty but that Buhari would right the wrongs so that poverty would vanish. Alas! That is the extent of religious sentiment in politics.

Although the leading candidates in the 2019 election (PMB and former Vice President Atiku Abubakar) are both Muslims, another dimension of the religious sentiment may emerge in terms of which sect any of them belong to or how religious they are and simply how they fulfil an individual voter's sentiment in that regard. If the experience of the past is anything to go by, religion has factionalised the polity such that any party has to consider religion when fielding candidates for elections. But does that serve the country? The answer is no! There is a great lesson for Nigeria to learn from other jurisdictions on how to manage this potential threat. For example, South Africa and Singapore were at one time the same as Nigeria with regard to multiplicity of tribes and other diversities, but over time they were able to stabilise their systems and now mundane issues as religion or ethnicity carry no risks to their democratic development.

**Regionalism:** Nigeria is informally divided into six geopolitical zones for expediency, but the real division and alternation of political power is between the North and the South. This arrangement, though not legally binding, has subsisted since independence and has helped in promoting a sense of unity and inclusiveness. However, the trend towards regional sentiment seems to be now so far-fetched that it is affecting the unity and stability of the country, and this can be attributed to the way politicians are using it to satisfy their personal aggrandisement. While regional sentiment was more of a threat in the 2015 election, obviously because the two leading candidates came from different sides, the 2019 one seems to be different as both leading candidates are from the North. However, typical of politicians, even within the North, PMB is from the North-West and Atiku is from the North-East, and this may affect the outcome of the election.

If regional sentiment is to be an option for the electorate, then they need to assess how each of the candidates has contributed towards the progress of the North. While Atiku's business profile and record of empowerment in the North may tilt in his favour, PMB's record of achievements in fighting Boko Haram, infrastructural development, education, health care and poverty reduction should be the benchmark for assessing his contributions to the North.

Overall, it would be risky to elect a candidate simply on the basis of his regional extraction. But since Nigeria is still in a learning stage of democracy, it is hoped that this consideration will be de-emphasised as we grow to promote national unity and cohesion.

**Ethnicity:** Nigeria is a multi-lingual, multi-cultural, multi-ethnic and multi-religious society. Each of these sub-groups competes for recognition, influence and dominance. Thus ethnicity, the feeling for one's ethnic group, has become one of problems of nation building. It is a potential threat to the 2019 election because politicians who struggle to outsmart one another talk loudly about ethnic sentiment –that is, where it suits them to win an election. As stated in Chapter 4, the outcomes of elections are determined by sentiment rather than objective factors. The danger is that unsuitable candidates are likely to be elected to public office based on nothing more than ethnic sentiment. Then what do you expect? Garbage in, garbage out!

The ethnic sentiment and its challenge in the 2019 presidential election have been mitigated to some extent, since both the leading candidates are from the same Fulani ethnic extraction. However, as the saying goes in Nigeria, if you want to know certain things which you did not know about your secrets in life, join politics and contest for a position; all the stereotypes about you will come out from your opponents. At one point some people started to complain that Atiku is not an 'original' Fulani. He seemed to have had foreknowledge of this and so, during the launch of his presidential campaign, he chose the centre of the Caliphate, Sokoto, and there he told the doubting Thomases that his father had migrated from Wurno in Sokoto State and that he is a full-blown Fulani man. In throwing back the salvo, he (Atiku) was reported to have accused Buhari of not being a true Fulani. That is politics!

Let me relate a personal experience here to buttress the point on ethnic sentiment in Nigerian politics. During the political parties' primary elections in October 2018, a friend of mine from Adamawa State tried to convince me that the incumbent governor had not performed and so did not deserve a second term, and that the majority of the people preferred another candidate, who had been my boss at one point. Because I know him personally and I commend his integrity and competence, I was happy to hear what the friend was telling me and hoping that the electorate would do the necessary to elect the most competent candidate. I asked my interviewee, what if my friend loses the primary election? Would they still elect the incumbent governor on account of being in the same party? He said not at all, but I could not fathom exactly why.

Then Atiku emerged as the candidate of the PDP and I asked the friend how the ethnic factor would play out, since both PMB and Atiku were Fulanis. He said that Atiku had not done anything to his state and local government areas when he was Vice President from 1999 to 2007. I observed that a Vice President does not have the full powers of a President and if he were given a chance this time around, didn't he think he would do more for his state? I further enquired what PMB had done to that state to mitigate Atiku's failure. My friend only said that the contract for construction of the road to Jada, Atiku's locality, had been awarded (not executed in three years under PMB). In the final conversation, my friend told me categorically that despite PMB's non-performance, he remained the preferred candidate of the people of Adamawa (he did not say the Fulanis, though it was implied from his analogy).

When I looked deeply into the two scenarios above, I discovered that my interviewee, a Fulani person, and his brothers and sisters simply did not like the incumbent governor because he was not a Fulani man. In the same vein, the sentiment swayed in favour of PMB because, as the source alleged, Atiku's real background was 'questionable', regardless of his capacity to lead, so many people from Adamawa, his home state, would not elect him. This is typical ethnic sentiment that goes far beyond religion and region. And as Aristotle found, 'most people are bad judges in their own case . . . they agree about the equality of things, but dispute the equality of the persons . . . because they are bad judges in their own affairs.'[133]

Writing more than two centuries ago, Usman Dan Fodio, the great Islamic scholar, reformer and leader of the Sokoto Caliphate, had warned of the dangers of promoting ethnicity: 'one of the swiftest ways of destroying a Kingdom (or a nation) is to give preference to one particular tribe over another, or to show favour to one group of people rather than another'. This message was reinforced by Abraham Lincoln, who observed that 'a house divided against itself cannot stand'.

**Illiteracy:** A good number of the voting population, especially from the northern parts of the country, are considered 'illiterate' or lacking in formal education, but they are politically conscious

133. Christian Breede, 'The Challenge of Nation-Building: Insights from Aristotle', The Royal Military College of Canada, 2012.

and can be vicious. Since PMB ventured into politics in 2003, this category of voters has been his main strength, and despite his alleged non-performance, there are many who would vote for PMB even if it were his dead body! While this portends a risk in leadership selection under a democratic system, its real effect may have been exaggerated in anticipation of the 2019 presidential election.

Commenting on the election and on the ignorance of some people, Saka Momodou, in an article titled 'Elevating Incompetence', obviously referring to the performance of PMB, remarked:

> I must confess that I have been struggling to understand the rationale and motive of some of these people for their wilful blind support for a man whose legendary lack of competence and capacity for the job of president of a diverse country as Nigeria has been established beyond a shadow of a doubt, not by murmurs of ill-feeling or whispers of rumours born out of partisan jealousy, but by loud evidence, albeit with the tragic consequences that have come through the massive decline in all facets of our national life. We are in strange times, an era where failure is hailed as excellence by a vocal group of revisionists hell-bent on continuing the path of destruction.[134]

He went on to catalogue PMB's failures and concluded that such sentiments can best be described as 'conscientious stupidity'. I am sure he would receive feedback that would counter his analysis.

For democracy to endure, a lot of social mobilisation and education is required on the fundamental and objective factors that should influence electorates' sentiments on their choices of candidates, and that is the lesson for Nigeria in the 21st century.

**Social Media:** technological advancement has created both opportunities and risks for society. While social media have become a potent tool for social mobilisation and education, they also carry the risk of being misused, and that can be a serious threat to electoral

134. Dele Momodou, 'Time to Re-Write the APC Manifesto', *Thisday*, 5 March 2016.

choices, as well as outcomes. Since the beginning of the political campaigns towards the 2019 elections, there have been competing opinions, mostly canvassing sympathy for one candidate or another or promoting some ideas over the others. People share information on social media, particularly Whatsapp, to promote their favoured views or to change perception regarding their disfavoured views. In this situation, some people have had cause to be irritated, leading to confrontation because one party exchanged unpleasant posts about others. I learnt about a jest from someone in one village which led to a fight and the person was killed.

Another aspect of the risk of social media is the circulation of fake news. People concoct stories that favour them, knowing full well that they are false and yet go ahead to spread it among social media counterparts to course disaffection. This is very dangerous and can undermine democratic choices in elections.

Having discussed the potential of the 2019 election and the immediate risks to it and to the future of democracy and good governance in Nigeria, I now turn to the more fundamental remote factors that could undermine elections and democracy. The obvious starting point is the issue of corruption.

## Corruption

Corruption is not peculiar to Nigeria, but while it exists in every society, its pervasiveness, deleterious effects and debilitating impacts have been obvious in Nigeria, reflected in the outcomes of most elections conducted in the past. Corruption manifests in various forms, but our concern here is on election-related corrupt practices (listed in Chapter 1). All these constitute potential risks to election and sustainable democracy, but I choose only a few to illustrate and draw examples from other jurisdictions on how these risks can be minimised or ameliorated.

## Election rigging[135]

Every election seeks to establish the legitimacy of the elected in any office. That is why credible election with integrity is the most essential quality for any democratic election. This essential quality can be undermined by corruption. Election rigging in the forms mentioned here is by far the greatest risk in all elections. In fact, the greatest fear expressed by any opposition party is not the fear of losing but the fear of losing an election because it was rigged. I have already discussed the impact of rigging on the electoral process in Nigeria in Chapter 1. It is understandable, however, that no matter how party leaders rig elections, it is voters who ultimately decide the outcome. Mobilising and educating voters on their rights in a long-term and sustainable way could mitigate the risk of rigging. But we must equally realise that those who are used as 'cannon-fodder' to rig elections or cause confusion are drawn from points of weakness.

One form of rigging which is often unrecognised is the deliberate delay or denial of electoral materials to voting centres believed to be the strongholds of the opposition. The risk of this method of rigging remains high in all elections in Nigeria. As stated in the previous chapter, harassment and intimidation of candidates and supporters of the opposition is yet another potential remote threat to elections.

It seems that rigging will be the highest risk in the 2019 elections. Never before have we had statesmen speaking publicly on the risk of rigging elections as now in 2019. In a lengthy statement dated 18 January 2019 but issued on the 20th, Obasanjo accused President Buhari and the APC Government of planning to rig the presidential election. A day after, Lai Mohammed, Minister of Information, alleged that the government had intelligence reports regarding plans by some opposition parties to foment trouble

---

135. There is a joke that says in Africa election malpractice is called rigging and is unacceptable, but in America it is called gerrymandering and so is OK.

or cause violence during the elections.[136] Two days later, on 23 January 2019, General Theophilus Danjuma alleged plans to rig the elections. Such openness is not common and something may be afoot with regard to the presidential election.

Perhaps a pattern of election fraud known as vote buying deserves special mentioning here.

**Vote buying**

Vote buying simply means the manipulation and inducement of voters to vote for certain candidates based on monetary or other incentives or inducement. This is one of the worst forms of election corruption and the risk in Nigeria remains very high. Vote buying exploits the needy conditions of voters, especially civil servants who have not been paid their legitimate entitlements for some months, or the poor who have little or no sustainable means of income. It is predicated on the vulnerable condition of the voter. It was alleged that vote buying was rampant, even though none has been proven, in the Ekiti and Osun States gubernatorial elections held sometime in August and September 2018. In a situation where citizens mortgage their electorate rights for a pittance or what has been described as 'stomach infrastructure', the future of democracy and good governance is in peril.[137]

Vote buying is a serious impediment to election integrity because it produces outcomes on a 'cash and carry' basis rather than merit. It undermines confidence in the electoral process and destroys democracy, because if unsuitable persons are elected into either the legislature or the executive arm of government, they would destroy the system with their incompetence and kill the morale of

136. The Minister was criticised by some commentators for acting like he was still in the opposition adding that if there was intelligence available to the government, who should be responsible for averting what is alleged rather than the government?

137. When receiving a election observers from the European Union and ECOWAS in his office on 21 January 2019, the Chairman of the INEC, Professor Mahmood Yakubu, revealed that the INEC has received intelligence report regarding a plot by some political parties to use food vendors at polling stations for the purposes of paying those who sell their votes the political parties.

credible candidates who cannot afford to pay a price on election. Of course good governance is the first casualty, and that leads to other negative threats such poverty, unemployment, corruption and other social vices in society.

## Poverty as a risk factor

The level of poverty in any society portends a threat not only to its electoral system but to its overall security and development. The habit of politicians of handing out money to people to vote for them can never be good practice, wherever it is found. In Nigeria, however, it has become entrenched, due to the level of poverty and the ubiquity of greed. The issue is whether the same people who bought their way into elective office can stop such practices. Despite the perception that money does not influence election choices, it remains a threat to election integrity and sustaining democracy.

Socio-economic realities are the single most important factor in ensuring that a state is stable and self-sufficient. Ibrahim Gambari drew attention to some of the socio-economic inequalities that are reflected in our nation building when he said:

If we take the level of immunization of children against dangerous childhood diseases, we note that while the South-East has 44.6% immunization coverage, the North-West has 3.7% and North-East 3.6%. If you take the education of the girl-child as indicator, you see a similar pattern of inequality with the South-East having an enrolment rate of 85%, South-West 89%, South-South 75%, North-East 20%, and North-West 25%. Only 25% of pregnant women in the North-West use maternity clinics, while 85% of the women in the South-East do. It is not surprising that 93% more women die in child-birth in the North-East, compared to the South-West. Education and poverty levels are also important dimensions of inequalities across Nigeria.If we take admissions into Nigerian universities in the academic year 2000/1, we see that the North-West had only 5% of the admissions, while the South-East had 39%.As for poverty, while 95% of the population of Jigawa State is classified as poor, only 20% of Bayelsa State is so classified.While 85% of Kwara State is classified as poor, only 32% of Osun is in the same boat.[138]

The elite class in particular take advantage of such vulnerabilities and further entrench the threat to democracy and good governance through their indiscipline, greed, impunity and vested interests. Therefore, the most important improvement required to strengthen the electoral system is to block all avenues for rigging, which seems to be a major challenge not only in Nigeria but in most developing countries. How can this be done?

The Global Commission on Election has documented a number of case studies which serve as lessons for any country that seeks to improve its electoral systems and Nigeria, despite the observable weaknesses in its system, is singled out as a good example. At the risk of repetition but stating the obvious, the Global Commission observed that:

Important progress was made in the 2011 elections towards professionalizing the country's Independent National Electoral Commission (INEC), most importantly through the appointment of a respected academic as chairman. Professor Attahiru M. Jega, who became known as 'Mr Integrity', revamped the voter registration process, improved transparency at the Commission and for the first time prosecuted electoral government officials (including INEC officials) for electoral malpractice. Unfortunately, improved electoral administration and transparency were not sufficient to achieve major reductions in violence in some regions.

This means that the responsibility for election with integrity lies in

138. Ibrahim Gambari, 'The Challenges of Nation-Building', First Anniversary Lecture of the Mustapha Akanbi Foundation, Abuja, 7 February 2018.

the hands of the electoral body and the competence, professionalism and non-partisanship of its staff. If there is anything, perceived or real, that could undermine the integrity of an election, it should be eliminated as a way of assuring the electorate of fairness and transparency. Unfortunately, not long ago and in preparations for the 2019 elections, some opposition parties had accused the electoral body in Nigeria, the INEC, of bias and/or lack of capacity or trust to conduct a credible election. Whatever may be their reasons, it is important to note that every human being is fallible in some ways and no 'Jupiter' can come from 'heaven' or anywhere to conduct elections for Nigerians. While the opposition parties must learn to give the benefit of the doubt to the electoral body, the incumbent must also demonstrate the utmost fairness, inclusiveness and transparency in constituting the electoral body as determined by law.

A recent controversy over the 2019 election is the appointment of Mrs Amina Zakari, a Federal Commissioner in the INEC, as Chairperson of the Committee on the collation centre. On the one hand, Mrs Zakari, whether she is a blood relation of the President or anyone else, has a right as a citizen and has responsibility for the nation. If by providence she found herself as the Commissioner in charge of Logistics in the INEC and therefore most suitable to provide logistics for the election, such suitability should be determined with some sensitivity to the feelings of other Nigerians who may assume that based on certain antecedents, she could favour one candidate over the others. Perhaps, in conducting our affairs, we may have to learn the lesson of leaving what is doubtful or could generate controversies, choosing instead what is without doubt and more straightforward, since there are many suitable persons to perform any national assignment. To this extent, one might conclude that while corruption is a major threat to credible elections, Nigerians seem to abhor corruption only when it does not benefit them directly or indirectly.

Other jurisdictions have had to improve their electoral systems, and Nigeria may learn some lessons from this. A few examples drawn from the Global Commission on Elections, Democracy and Security[139] are shown below:

## Case Study 1: Transparency and Institutional Strength in Ghana

In many ways, Ghana's 2008 presidential elections were strikingly similar to the Kenyan elections the year before. Each featured a hotly-contested race with ethnic undertones in countries widely known for their political stability. But whereas the manipulation of electoral institutions in Kenya precipitated widespread violence, a history of sound electoral management and transparency allowed Ghana to navigate a tense political situation with relatively little violence, leading to a legitimate transfer of power and continued stability.

In 2008, the two main presidential candidates, Nana Akufo-Addo of the New Patriotic Party and John Atta Mills of the National Democratic Congress, were running very close to each other in opinion polls. Akufo-Addo fell less than 1 percentage point short of a first-round majority in early December, forcing a run-off election at the end of that month. Rhetoric escalated in the intervening weeks, and many feared the heated campaigning would lead to violence, but the Electoral Commission took a number of steps to reduce tensions and build confidence in its performance and the integrity of the results, for example by replacing poll workers who had failed to follow procedures in the first round. When the run-off ballot resulted in Mills winning by less than 50,000 votes, these steps helped persuade the losing party to accept the results.

In addition, civil society conducted what is regarded as a highly successful monitoring effort, which included parallel vote

---

139. Global Commission on Elections, Democracy and Security 'Deepening Democracy: A Strategy for Improving the Integrity of Elections Worldwide, September 2012, pp. 23, 43.

tabulation for both rounds of the election. Ghana's Electoral Commission Chairman, Dr Kwadwo Afari-Gyan, publicly praised the citizen election-monitoring efforts of the Ghana Center for Democratic Development, and its partners in the Coalition of Domestic Election Observers, as important factors that reinforced the Electoral Commission's work and reduced volatility in the election environment.

Fundamentally, the ability of the Ghanaian Electoral Commission to manage such a close election successfully was rooted in years of respect and independence from other political actors in the country. By establishing a track record of competence and professionalism, while simultaneously maintaining its independence from improper influence, the Commission was able to build political capital that it could draw upon when needed in 2008.

## Case Study 2: NAMFREL in the Philippines

One of the earliest and best-known examples of bottom-up electoral reform comes from the National Citizens Movement for Free Elections (NAMFREL) in the Philippines. Philippines President Ferdinand Marcos called snap presidential elections in 1986, just two years after parliamentary elections that were widely viewed with suspicion.NAMFREL, a non-partisan election watchdog, had organised observers for the 1984 elections, and in 1986 it was able to build on this experience to effectively expose the electoral manipulations of the Marcos regime. With the help of the Catholic Church, NAMFREL mobilised half a million Filipinos to observe the polling process. The centrepiece of their work was Operation Quick Count, an effort to provide a comprehensive tally of the results from all 85,000 polling stations in the country as a check on the official count provided by the election commission. In the end, NAMFREL tabulated results from 70% of polling stations, showing enough of a discrepancy from the official results to convince the Filipino public of fraud, thus helping to kick off the People Power revolution that forced Marcos from power.

The 1986 elections in the Philippines were the first in a series of electoral revolutions over the next two decades that ranged from Chile in 1988 to Ukraine in 2004 and beyond, all of which featured domestic observation groups organised to promote electoral integrity in their own countries. These groups show the power of domestic advocacy from civil society groups and the broader public to support the cause of elections with integrity.

## Security

Security, simply defined as the absence of threat, is an important requirement for a credible election and the future of democracy and good governance. With respect to election, the requirements for security can be categorised into a national security environment that would guarantee a peaceful election, and the security of any particular election, in this case the security of the electoral materials, personnel and voting centres. While the ravaging insurgency in the north-east of Nigeria affected the conduct of the 2015 elections, leading to a six-week deferment of the presidential election, its likely impact on the 2019 elections, especially with regard to security in large parts of the country, is minuscule; even less so other potential threats. The main concerns with regard to security in the elections are the misuse, abuse or partisanship of security personnel, and the security of the electoral process itself.

Obviously, violence is a potential threat to the 2019 elections. To curtail the spate of electoral violence, it must first be understood that violence is a reaction to actions which are considered unethical, irregular and unjust. Election rigging is the principal cause of violence in any election. When people are convinced that an election was conducted freely and fairly, no one raises the alarm. During the run-up to the 2011 presidential election in Nigeria, at least 165 people were killed in violence related to political campaigns and voter registration. Another 800 to 1,000 died after widespread protests broke out in the North on the announcement of incumbent President Goodluck Jonathan's victory. More than 65,000 were displaced.[140]

This violence, according to the Global Commission on Elections, Democracy and Security Report,[141] 'represents a political failure in the face of what was largely a technical and administrative success. Losing candidates and party leaders failed to meet their responsibilities to restrain their supporters and accept the election results.'

With respect to the alleged involvement of security personnel, especially the police who are supposed to ensure a level playing field, their roles in the Ekiti and Osun elections, and other by-elections in Kwara, Katsina and Bauchi States in 2018 have been criticised for being biased in favour of the ruling party. This is not new of course, as the ruling party also accused them of bias during previous election when it was in the opposition. So, it's a matter of one thief giving another a bad name.

The electoral body is responsible for the conduct of elections, but it must be assisted by the police and other security agencies to ensure that there is an environment conducive to the conduct of elections. But quite frankly, the role of security agencies in conducting elections in Nigeria leaves many aspects to be desired;

140. Following this violence, a Presidential Committee was established under the Chairmanship of a renowned Islamic scholar, Sheikh Lemu, to investigate the immediate and remote cause of the violence and proffer remedial solutions. The report of this Committee was not made public, but it is believed the number of deaths and properties destroyed are more than the estimates provided here. None implementation of the recommendations of the Committee is also a setback in addressing the problem of electoral violence in Nigeria. Over 21,000 post-election violence deaths were reported after the 2011 elections in Nigeria.

141. Global Commission on Elections, Democracy and Security, 'Deepening Democracy: A Strategy for Improving the Integrity of Elections Worldwide, 2012, p. 25.

there is ample room for improvement. Perhaps Nigeria needs to develop its electoral system such that the role of the police and other law enforcement agents could be regulated by the electoral body rather than by the Police High Command.

The specific risk of police bias has already been expressed towards the 2019 elections as the opposition parties alleged the potential bias of the Inspector General of Police, Ibrahim Idris, based on his fractured relationships with some members of the opposition, especially those in the NASS. The Coalition of United Political Parties issued a threat to embark on a protest from 15 January 2019 to press for the retirement of the IGP.[142]

Given the outlook for Nigeria 2019-23, and specifically forecasting the 2019 presidential election, the Economic Intelligence Unit of *the Economist* magazine had on 17 October 2018 predicted that there will be 'severe outbreaks of instability, given slow progress on tackling numerous security and societal challenges at a time of economic difficulty... The election period itself will be a time of high risk; as a recent by-election in Osun demonstrated; small scale violence at the polls is highly likely, as is disputation of results... It will prove hard to build a more effective security apparatus while also creating economic opportunities for local populations; poverty is at the root of much of the instability.'

The United States government, through a representative of the American embassy in Nigeria, David Yong, at a meeting with the INEC in Abuja on 16 January 2019, expressed concern over the neutrality of the security services ahead of 2019 elections in Nigeria. That leads me to the role of the international community and supporting and promoting democracy and credible elections.

---

142. Following his retirement upon attaining the mandatory age of 60 on 15 January 2019, the President appointed Adamu Mohammed Lafia as the 20th Inspector General of Police in acting capacity pending confirmation by the National Council of State. His appointment was hailed by a cross-section of the civil society and opinion leaders.

## The Role of the International Community and Development Partners

As democracy is a global phenomenon, there has been renewed interest in elections all over the world by both governmental and non-governmental bodies. While the involvement of foreign observers is encouraged to enhance the transparency and credibility of the electoral process and democracy as a whole, it seems that there is a potential threat when some international bodies overstep their limits to dictate to countries what they should do or what they shouldn't in their electoral processes.

During a meeting of delegates of the international partners with the INEC on 16 January 2019, the US representative assured the INEC of its support; while the EU Ambassador to Nigeria and the ECOWAS, Ketil Karlsen, was quoted as saying 'Our only real mission here is for Nigeria to succeed in having free, fair, transparent and credible elections'. He emphasised that they do not support any candidate, party or ideology, adding that any candidate who emerges victorious in the election will become a partner of the EU countries.

In recent years, opposition parties in Nigeria have been prone to taking their complaints regarding lack of transparency in the process to foreign bodies or civil society organisations that are seen as the only capable bodies that could exert pressure on any government to do the needful. It seems that the opposition in every country believes that their last resort to getting credible and acceptable elections is only through international observer bodies. On the other hand, such bodies have their own prejudices and sometimes limitations.

Regardless of the perception of the role of international bodies and election monitors, they serve certain purposes which individually or collectively help in ensuring that electoral processes are free, fair and credible:

- They are physically on the ground to observe the election processes

- They meet and discuss with all stakeholders, including the political parties, CSOs, the security agencies and the electoral bodies, with a view to sharing their concerns and proffer solutions and support where necessary.

- They voice observable grievances without taking sides.

- They produce reports with succinct recommendations that would assist the responsible national authorities to improve in future elections; as well as provide development partners with potential areas of support and assistance.

Managing the electoral process is, however, a difficult task which only those who are directly involved can really understand. In order to mitigate the risk of direct interference by foreign bodies and election observers, therefore, acceptable standards have been adumbrated and adopted by recognised bodies, such the UN Global Commission on Election Integrity.

## Conclusion

The future of democracy and good governance in Nigeria, and indeed anywhere, depends largely on the credibility and integrity of elections. The greatest threat to election integrity the world over is corruption, manifested in different forms of malpractice. Dealing with such malpractice remains a challenge because often opposition parties who accused incumbents of certain malpractice or irregularities turn out to do the same when they are in power, thus suggesting that they only dislike corruption when it benefits their opponents. I have attempted to identify some specific risks that could threaten the 2019 elections in Nigeria and subsequent elections to serve as lessons and open a vista of opportunities to keep on improving the electoral system. That requires a strategic synergy among the beneficiaries of elections, those in the legislative and executive arms of government. Nonetheless, when it comes to entrenching democracy and good governance, the judiciary also has a crucial role to play because as the saying goes 'when politics enters the palace of justice, justice leaves through the back door'. It has become acceptable norm that 'justice is the bond of men in states, for the administration of justice, which is the determination of what is just, is the principle of order in political society'.[143]

The electorate may accept overtures, including offer of money by politicians, but ultimately the onus is on them to make their choices according to informed and objective criteria, not on influence and sentiment.

Let me conclude with some words of wisdom and recommendation on the way forward from my mentor, Dr Buakar Usman:

> Only very few countries in the African continent have gotten their electoral systems right. Therefore, to stabilize democracy as a primary condition for security and national development in a society of great diversity such as the case in most African countries, decision makers in positions of leadership at all levels should always strive for a workable formula, known by whatever name, that ensures an inclusive system of governance. It is imperative that such arrangements which require great individual and group sacrifice remain firmly planted in their minds whether or not it is constitutionally provided. The overall aim should be to foster strong institutions to check the excesses of everyone under the law.[144]

---

143. Christian Breede, 'The Challenge of Nation-Building: Insights from Aristotle', The Royal Military College of Canada, 2012, p. 5.

144. Bukar Usman, 'Leadership, Security and National Development'. Lecture Delivered at the Faculty of Arts, Ahmadu Bello University, Zaria, on 20 January 2015.

CHAPTER 6

# Democracy and the
# Future of Nigeria

It is now obvious that the future of Nigeria depends on democracy that produces dividends in the form of good governance: rule of law, access to justice, equity, freedom, security, welfare and accountability. While the theoretical issue of whether democracy should be fully established before a society can have good governance or vice versa remains unresolved, the analysis of the issues and options discussed in this book suggest that Nigeria, and indeed any country for that matter, must strengthen its democratic institutions before it can experience good governance. Because *democracy is an ideal*, its meaning consists in the content of the normative arguments that can be adduced to defend it.

I believe the key to ending poverty in Africa is to improve the quality of human resources through *democracy* and *good governance*. In my opinion, without the motivation and hard work of people, the process of development will not be smooth and rapid. One needs only to look at the lessons learned from developed, rich countries and those newly emerging rich countries. They are conscious that their development can only be sustained through the high quality of their people, i.e. good human capital. My argument will be that Africa cannot develop without democracy, and that democracy in Africa ultimately cannot be sustained without development.[145] Here lies the challenge for Nigeria.

This chapter therefore examines what are Nigeria's challenges in nation building, and, drawing inspiration from other jurisdictions, I will suggest how the pattern of politics and leadership might be turned towards nation building and greatness. Let me begin by explaining what nation building is all about.

## What is Nation Building?

I have argued elsewhere[146] that nation building is the ultimate objective of any nation. Yet, our understanding of the process remains skewed, if not blurred by sectional, tribal, ethnic and religious bigotry and loyalty. While we may agree that we want to develop our nation, we still lack a proper understanding of whether we want to build nations in our various tribes, since those tribes in practice are referred to as nations or nationalities. For example, the agitation for relevance, if not dominance, of the Oodu'a Peoples' Congress, the resource control clamour by the Niger Delta or Ijaw nation, the Arewa Consultative Forum; the MOSSOB and Middle Belt Forum, etc. all aim to promote sectional interests. Would they be considered to be aspiring to nation building? In my opinion, yes, they are building their own nations, but they are not building a nation-state. We have to make the distinction clear from the outset so that we can appreciate what sort of actions are required to build a nation-state and not a nation, because the state is the medium

145. For details, see Shehu, *Nigeria: The Way Through Corruption to the Well-being of a People*, p. 7.

146. A.Y. Shehu, 'The Fight against Corruption in Nigeria: Old Wine in a New Bottle', Keynote presentation at a two-day policy roundtable on the Future of the Anti-Corruption Campaign in Abuja, 28 February–1 March 2018, p. 4.

through which political power is exercised in furtherance of social order. We can say that Angas, Bogghom, Hausa, Yoruba, Igbo and Tiv are all nations, but Nigeria is the only nation-state in which they exist. So to understand nation building, we must first understand the people and the state institutions.

Nation building is about developing a common sense of purpose – a shared view of the society that belongs to 'us' as stated in the relevant sections of the Constitution. It is the process by which citizens collectively harness their resources, both human and material, to improve their standard of living. Nation building incorporates both the state and nations, both of which evolve out of a historical process. In short, it is a dynamic process. This can be by way of developing institutions, systems and infrastructure. Scholars of comparative politics like Francis Fukuyama argued that nation building encompasses two types of activities, reconstruction and development.

Technological advancement, in tandem with globalisation, have spawned significant changes, thus making any meaningful process of nation building dependent on the skills, industriousness, productivity and competitiveness of citizens. In other words, human capital constitutes the embodiment of nation building. Nations attain greatness not by the size of the wealth of their leaders, but by the productivity and competitiveness of their population in the comity of nations.

## Nigeria and the Challenges of Nation Building

Since 1960, when Nigeria became an independent state, it has been engulfed in many crises of development. In Gambari's words, the challenges of nation building in Nigeria include: (1) the challenge from our history; (2) the challenge of socio-economic inequalities; (3) the challenges of an appropriate constitutional settlement; (4) the challenges of building institutions for democracy and development;

and (5) the challenge of leadership. He concluded that 'in our quest for nation-building, we have recorded some successes, such as keeping the country together in the face of many challenges. But these challenges continue to keep us from achieving our full potential'.[147] My intention here is to contextualise these and other challenges to democracy and good governance as a way to finding a remedy for the obstacles to Nigeria's development.

## The Challenge of Colonialism

The challenge of our colonial experience is what Gambari referred to as 'the challenge from our history'. While it may be true that Nigeria suffered some setbacks as a result of its colonial experience, it is about time that we stop blaming our failures on colonialism. Nigeria was under colonial rule effectively from 1914 to 1960. And from 1960 to now, the period that Nigeria has been under 'self-rule', is far longer and the opportunities are many compared to the opportunities during the colonial era. Besides, Nigeria is not the only country in the world that experienced colonialism. Even the USA, which is the great world power today, was colonised at one time. We can draw references from other British colonies, including India, that were colonised, but today, despite its challenges of population and poverty, India's level of development is not comparable to Nigeria, which is more endowed with natural resources than India.

We can draw examples from jurisdictions that faced similar challenges with Nigeria, namely Malaysia, Singapore, China and Dubai (United Arab Emirates). All these shared similar historical circumstances.[148] They were considered Third World countries, but today they have joined the First World; only Nigeria remains

147. Ibrahim Gambari,'The Challenges of Nation-Building', First Anniversary lecture of the Mustapha Akanbi Foundation, Abuja, 7 February 2018.

148. Sam Nda-Isaiah, 'Moving Nigeria forward: lessons from Malaysia, Singapore, China and Dubai', First City People Monthly Lecture, Lagos, 17 August 2014, p. 4.

a 'Third World' nation. Out of those countries, only the UAE is homogeneous; the others are even more complex than Nigeria in terms of religion and race, yet they were able to achieve a considerable level of development. So, to be very frank, blaming our past failures on our colonial heritage is misplaced. We should look for solutions to our national development from within ourselves. No nation has experienced development from outside; it is driven from within.

## The Crisis of Legitimacy

Since independence, one of the persistent crises in Nigeria has been that of legitimacy. Under the military, every regime contended not only with the threat of a coup but also with the threat of ethnic agitation, religious upheavals, regional instability, including problems of succession or declaration of war, corruption, and lack of accountability to the people. Democracy, which is seen as a way of legitimising an elected government, has unfortunately carried these crises over in different dimensions, including the high cost of governance, the difficulty of revenue generation, allocation and appropriations, insurgencies and many forms of criminality.

All these crises led to what Gambari described as the challenge of socio-economic inequalities, which pose two immediate problems: one, different Nigerians live different lives in different parts of the country, and yet they are supposed to have a common sense of citizenship; two, even in those parts of the country that may be considered better off in means of livelihood, the quality is far below acceptable world standard.

There is now evidence that the way democracy is practised in Nigeria can address those challenges and the crises of legitimacy without changing the narratives by those who practise democracy. I shall attempt to make some recommendations in this regard in the subsequent section in this chapter.

## The Crisis of Transition and Constitutional Development

Closely related to the above is the crisis of constitutional development, which has been the bane of Nigeria. From the 'mutual suspicion' between the different ethnic groups and regions of Nigeria that characterised the struggle for independence, to the clear expression of disagreement on how the country should be governed in the various constitutional conferences, up to the last one in 2014, Nigeria has remained divided on almost all issues that should bind the people together as a strong, united, indivisible and indissoluble nation as contemplated by the Constitution.

Before and after independence, our political leaders have been struggling to find the right bearing for nation building through the processes of constitution making and the development of political systems. In the end, they settled for federalism as the building block for our nation-state. Unfortunately, up to this moment we do not have a consensus on the definition of this federalism, and even when we pretend to have one, its application has been characterised by oscillation, pretence or inertia.

Federalism, which remains the main thrust of Nigeria, has had its own challenges of endurance. As Gambari rightly observed:

> related to the problem of federalism is the question of fiscal federalism. What is the appropriate and just basis for sharing revenue? Should the federal government have the right to deduct monies due to states without their permission? Should state governments continue to control local government allocations? These are all fundamental principles on which we have no clear consensus… the worst enemies of Nigerian federalism are those who speak of federalism, but act in a unitary fashion by brushing aside all the divisions of powers between different levels of our federation.[149]

149. Gambari, 'The Challenges of Nation-Building'.

The problem of Nigeria is not with the Constitution but with those who implement it, the elected representatives of the people who are supposed to adhere to its provisions and enforce them to the letter. The question that has been gasping for an answer is, can democracy as practised in Nigeria provide the solution to its constitutional challenges? Although Nigeria's problems are unique to Nigeria, there are some lessons to learn from other jurisdictions with regard to managing Nigeria's constitutional crises within the framework of democracy. Other societies have established systems and strong institutions that can absorb the socio-economic shocks that undermine stability and development in Nigeria.

## The Challenge of Building Democratic Institutions

During his Africa tour in 2008, then US President Barack Obama emphasised the need for Africa in its quest for democracy and development to build strong institutions, not strong individuals. It is true that democracy and development can only be sustained through strong institutions, but it is also the case that strong institutions can only be built by strong individuals. Therefore, the emphasis should not only be on the institutions but also on how the institutions are built and by whom.[150] There are many components of building institutions, including setting the rules on how the institutions should be built and run; the processes for hiring the technical expertise, as well as integrity and moral competence, to make sure the institutions work as independent and non-partisan as desired; and ensuring that the institutions deliver on their mandates in a transparent, accountable, professional and consistent manner. The reflections on the experiences of our jurisdictions on how they managed some of these challenges are discussed below.

150. In the context of democracy and development, the institutions required include those for fighting corruption, promoting integrity, ethnics and good governance, such as law enforcement, oversight and accountability institutions; those responsible for public service delivery in the form of the rewards of democracy, including the civil service, economic governance and utilities institutions; and judicial institutions, such as courts for the adjudication of justice and enforcement of rights and privileges.

## Democracy and the Crisis of Leadership

Democracy seeks to create the avenues for selecting credible leadership that would steer the affairs of society based on the principles of participation, fairness, justice, equity, transparency, accountability and freedom of choice. Unfortunately, the crisis of leadership seems to be what most affects the stability and progress of the country. While leadership is not everything and cannot on its own allow society to develop, it is important if that society seeks an orderly and sustainable process of development. Leadership should be conceptualised at both individual and collective levels, involving the leaders and the led. In Nigeria, the problem has to do with the shifting of blame. In other words, all the mistakes are blamed on the leaders, while the led pretend to be blameless. This may be understandable when leaders are blamed because they have the mandate of the governed to design policies and programmes that would improve the living standards of the people, regardless of the challenges they face. After all, the test of leadership is in the way such challenges are met and the right policies set in place that can produce the desired outcomes.

Nigeria is blessed with such material and human resources that many thinkit should not have the problems of leadership it is having. Economically, Nigeria is potentially a rich country by all comparative indices, with significant crude oil production and export amounting to about 2.34 million barrels per dayand natural gas exports of about 25.96 million cubic metres in 2015. Following a 'rebasing' of the economy in April 2014, Nigeria has emerged as Africa's largest economy, with an estimated GDP of US$540 billion and an estimated growth rate of 6.7%.[151] The Nigerian economy is heavily dependent on petroleum, which constitutes about 97% of its exports earnings and about 80% of total federal (collectable)

151. For details, see Shehu,*Nigeria: The Way Through Corruption to the Well-being of a People.*

revenue. Oil dependency and the allure it generates of great wealth through government contracts have spawned distortions in the economy of Nigeria.

The exploitation of oil resources and the (mis)management of oil windfalls have dominated the progress and decline of Nigeria's economy over the years, and have significantly influenced the growth of poverty. Despite these potentials, however, Nigeria presents a paradox of 'poverty in prosperity'. According to the Central Intelligence Agency World Facts Book (July 2014) the incidence of poverty and unemployment are simultaneously very high, with poverty estimated at 71% in 2011 and unemployment at 23.9%. The Director General of the National Bureau of Statistics revealed in his press conference statement in 2011 that about 112 million Nigerians were living in poverty, while a few privileged elite live in affluence. Infant mortality is estimated at 630 per 100,000 live births with a death rate of 13.16%, yet the population is estimated to grow exponentially at a birth rate of 38.03% without commensurate growth in infrastructure and employment opportunities to absorb the shocks.[152]

Professionals such as lawyers, teachers and the military have been involved in the leadership of Nigeria, yet it remains as if competence is still lacking. While some countries had exemplary leaders who served as rallying points for their own nation building, Nigeria never had such leaders like Kwame Nkrumah of Ghana, Nelson Mandela of South Africa, Lee Kuan Yew of Singapore, Deng Xiaoping or Mao TseTung of China, Mohammed Bin Rashid Al Maktoum of UAE and Mahathir Muhammad of Malaysia.[153] Leadership is crucial for nation building; it is the personal qualities of integrity, honesty, commitment and competence and the collective

152. Ibid, p. 8.
153. That is not to say that I do not recognise the exemplary vision and leadership of our own Tafawa Balewa, Nnamdi Azikiwe, Ahmadu Bello and Akintola, just to mention a few, who struggled for our independence and laid a good foundation for our nationhood until it was aborted by the military in 1966.

attributes of vision and capacity that will bring the rewards and wellbeing to Nigeria that the facts and figures demand.

To further examine the leadership failure in Nigeria, reference is often made to other jurisdictions which should provide models for Nigeria to change the course of its leadership and development.

## Democracy and Crisis of Expectations

One of the challenges of nation building is the crisis of expectations, where the citizens expect more than the government can deliver. This is a true reflection of the situation in Nigeria, especially under the democratic system. Democracy is defined as 'government of the people, by the people and for the people', because the expectation is that the people will be active in deciding who should rule, when and how. Because of the crisis of political development, including the role of the political parties in developing countries, expectations remain unfulfilled and citizens feel frustrated, their patriotism eroded, especially where merit is replaced by mediocrity and nepotism. Ultimately citizens do not feel that they have a stake and therefore are not obliged to participate in nation building.

## The Way Forward for Nigeria

There is, however, a way forward in which democracy can be sustained and the challenges of nation building addressed. I have some recommendations to offer on this, and since the purpose of this book to create awareness of the issues for the electorate, I intend to be as brief and straight to the point as possible. My recommendations can serve as an action plan for reforming the critical areas towards meaningful nation building. In the problem areas that I have identified, the 1999 Constitution has provided the necessary legal framework for reform. In other words, the bedrock of nation building is the participation of the citizenry, and the need for them to have faith in the constitution of their country.

## Fighting Corruption

I have talked about corruption several times in this book because in my view it is the greatest threat to Nigeria's democracy and development. Every administration since 1960s, military or civilian, realised the negative impact of corruption and promised to fight it. Unfortunately, virtually all the administrations were themselves accused of corruption, including the First Republic, which should have been a starting point on a clean slate. The allegations of corruption have become worse since the inception of the civilian administration in 1999. It should of course be noted that not every rich person is corrupt and not every person belonging to the elite.

Corruption manifests in different forms and types; and while some people think that bribery of public officials or embezzlement of public funds impact more on the society, others may argue that nepotism is even worse because it undermines or shortcuts merit, which should be the main criterion for leadership selection for nation building. Every person is entitled to their perspective, but the most important issue is that corruption has undermined the fabric of Nigerian society and it must be dealt with seriously for any meaningful development to happen.

The Constitution defined the relationship between the citizens and the government as a contract. In section 14 it is stated that 'the Federal Republic of Nigeria shall be a State based on the principles of democracy and social justice'; and that

(a) 'sovereignty belongs to the people of Nigeria from whom government through this Constitution derives all its powers and authority;

(b) the security and welfare of the people shall be the primary purpose of government; and

(c) the participation by the people in their government shall be ensured in accordance with the provisions of this Constitution'.

The Constitution is the bond between the state and the citizens. Accordingly, Chapter II concerned the Fundamental Objectives and Directive Principles of State and outlined the obligations of the government in section 13 to take full responsibility and exercise power and apply the provisions of the Constitution. With regard to corruption, section 15(5) provides that 'The State shall abolish all corrupt practices and abuse of power'.

While acknowledging and commending the efforts that have been invested in fighting corruption, it appears that all imaginable solutions have been deferred and only a democratic revolution can effectively tackle it. The fundamental steps that can be taken honestly, sincerely, comprehensively, courageously and inclusively to tackle corruption for any government includes the following major actions:

● Make the asset declarations of all public office holders open and accessible to the public as part of accountability. This would enable the public to monitor their elected representatives and anyone who does not want his assets to be known; then such a person should not make him/herself a public official. When infractions are investigated and confirmed, defaulters should be severely punished. This method has worked effectively in all societies that have fought corruption, such as Singapore, Hong Kong and China.

● The existing anti-corruption legislation is sufficient to address the problem. What is lacking is political will, which has been constrained by vested interests and impunity. New legislation may be needed in a few cases, while existing laws can be amended to improve identified deficiencies. Impunity and vested interests must be removed at all levels of society.

- Strengthening the anti-corruption agencies, including the provision of technical equipment and infrastructure, should be a priority. But the most important change required is in the method of selecting the heads of those agencies. The quality of leadership is extremely important, especially in the technical areas of investigation and prosecution of corruption. Again, the method of selection must be based on 'observable and measurable' merit before any other consideration. The definition of merit should be comprehensive enough to include academic and professional knowledge, aptitude and attitude, capacity to deliver results in the circumstances and most importantly, managerial ability. A situation where the essential criteria for recruitment of corruption fighters are where you come from, whom you know, your political sympathy or potential for compromise, would only produce business as usual, with more noise about achievements but without real achievements in concrete and measurable terms.

- The fight against corruption should seek to make the maximum impact. We may begin with a census of the houses in the streets of Asokoro and Maitama and determine who owns them, how the pieces of land were allocated or when the structures were built. What was their value at the time of construction? What are their values at the time of assessment? And so on. All these would reveal a tangled nest of corrupt practices. Only a courageous government committed to truly routing corruption would say that the owners of such properties, if they were public officials, should account for how they acquired them, and failure to do so should result in their confiscation in a court of law. Another idea, which may sound impossible but is very practical and impactful, is for the citizenry to rise up and say that anybody who has no house in Abuja should go and occupy any of the estates that have stayed for more than five years without occupants; anyone who claims ownership should go to court and prove the source of the wealth with which the estates were built, their beneficial owners, etc. What is being advocated here is that since many people are homeless, yet some people gained illegal wealth and laundered it through real estate, the law of the land should assist them to earn a living that is as fair as contemplated in the Constitution. After all, in the UK, such action may be allowed under UK law. Why should it not be so in Nigeria, where we copy what obtains in other countries?

- As an immediate step, a list of all pending cases involving politically exposed persons (PEPs) should be compiled and a task force set up under the law, if possible with modified extra powers to conclude their investigation and prosecution within three years. The government should not interfere to protect any of its party members or members of the opposition. The Administration of Criminal Justice Act (ACJA) of 2015 has provision for fast-tracking cases and remains a very powerful anti-corruption tool in Nigeria. The problem, however, has to do with the lack of capacity for investigating and prosecuting agencies to meet the standards required in the Act.[154]

- Another powerful tool for prosecution is the case of *Gabriel Daudu vs FRN (2018) 10 NWLR (Pt.1626) 169, 183 E-F (2018) LPELR – 43637 (SC)* in which the Supreme Court made a significant pronouncement on burden of proof in corruption cases. The apex court held: 'The burden lies on an accused person to explain properties he acquired which are disproportionate to his KNOWN legitimate earnings.' The implication of this

---

154. Including trial on a day-by-day basis if witnesses can be brought to court and all other delays removed by strict adherence to the Act without compromising the rights of defendants. For example, if government would like to measure the level of success in the prosecution of cases that can be determined by analysing the reasons for adjournments, which often is blamed on members of the Bar or the Court.

judgment is that once it is shown that you have much more than you should have had, then it is your responsibility to explain the source of such wealth. This is a major contribution by the judiciary, particularly the Apex Court, to the war against corruption.'[155]

- This leads to the very important matter of prioritisation. It is no use for many cases to be half-heartedly investigated if when such cases are taken to court, they are lost even at the preliminary stages of prosecution. Fighting corruption cannot be a one-day or one-year affair, and neither can it be completely eradicated; but when critical cases are given priority, the potential impact from the outcome would be higher. Therefore, efforts must be put on taking the highest risks, in terms of the volume of losses and the class of offenders, to make the maximum impact by investigating and prosecuting such cases well enough to send a credible deterrence, even if they are fewer in number.

- No two societies can be the same. Nevertheless, we have seen elsewhere that transparent, purposeful and committed leadership can perform the wonders, such as Lee Kuan Yew in Singapore, who used the structures he inherited to achieve landmark results in fighting corruption. Lee Kuan Yew's experience has proved that 'ordinary calculations can be overturned by extra-ordinary personalities'. Lee used the Corrupt Services Investigation Bureau (CSIB) he inherited from a past administration and launched a new approach to the fight against corruption by empowering the CSIB to investigate corruption cases without relying on the 'untrustworthy' police. Over time the CSIB became one of the most efficient and effective anti-corruption agencies in the world. Where what Lee inherited proved inadequate, he created new structures to overcome challenges.

155. Wahab Shittu, 'EFCC Convictions and the Role of the Judiciary', The Nigeria Lawyer, *Thisday*, 24December 2018, p. 1.

For example, he introduced the Prevention of Corruption Act (POCA) which criminalised all forms of corruption, particularly bribery, and extended such offences to the private sector. To make his anti-corruption war effective, he started from the top with high-profile targets, including some of his Ministers' allies who were accused to show that no one is above the law and it would not be a selective war.

Perhaps the most effective change Yew made in 1960 was to 'allow the courts to treat proof that an accused was living beyond his or her means or had property his or her income could not explain as corroborating evidence that the accused had accepted or obtained a bribe'.[156] But most importantly, Yew was himself incorruptible and he demonstrated open examples in that regard. That is possible in Nigeria only if political interests are set aside.

My intention is not to provide a comprehensive strategy for combating corruption here but to highlight a few practical steps that can be taken by any well-intentioned government to make the maximum or desired impact in reducing corruption.

Nigeria is not the only country in the world that has experienced corruption. Let me explore a few examples where some of the principles suggested above might have worked in other places, even though those places may not be comparable to Nigeria in terms of size, political, economic and socio-cultural complexities.

### Reforming the Electoral System[157]

There is no doubt that corruption has a deleterious effect on the electoral system. And since election is the most important element of democracy, every country that seeks to entrench democracy,

156. Lee Kuan Yew, *From Third world to First World: The Singapore story: 1965-2000,* Harper Collins, 2000, p. 159.

157. For clarity, I will discuss reforms of the electoral system separately from reforms of demo-cratic institutions, including the electoral body for obvious reasons.

good governance and development must seek to improve its electoral system. It is because of the flows and weaknesses in the electoral system in Nigeria that all presidential elections, except that in 2015, have been contested in court. The 2007 election, which was described by many people as the worst in terms of credibility, produced Umaru Musa Yar'adua as President, who accepted the criticisms and courageously took steps to improve the system by setting up the Electoral Reform Committee under the Chairmanship of former Chief Justice of Nigeria, His Lordship Mohammed Lawal Uwais. The report of this Committee, together with that of the Ahmed Lemu Panel on Electoral Violence under President Jonathan, made far-reaching recommendations that if implemented to the letter would have significantly addressed most of the flaws in the electoral system.

It should be recalled that President Goodluck Jonathan signed the Electoral Amendment Act 2015, which introduced the use of the card reader machine which was acclaimed as the greatest improvement in the electoral system; President Buhari declined assent to this Act four times in a row in 2018.[158]

Many African countries have not changed their electoral systems for the better, but in a few cases where meaningful improvements were made as in Nigeria, Ghana, Sierra Leone and a few other countries, the outcomes of elections have been better, though there is still room for improvement. For the sustenance of democracy, therefore, taking meaningful, fair, transparent and non-partisan steps to improve the electoral system in Nigeria, taking advantage especially of new technology would greatly change the narrative of flawed or dented elections, would not only legitimise the government but also reinforce the confidence of the people in democracy.

158. Reasons for refusal have already been discussed in Chapter 2.

## Reforming Democratic Institutions

Democracy cannot endure without strong institutions to support its tenets. It is in recognition of this that the Constitution of Nigeria (1999) in Part II section 4(1-9) confers the legislative powers of the Federation on the NASS; section 5(1-5) confers the executive powers in the President and subjects such powers to any laws made by the NASS; while section 6(1-6) provides that the judicial powers are vested in the judicial courts which are established by the Constitution and for the Federation. The separation of powers of these arms of government is implicit. There is great wisdom in these constitutional arrangements. Over time, however, there has been friction between the arms of government, not because the Constitution is ambiguous but simply because of the greed, impunity and vested interests of the elite – the miserable basket of obstacles that Nigeria carries.

Removing corruption is by far the most important step in reforming democratic institutions so that they can perform their functions according to the Constitution. The NASS has come under attacks due to certain practices that are believed to be corrupt or promote corruption. Many commentators have accused the NASS of making the cost of governance very high through most of their 'opaque and illegal allowances', including the so-called constituency projects, most of which leave no trace after their budgets have been reported as executed. In a letter addressed to Members of the NASS through the Senate President and Speaker of the House of Representatives on 23 January 2016, former President Obasanjo, in his usual manner of speaking against corruption 'no matter whose ox is gored', challenged that 'the National Assembly should have the courage to publish its revenue budgets for the years 2000, 2005, 2010 and 2015. That is what transparency demands. With the number of legislators not changing, comparison can be made. Comparisons in emoluments can also be made with countries like Ghana, Kenya, Senegal and even Malaysia and Indonesia who are richer and more developed than we are.'

The Executive and Judiciary are equally not immune to corruption, suggesting that while reforming all these arms of government remains a challenge, it must be a priority for any government that seeks to provide a unique legacy of leadership to the country. Whether the elite class can do that remains to be seen. This problem transcends the federal government to all the other tiers – state and local governments.

But one important institution that requires specific mentioning with respect to reform is the electoral body, which has responsibility for conducting elections. While significant improvements have been made and landmark successes have been recorded in the operations of the INEC, there are still considerable reforms that call for urgent attention, including the procedure for the appointment of the head of the electoral body and other key staff, its funding and the guidelines governing elections. Just as the issue of amendment to the Electoral Act was discussed in Chapter 1 when the matter was current at the end of 2018, one of the immediate concerns expressed during the meeting of the INEC with political parties in January 2019 was a proposed new guideline, which the INEC produced without the inputs from political parties. The bone of contention has to do with the method of accreditation, which the INEC changed from 'accreditation before voting to accreditation and voting simultaneously'. The motive for such change could be a groundswell of public opinion, but the process, which lacks transparency and inclusiveness, may be questioned. These are critical issues for politicians and other citizens if they are to find solutions as a way of safeguarding the future of democracy and the country at large.

The electoral body does not work in isolation, and therefore, to make the system more transparent, credible and acceptable, all public service institutions would also require some reforms. For example, the INEC cannot conduct peaceful elections without the support of the law enforcement and security agencies. While it is responsible for all elections, it has no absolute control over the police that are deployed for election support; if it has, such command is limited to a large extent. Without going into the details of all the issues that require reforms to make the electoral system more efficient, credible and accountable, suffice it to say that government ought to demonstrate sincerity in implementing meaningful reforms that were recommended in technical committees which were set up and which made far-reaching recommendations for reforms.

## Population Growth and Unemployment

The quality of human capital is an important asset for any nation and Nigeria is no exception. However, the trend of population growth without concomitant growth and expansion in opportunities to make the population truly productive constitutes a real threat to democracy and development. Nigeria's population is estimated at 200 million and rapidly growing, heading for 400 million in the next 30 years. About 1.8 million graduates are leaving the universities and other higher institutions of learning to join an unemployment market that is already saturated. Crime is becoming more sophisticated with technology and globalisation, yet the economy is not expanding to accommodate this. The result is the inequalities earlier discussed in this chapter, which if not addressed can lead to a failed state – that is, if Nigeria is not already in that category.

Well-meaning Nigerians and concerned institutions globally have expressed their fears if this trend is not curtailed. While this remains a challenge, the political elite are only concerned with grabbing and retaining power. Under the Fundamental Objectives and Directive principles of State Policy, Section 14 of the

Constitution says:

(1) *The Federal Republic of Nigeria shall be a State based on the principles of democracy and social justice.*

(2) *It is hereby, accordingly, declared that:*

(a) *sovereignty belongs to the people of Nigeria from whom government through this Constitution derives all its powers and authority;*

(b) *the security and welfare of the people shall be the primary purpose of government: and*

(c) *the participation by the people in their government shall be ensured in accordance with the provisions of this Constitution.*

If this is the basis of legitimacy of any government, such legitimacy would be questioned in relation to the wellbeing of the people under democracy today. Whatever effort the government has put into generating employment, the stark realities suggest that such efforts must be doubled to cope with the challenge. Singapore under Lee Kuan Yew emerged as a model because it chose to 'distribute wealth by asset enhancement, not by subsidies for consumption'. The distribution of 10,000 naira to traders in the market in Abuja and Lagos under the APC Social Investment Programme, specially called 'trader-moni', has been described as an unsustainable and 'at best idiotic' programme.

### Infrastructure

The developmental objective and the future of Nigeria depend largely on the state of its infrastructure. Again, no other sector deserves reforms more than this one. As a result of corruption, many projects have not been executed, yet some have been paid for several times and no one can account for such payments. Can we therefore hope that the fight against corruption will succeed without doing something in a different way with regard to failed projects? The major reasons why there are many abandoned, uncompleted or non-executed projects is because either the elite conspiracy grounded those projects through corruption or no one is held to account for failed projects; and there is no effective monitoring mechanism to track the stages and number of projects from the start of implementation to finish. Or all of these and other reasons.

It is impossible to overstate the risk and threat to the future of Nigeria of failed, poorly executed or non-executed infrastructure programmes. Like it or not, government has a responsibility to review and make sure all important projects that were paid for and abandoned are completed: no matter who was involved and no matter how high the cost, they must be brought to justice. That would be the beginning of a revolution that would sustain and propel Nigeria into the comity of developed nations. Anything short of this would mean doing the same thing and expecting different results. But that has to be carried along with current plans of infrastructure development.

## Education and Health

Nigeria's education and health systems have collapsed, and the decline does not seem to command the attention of policymakers as a serious threat to the future of the country. This decline is also reflected in the Human Capital Index (HCI). With an HCI of 34%, according to the World Bank, Nigeria was rated 152 out of 157 countries surveyed,[159] meaning that children born in Nigeria could only realise 34% of their potential. Nelson Mandela warned that the first signal of the destruction of a country is seen in its educational system. Today, Nigerians spend several millions in foreign currencies in search for quality education and good health care. Many talented Nigerians are leaving for greener pastures abroad,

159. Only better than Niger, Chad, South Sudan and two other smaller African countries.

and all these seem not to send a signal to the political leaders that the country's future is under threat. I shall again turn to the issue of leadership as the solution to all these challenges.

## Leadership as the Solution

Leadership, as stated earlier, is not everything, but it is an important, if not the most important, factor to address the various challenges of nation building as well to rigorously implement the tough recommendations above. Of the many types of leadership, that of legacy and production is by far the best kind of leadership required to progress Nigeria to greatness. Leadership of legacy and production simply means a leadership that is conscious of history and whose aim is not to retain power but make an impact through tough policy choices that would bring a meaningful and sustainable change in society. It is also a leadership that is conscious of empowering new generations that share the same vision, courage, determination and accountability to the people. All leaders in Nigeria have the same potential as those who have changed their societies, and they have travelled far to learn from other jurisdictions. Let me illustrate how leadership has been the solution for the problems of democracy and development with a view to drawing some lessons for Nigeria.

## Mandela and Nyerere

Mandela, who was the first Black President of South Africa from 1994 to 1998, led the liberation struggle in his country through the African National Congress (ANC) and in 1962 he was jailed for 27 years. He was released from jail in 1990 and the ANC fielded him as its candidate in the first democratic election in South Africa and he became President in 1994. He is a shining example of uniting a post-apartheid South Africa through his leadership ethos and conduct. First, after gaining his freedom, he never expressed bitterness against those who jailed him. He was seen as a bridge builder. When he assumed the presidency many Black hardliners wanted justice from 'the sins of apartheid while many White South Africans were apprehensive of their fate under Black majority rule'. Rather than taking sides with his Black brethren, Mandela opted for reconciliation among the fractured populations of his country, thus espousing the ethos of leadership, good governance and nation-building. He set up the 'Truth and Reconciliation Commission with emphasis on reconciliation in sharp contrast to the approach in the Nuremberg Trials and other de-Nazification measures'.[160] Mandela's legacy was his ability to save South Africa from all the crises one could imagine in its journey to nation-building from its birth as a sovereign democratic nation.

Another example is Mualimu Julius Nyerere, first President of Tanzania from 1962 to 1985, whose democratic ethos was espoused through his *Ujamaa* philosophy – the quest for a just social order based on community solidarity. His commitment to nation building was the driving force throughout his tenure and he was very conscious of this in all his endeavours, to the extent that he reminded the Parliament that social justice was what he promised and he bequeathed it to Tanzania. While some may argue that his nation-building strategies were not unique, his legacies propelled Tanzania, despite its poor economic and social indicators, into becoming a democratically stable country. Comparatively, he introduced Swahili as a national language, although similarly, Emperor Haile Selassie introduces Amharic as the national language in Ethiopia and Sa'id Barre standardised the Somali script in Somalia and made it the sole national language. While the Swahili language helped to further Nyerere's nation-building in Tanzania, the same introduction of a national language in Ethiopia and Somalia failed to prevent the fragmentation of both countries. The crucial difference between

160. Jideofor Adibe, 'Nation-Building: The Mandela and Nyerere examples', 2016.

the nation-building efforts in Ethiopia and Somalia and the one in Tanzania was simply Nyerere's leadership.

In fact, despite the continuing challenges of underdevelopment, Tanzania has largely avoided the tumultuous ethnic politics of most African states. The country's sense of national identity is legendary and a matter of pride in Africa. For instance, a 2011 Afrobarometer survey by the London School of Economics, in which some Africans were asked if they identified more with their national or ethnic identity, showed that 88% of Tanzanian respondents said they prioritised their national identity over their ethnic identity. This contrasted with the continental average of 42% who prioritised their national identity over their ethnic identity. The figure for Nigeria was a paltry 17%.[161]

The lessons in these two examples are that first, a leader has to make a conscious decision as to whether he wants to serve the narrow interests of his ethnic group, region or section, or bridge these fault lines to serve and preserve the national interests, and so leave a legacy that would enhance nation building; this is not an easy choice for any leader, especially in Africa. Second, a leader has to be conscious that in a society of many ethnicities, religions and cultures, 'his intentions count for little and often perception is everything'. So the leader has to navigate with his eyes open as every policy option involves some politics and such politics has to be managed carefully. Third, nation building is not necessarily doing the wrong and right things even if they are in the overall interest of the people, but it is about being sensitive to actions or inactions and how they could be perceived and interpreted across the various fault lines. Finally, it is not what the leader says he is or his intentions are that count, but his actions and how he manages the sensitivities of the fault lines through policies that promote oneness of a nation.

In another view, Gambari observed succinctly that 'Botswana and Somalia are similar in terms of their fundamental characteristics':

161    Ibid., p. 3.

Both have: (1) one large dominant ethnic group divided into clans; (2) both are sparsely populated in semi-arid conditions; (3) at independence, both depended on livestock for the livelihood of a majority of the population. While the Botswana leadership was collectively focused and had a vision of what it wanted to do with the country, the leadership in Somalia was divided against itself. As a result, Botswana learned to harness its limited resources for generally agreed objectives. It learned to survive under the shadow of apartheid South Africa. And it learned to manage its diamond resources well when those resources started flowing in. Somalia, on the other hand had a divided leadership, some of whom wanted to build Greater Somalia by military means, while others simply wanted to get on with running the country they inherited from colonialism. As a result, the Somali leadership lacked focus and vision, and often fought itself through conspiracies and military coups. Somalia also went to war with its neighbours. For anybody looking at these two countries today, the difference is clear. That is the dividend of good leadership. The comparative histories of Botswana and Somalia suggest that we should be concerned not just with the quality of leadership of our Presidents, Governors, Senators and Judges; we should also be concerned by the quality of leadership which we all bring to our professional and personal responsibilities.[162]

In Singapore, though a much smaller society than Nigeria in size and population but no less complex and variegated with different ethnic groups, Lee Kuan Yew has proved that every achievement was a dream before it became a reality. His vision for Singapore was a state that would excel with superior intelligence, discipline and ingenuity, and that would maximise resources. With this vision, he was able to increase the annual per capita income of his country from $1,000 at independence to over $30,000 by the year 2000. The per capita GDP rose from $400 in 1959 when Lee took over

162       Gambari, 'The Challenges of Nation-Building', p. 11.

as Prime Minister to more than $12,200 in 1990 when he stepped down. Today, Singapore is one of the 'cleanest' countries and a world financial centre, because Lee Kuan Yew laid the 'foundation on rule of law, independent judiciary, and a stable, competent and honest government that pursued sound macroeconomic policies, with budget surpluses every year.'[163]

Nigeria needs to develop a national vision consisting of leaders ascending to higher values with a clear communication strategy to inspire confidence and acceptability of leadership by the citizens. The Constitution has already provided the framework.

We need to develop an elite consensus on how Nigeria should be moved forward. This consensus can only emerge if the elite put the national interest over personal, sectional, regional interests and sacrifice personal power and wealth for the common good of all.

## In conclusion

There are more positive sides to Nigeria's history than its misfortunes. Nigeria has great potential, not only in its natural resource endowment but also in becoming a regional leader. Nigeria cannot afford to fail in this regard. Consolidating democracy is critical to the building and development of Nigeria. There are many challenges, but it appears that most of these are man-made and can be overcome through a charismatic, dedicated and purposeful leadership. After almost sixty years of political independence, the experience of colonial rule, which was less than sixty years, is still being blamed for the failures of Nigeria. Although developed countries make a mistake of interpreting the problems of other countries from their own point of view, the peculiarities of every society must be properly understood before its development course can be charted meaningfully.

The challenges of nation building discussed in this chapter are

163. See Lee Kuan Yew, *From Third World to First World*, p. 73.

surmountable and the hope is that the democratic process can do that. Societies change either by peaceful or violent means. Nigeria has chosen the pathway of peaceful change and that process must be managed very well through free, fair, and credible elections.

# CONCLUSION

In concluding, I would recall that the 2019 presidential election in Nigeria is the motive for writing this book. While the 2015 election was a landmark development in Nigeria's political history and in its quest for a sustainable democracy; the 2019 election promises to be a test of the consolidation of that breakthrough. Unlike in 2015, when the chapter of failures of the PDP was the only one opened for assessment, today Nigerians have two chapters to assess and compare the performances of the PDP and the APC. Not only do they have a choice in the two chapters, but the sentiments that drove the 2015 election were different from those that may shape the 2019 election. For example, while many voters in the North preferred PMB because of the zoning of the presidency to the North, others were persuaded by religious, regional and ethic sentiments. Former President Jonathan's main mistake was his insistence to hold on to power, contrary to party agreement and when the mood of the nation was to rotate power to the North. Furthermore, his handling of the insurgency situation in the north-eastern parts of Nigeria and the pervasive corruption were also his undoing.

The political ground looks slightly different in terms of personal factors: both candidates of the APC and PDP are Muslims, Fulani and from the North, but they share common perception of the objective factors, including the lingering issues of insecurity, poverty, unemployment and corruption. This book has therefore attempted to highlight the likely campaign issues with a view to raising awareness among voters on their choices for the suitable candidate to be President of Nigeria.

I have underscored the importance of election in democracy. The emphasis has been not only election per se, but election with integrity as the bedrock for sustaining democracy and good governance. One of the major concerns regarding the fairness and credibility of the election is the fear or allegations of rigging, in which all parties are pointing accusing fingers at each other. Then who is doing the rigging and how? Elections can be rigged by various means. In most cases in Africa, the rigger must have the resources, including the strategy, money and logistics to mobilise the electoral officials and security agents to agreeing to compromise. However, even with all the resources at their disposal, sometimes it is difficult to rig elections when there is overwhelming support for a particular candidate. Rigging can only be possible when there is a passive electorate who show no interest in how their votes are counted. This reinforces the message that the electorate must protect their votes by being vigilant throughout the election period.

In reality, it is the incumbent government that has the wherewithal, including control over security and electoral officials to rig an election. Despite promises of non-interference, free, fair and credible elections during previous elections, at least some malpractice were observed. No election is entirely free and fair; but depending on the margin of observable malpractice or deficiency, an election can be described as relatively fair and credible, as was the 2015 presidential election in Nigeria. In recent times, PMB has been preoccupied with giving assurances that if there is any legacy he would like to leave, it is ensuring that he does not interfere in the election, thus making it free, fair and credible. As elections are not usually rigged by presidents themselves but by their cronies, Nigerians wait to see how truthful this assurance will be as the election approaches.

While the major opposition party is known for its manipulation in past elections, some of the steps taken by the APC Government were ethically inept, such as the appointment of a Chief Electoral Officer from the same region as the President. Among the concerns of many political parties over the credibility of the election are the following: the President's refusal to assent to the amended Electoral Act; the alleged use of the police in recent elections in Ekiti and Osun States, as well as the police crackdown on some vocal opposition members; the appointment of one of the National Electoral Commissioners, who is alleged to be related to the President (by marriage) to the sensitive role of coordinating the collation centre for the presidential election; and the issuance of the election Guidelines by the INEC without the inputs of the political parties.

No matter how interested a president is in influencing elections, the electoral body has full responsibility for the credibility of elections. The INEC had set a standard for credible elections in 2015 and the next elections provide a litmus test for the independence, capacity and credibility of the INEC to conduct similar elections. While many would have loved to have an amended electoral law that would improve the standards, it is the same law that was used for the 2015 elections that will prevail in 2019.

There are potential risks and threats that could affect the outcome of the election, but while the security risk is less obvious than that in 2015, the risk of violence can be mitigated through a transparent and fair process. The other potential risks identified in

Chapter 4 are all part of the challenges of nation building and they too can be surmounted as people embrace the ethos and principles of democracy.

With regard to the outcome of the election, several predictions have been made, but the analysis remains largely theoretical. Each of the major contenders has his own unique strengths and weaknesses. And as observed in Chapter 4, election outcomes are not necessarily determined by objective factors but by the sentiments of voters, and this is most likely to be the case in this election. While the competition is stiff, only one candidate will emerge victorious. However it turns out, Nigerians will be left with the choice they make in the leadership of the country.

Overall, however, the election will further consolidate the practice of democracy in Nigeria, but it will take some time for elections to have an impact on good governance. The same campaign issues, including security, corruption, poverty and unemployment, economy and restructuring will remain for at least the next twenty years because they are the issues that affect the fabric of this society.

With regard to the way forward, I have made some recommendations, including ways to improve the electoral system, fighting corruption more effectively, strengthening democratic institutions and reforming the public service. The dividends of democracy should be seen in the improved standards of living of the citizens, and that would require greater attention to education, health, agriculture and infrastructural development. Perhaps the most important recommendation is that there has to be a visionary, purposeful and committed leadership that would strive for legacy not legitimacy.

The one important thing in relation to leadership which I did not discuss is the role of state governors in consolidating democracy in Nigeria. While I have no intention of opening a debate on that in this concluding chapter, I can say that for democracy to be properly entrenched, accountability of the state governors must be paramount. President Buhari deserves commendation for assenting to the Constitutional Amendment Act which provided for the financial autonomy of the Judiciary and the state assemblies. Unfortunately, due to the weaknesses of the State Houses of Assembly, but more of the vested interest of the state governors, this significant change has not been enforced and this is worrying.

Finally, in the hope that this book will be published prior to the presidential election on 16 February 2019, I wish Nigerians a peaceful election season and better alternative choices.

# INDEPENDENT NATIONAL ELECTORAL COMMISSION

## REGULATIONS AND GUIDELINES FOR THE CONDUCT OF ELECTIONS

In exercise of the powers conferred by the Constitution of the Federal Republic of Nigeria 1999 (as amended) and the Electoral Act 2010 (as amended), the Independent National Electoral Commission (INEC) herein referred to as "the Commission" issues the following Regulations and Guidelines for the conduct of Elections (General Elections, Bye- elections, Re-run Elections and Supplementary Elections). These regulations and guidelines are issued as a Decision Extract of the Commission of the 12th day of the month of January 2019. These Regulations and Guidelines supersede all other Regulations and/or Guidelines on the Conduct of Elections issued by the Commission and shall remain in force until replaced by new regulations or amendments supported by a Decision Extract of the Commission or an official gazette.

1. These regulations and guidelines shall apply to the conduct of elections to the following offices:

Elections to which these Regulations and Guidelines apply

(i) President and Vice President;

(ii) Governor and Deputy Governor;

(iii) National Assembly (Senate and House of Representatives);

(iv) State Houses of Assembly;

(v) Chairmen and Vice - Chairmen of the Federal Capital Territory (FCT) Area Councils; and

(vi) Councillors of FCT Area Councils Legislature.

(a) Election to the office of President and Vice President as well as National Assembly shall hold on the 3rd Saturday in February of any General election year, while election to the office of Governor and Deputy Governor and the State Houses of Assembly shall hold two (2) weeks thereafter.

Date of General Elections

(b) Whenever the end of tenure of FCT Area Council coincides with a General election year, election into the office of Chairman and Vice Chairman and Councillors of the Area Councils shall be combined with election for Governor and Deputy Governor and the State Houses of Assembly.

(c) Where the end of tenure of FCT Area Council does not coincide with a General election year, the election to the office of Chairman and Vice Chairman and Councillors of the Area Councils shall hold on the Saturday closest to 100 days to the end of tenure of the elected officials of the Area Councils.

2. A person is eligible to vote at an election conducted by the Commission if:

Who can vote

(i) he/she is a Nigerian;

(ii) he/she is registered as a voter;

(iii) his/her name appears on the Register of Voters; and

(iv) he/she presents a valid Permanent Voter's Card (PVC) at his/her Polling Unit.

3.  (a) Voting in any election to which these regulations and guidelines apply shall take place at Polling Units and Voting Points. In the case of the FCT, voting takes place at Polling Units, Voting Point Settlements (VPS) and Voting Points. *Who can vote*

(b)  Voting Points (VPs) are created out of Polling Units based on multiples of 500 and a maximum of 750 registered voters or as may otherwise be determined by the Commission. *Polling Station/ Voting Point Settlements / Voting Points*

(c)  Where a VPS is created, it shall be treated as a Polling Unit.

(d)  As much as practicable, all voting locations shall be located within enclosures in public places accessible to every voter, including Persons With Disability (PWDs). Where they are in open spaces, canopies will be provided.

(e)  Public facilities include public schools, civic centres, town halls and communal open spaces. They do not include places of worship, palaces of traditional rulers and private homes.

4.  Each Polling Unit (PU) will be manned by a Presiding Officer (PO) and three (3) Assistant Presiding officers (APOs) namely, APO I, APO II and APO III. *Appointment of Presiding Officers/ Asst. Presiding Officers*

5.  (a) Where Voting Points are created, there will be for each Voting Point an APO (VP) and 3 APOs appointed by the Commission under the supervision of the Presiding Officer.

(b)  The Presiding Officer shall delegate the responsibility of accreditation, preparing and issuing of ballot papers to the Assistant Presiding Officer APO(VP) in-charge of a Voting Point.

6.   (a) A political party sponsoring a candidate may by notice appoint one person as its polling agent for each Polling Unit, one polling agent for each collation centre and a representative at each point of distribution of electoral materials in the constituency where it is sponsoring candidate(s) for an election.

*Appointment of Polling Agents*

(b)   Where Voting Points are established, political parties may appoint polling agents for each Voting Point.

(c)   The notice referred to in sub-Clause (a) of this Clause shall be in writing, signed, addressed and delivered to the:

i.    Chairman of the Commission in the case of polling agents for collation at the Presidential election;
ii.   Resident Electoral Commissioner in the case of polling agents for Collation at the Governorship election; and
iii.  Electoral Officer in all cases of polling agents for Polling Units/Voting Point Settlements/Voting Points, and polling agents for Registration Area/Ward and LGA Collation;

(d)   The notice shall contain the names, addresses and recent passport photographs of the polling agents and the respective Polling Units/Voting Point Settlements/Voting Points or Collation Centers to which they have been assigned and to be submitted not later than 14 days before the election. Any notice sent in late will be rejected.

(e)   Only a Polling Agent whose name had been submitted to the Commission in the prescribed manner shall receive a copy of the result sheet at a Polling Unit or Collation Centre.

7.   (a) No person shall be qualified to be appointed or serve as a polling agent of any political party if, being a person employed in the public service of the Federation or of any State or Local Government/Area Council, he/she has not resigned or withdrawn or retired from such employment at least 90 days before the date of the election.

*Disqualification of certain categories of persons from being Polling Agents*

(b)   A Polling Agent who aids and abets election malpractices at a Polling Unit or Collation Centre shall be disqualified and on the instruction of the Poll Official/Collation Official shall be removed from the Polling Unit/Collation Center and shall be liable to prosecution. *Disqualification of a Polling Agent*

## ACCREDITATION AND VOTING PROCEDURE AT ELECTIONS

8.   (a) Voting shall be in accordance with the Continuous Accreditation and Voting System (CAVS) procedures as specified in these Regulations and Guidelines, the Election Manual and any other Guide issued by the Commission. *Method of Voting*

(b)   No person shall be allowed to vote at any Polling Unit/Voting Point Settlement/Voting Point other than the one at which his/her name appears in the Register of Voters and he/she presents his/her permanent voter's card to be verified by the Smart Card Reader (SCR), or as otherwise determined by the Commission. *Voting at appropriate PU*

(c)   Each Voter shall cast his/her vote in person at the Polling Unit/Voting Point Settlement /Voting Point where he/she registered or was assigned, in the manner prescribed by the Commission.

(d)   The Presiding Officer shall regulate the admission of voters to the Polling Unit/Voting Point Settlement/Voting Point and shall exclude all other persons except candidates or their Polling Agents, election officials, security personnel, accredited observers and any other person who in his opinion has lawful reason to be admitted. *Persons allowed into the Polling Unit*

(e)   Attendance Register in PU booklet will be signed by these categories of election personnel: POs, APOs, Polling Agents, Security Personnel, Accredited Media and Accredited Observers.

9. (a) At 7:30am, the Presiding Officer of a Polling Unit/Voting Point Settlement, or the Assistant Presiding Officer (VP) in the case of a Voting Point shall cross-check the adequacy of materials. Opening of poll

(b) At 8:00am, Presiding Officer shall:

   (i) declare the Polling Unit open for accreditation and voting;
   (ii) allow voters into the Polling Unit in an orderly queue;
   (iii) introduce the poll officials, polling agents and observers present;
   (iv) separate the queue between men and women, where the culture does not allow the mingling of men and women;
   (v) create a separate queue for PWDs; and
   (vi) explain the accreditation and voting procedures to all present.

10. (a) In accordance with Section 49 (2) of the Electoral Act, a person intending to vote shall be verified to be the same person on the Register of Voters by use of the Smart Card Reader (SCR) in the manner prescribed in these Regulations and Guidelines. Mandatory use of Smart Card Reader (SCR)

(b) Any poll official who violates the provision of Clause 10 (a) shall be deemed to be guilty of an offence and shall be liable to prosecution.

(c) Accreditation and voting shall commence at 8.00am and close at 2:00pm, provided that all voters already on the queue by 2:00pm shall be allowed for accreditation and voting. Accreditation and voting

(d) The accreditation process shall comprise reading of the Permanent Voter's Card (PVC) and authentication of the voter's fingerprint using the SCR; checking of the Register of Voters and inking of the cuticle of the specified finger of the voter.

(e)    The voter shall present himself/herself to the APO (III) for the Polling Unit, Voting Point Settlement or Voting Point who shall:

    i.   determine that he/she is at the correct Polling Unit or Voting Point Settlement or Voting Point;

    ii.  confirm that the voter has not voted anywhere by inspection of the cuticle of the fingernails, and if satisfied direct the voter to the APO I; and

    iii. upon inspection of the PVC held by the voter, if the APO III discovers that the PVC is not for the Polling Unit, the APO III will advise the voter to proceed to the appropriate Polling Unit or Voting Point Settlement or Voting Point.

The APO I shall:

    i.   request for the PVC from the voter;

    ii.  read the PVC using the Smart Card Reader to ascertain that the photograph on the permanent voter's card is that of the voter and that the Polling Unit details correspond with those of the Polling Unit;

    iii. request the voter to place the appropriate finger in the place provided on the Smart Card Reader for authentication; and if the fingerprint matches, request the voter to proceed to APO II.

(f)    The verified voter shall then proceed to theAPO II who shall:

    (i)   request for the permanent voter's card;

    (ii)  check the Register of Voters to confirm that the voter's name, details, and Voter Identification Number (VIN) are as contained in the Register of Voters;

(iii) tick the appropriate box of the horizontal boxes on the right margin beside the voter's details on the Register, showing the category of election, if the person's name is on the Register of Voters;

(iv) tick the appropriate box at the left margin of the Voter details in the case of SCR failure to read (FR) or failure to authenticate (FA);

(v) document the status of the voter; if the voter is a PWD by completing the PWD Form EC 40H as prescribed; and    PWD status

(vi) apply indelible ink to the cuticle of the specified finger on the left hand to indicate that the voter has been accredited to vote in that election.

11. (a) The accredited voter shall proceed to the PO who shall:

    (i) Check the cuticle of the appropriate finger/thumb-nail of the voter to confirm that he/she has been accredited;

    (ii) On being satisfied that the person before him/her has been duly accredited, stamp, sign and write the date on the back of the ballot paper(s)for the respective categories of elections;

    (iii) Pre-fold the endorsed ballot paper(s) using the roll and flatten method;

    (iv) Issue the pre-folded and endorsed ballot paper(s) to the voter;

    (v) Request the voter to remove his/her cell phone or any photographic device before proceeding to voting cubicle;

    (vi) Direct the voter to the voting cubicle to mark his/her choice on the ballot paper; and

    (vii) Ensure that the voter deposits the marked ballot paper in the appropriate ballot box.

(b) Where a voter's PVC is read but his/her fingerprint is not authenticated, the APO I shall refer the voter to the APO II who shall:

*Failure to Authenticate*

&#x20;   (i)   request the voter to thumbprint the appropriate box in the Register of Voters;

&#x20;   (ii)  request the voter to provide his/her phone number in the appropriate box in the Register of Voters;

&#x20;   (iii) continue with the accreditation of the voter; and

&#x20;   (iv)  refer the voter to the PO or APO (VP) for issuance of ballot paper(s).

(c) Where a voter's PVC is read but the name of the voter is not on the Register of Voters, APO II shall refer the voter to the PO or APO (VP) who shall politely request the voter to leave the Polling Unit.

*Absence of name from Register of Voters*

(d) In the event that the PVC fails to be read by the Smart Card Reader, the APO I shall refer the voter to the PO or APO (VP) who shall politely request the voter to leave the Polling Unit.

*Failure to Read PVC, but details on Register match those on PVC*

(e) Where a voter's PVC is read and the SCR shows the details of another person, rather than the details of the cardholder as printed on the PVC, the APO I shall:

*PVC is read, Smart Card shows wrong details, but correct details are in the Register of Voters*

&#x20;   (i)   Refer the voter to APO II to confirm that the details of the voter in the Register of Voters correspond to those on the PVC;

&#x20;   (ii)  APO II if satisfied that the holder of the card is on the Register of Voters, shall record the phone number of the voter in the appropriate box on the Register of Voters; and

&#x20;   (iii) Proceed with the accreditation of the voter.

(f) In all cases from 11(b) to 11(e) the Presiding Officer shall fill the appropriate forms in the PU booklet and make a report. Affected voters in 11(b) and 11(e) qualify to be issued ballot papers after consultation with Polling Agents.

*Consultation with Polling Agents before issuing ballots to voters with verification problems*

273

12   (a) Where the Permanent Voters' Card (PVC) presented by the voter is not for the Polling Unit, the APO I shall politely inform the voter and advise him/her to proceed to the appropriate Polling Unit.

PVC for the wrong Polling Unit

(b)   Any person who presents the PVC of another person with an intention to use it to vote, shall not be allowed to vote and may be liable to arrest and prosecution.

Presentation of someone else's PVC

13   (a) In the event of sustained malfunction of the Smart Card Reader (SCR), the Presiding Officer (PO) shall:

Sustained SCR malfunction/ conti nuation of elections

(i)   immediately inform the Supervisory Presiding Officer (SPO), the Electoral Officer (EO), and the Electoral Operations Support Centre (EOSC) for replacement;

(ii)   suspend Accreditation and Voting until a new Card Reader is made available;

(iii)   file a report of the incident; and

(iv)   inform the voters and polling agents of the situation.

(b)   Where a replacement Smart Card Reader is not available by 2:00pm, the Presiding Officer or APO(VP) as the case may be shall:

i.   inform the SPO, EO, and EOSC of the situation;

ii.   file a report of the incident; and

iii.   inform the voters and polling agents that accreditation and voting for the affected Polling Unit, Voting Point Settlement, and Voting Point shall continue the following day.

(c)   Where a Smart Card Reader (SCR) is replaced in the middle of an election, the data of verified voters in the faulty SCR shall be merged with data in the replacement SCR for purposes of determining the number of verified voters.

14. The Presiding Officer shall allow a voter who is visually impaired or blind or is unable to distinguish symbols or who suffers from any other physical disability to be accompanied into the Polling Unit/Voting Point Settlement/Voting Point and be assisted to vote by a person chosen by him/her, other than an election official, a polling agent or a security personnel on election duty.

Visually Impaired/ Blind or incapacitated Voter (PWDs).

15. Visually Impaired/Blind registered voters may, where available, use the Braille Guide or magnifying glass.

16. PWDs, visibly pregnant women and the aged, shall be granted priority access to voting at the Polling Units, Voting Point Settlements and Voting Points.

17. A voter shall not make any mark on the ballot paper by which he/she may be identified. If he/she does so, such ballot paper shall be rejected provided that any print resulting from the staining of the finger-print of the voter in the voting compartment shall not be deemed to be a mark of identification.

Voter not to make a mark for identification

18 A voter who by accident spoils his/her ballot paper such that it cannot be used for voting may present it to the Presiding Officer and if satisfied that the ballot paper is spoilt, the Presiding Officer shall issue another ballot paper to the voter in place of the spoilt ballot paper and the spoilt ballot paper shall be marked "cancelled" by the Presiding Officer, and recorded in appropriate form in the PU booklet.

Accidental destruction of ballot paper

19. If a person claiming to be entitled to vote applies for a ballot paper after another person has voted in the name given by the claimant, he/she shall, upon satisfactory answers given to any questions put to him/her by the APO II, shall be entitled to receive a ballot paper in the same manner as any other voter; but the ballot paper shall be a tendered ballot paper and deposited in the Tendered Ballot envelope in accordance with the procedure in the Electoral Act.

Tendered ballot. Section 60 of Electoral Act

20. (a) Telephones and other electronic devices capable of taking pictures are not allowed in voting cubicles. Voters may come to the Polling Unit with telephones and other electronic devices provided that they do not take them to the voting cubicles or take pictures of other voters while they are voting.

*Use of telephones and other electronic/ photographic devices*

(b) After thumbprinting the ballot, while still in the voting cubicle, the voter shall carefully fold the marked ballot paper in the same manner that the Presiding Officer had pre-folded the ballot before issuing it to the voter and proceed to drop it in the appropriate ballot box. Additional ballot boxes will be provided where necessary.

(c) Presiding Officers shall place the ballot boxes not more than two meters away from the voting cubicle, in the direction of the Presiding Officers and away from the Polling Agents.

*Proper placement of ballot boxes*

(d) After casting his/her ballot, the voter is free to remain within the vicinity of the Polling Unit to witness the sorting and counting of votes and the announcement of results, provided he/she is orderly.

*Leave to remain in the vicinity of the Polling Unit after voting*

21. After every voter on the queue has voted, the Presiding Officer shall declare voting closed.

*Close of voting*

22 (a) At the close of voting, the Presiding Officer shall:

(i) cancel all the unused ballot papers by crossing them out;

(ii) sort out the ballot papers by party and thereafter loudly count the votes scored by each political party in the presence of the Polling Agents and observers;

*Sorting and counting of ballot, and recording of votes*

(iii) allow recount of votes on demand by a Polling Agent, provided that such a recount shall only be allowed once;

*Recount of votes*

(iv) cross-check the scores;

(v) enter the scores of the candidates in both figures and words in the appropriate forms EC8A/EC8A(VP) series; and fill the Form EC 60E and paste it conspicuously. Pasting of Form EC 60E is mandatory and failure to do so may amount to dereliction of duty.

*Pasting of Form EC60E*

(b) Where Voting Points have been created the APOI shall:

    (i)    enter the result on form EC8A (VP); and

    (ii)   submit to the presiding officer who shall consolidate the result using form EC8A and attach theEC8A(VP) to form EC8A.

(c) The Presiding officer shall then:

    (i)    sign, date and stamp the appropriate EC8A forms;

    (ii)   announce loudly the votes scored by each political party;

    (iii)  request the candidates or their polling agents where available at the Polling Unit to countersign;

    (iv)  refusal of any candidate or polling agent to countersign the appropriate form EC 8(A) series shall not invalidate the result of the Polling Unit;

    (v)   keep the originals of EC8 series and the first pink copies for the Commission;

    (vi)  give to the polling agents and the Police, a duplicate copy each of the completed forms;

    (vii) post the completed Publication of Result Poster EC60(E) at the Polling Unit;

    (viii) complete the EC 40H(I) for PWD Information and Statistics;

    (ix)  Complete the PWD information boxes in the PU booklet;

    (x)   transmit the result as prescribed in the Electoral Act;    Transmission of Results

    (xi)  take the card reader and the original copy of each of the forms in tamper-evident envelope to the Registration Area/Ward Collation Officer, in the company of security agents; and

    (xii) The polling agents may accompany the Presiding Officer to RA/Ward Collation Centre.

23  (a) Where the total number of votes cast at a Polling Unit    Over voting
exceeds the number of registered voters in the Polling Unit,
the result of the election for that Polling Unit shall be declared
null and void, and a report in that regard shall be made to the
Collation officer.

(b)  Similarly, where the total number of votes cast at a Polling
Unit exceeds the total number of accredited voters, the
outcome of the election shall be declared null and void, and a
report in that regard shall made to the Collation officer.

24.  Where after a crosscheck and recount, the sum of spoiled
ballot papers, rejected ballots and valid votes is not equal
to the total number of used ballots, an anomaly exists, and
the Presiding Officer shall submit a written report to the RA/
Ward Collation Officer.

25.  The RA/Ward Collation Officer shall examine the report and
reconcile the figures. Where the figures cannot be reconciled,
the RA/Ward Collation Officer shall locate the source of the
discrepancy, rectify it and make a report to the LGA Collation
officer.

26.  For a Polling Unit where election is not held or is cancelled,    Where
or poll is declared null and void in accordance with these    election is
cancelled or
regulations, the Presiding Officer shall report same in writing    not held.
to the RA/Ward Collation Officer explaining the nature of the
problem and the Collation Officer shall fill form EC 40G as
applicable.

## COLLATION OF ELECTION RESULTS

27.  The collation and declaration of election results shall be done    Collation
of election
at the following levels depending on the type of election:    results

(i)  Registration Area - RA/Ward (Collation for all
elections) including that of Councillor in the case of
the FCT;

(ii) Local Government Area- LGA (Collation for all elections) including that of Chairman in the case of the FCT;

(iii) State Constituency (Collation and Declaration of State House of Assembly elections);

(iv) Federal Constituency (Collation and Declaration of House of Representatives elections);

(v) Senatorial District (Collation and declaration of Senatorial District elections);

(vi) Governorship (Collation and Declaration of Governorship elections); and

(vii) Presidential (Collation and Declaration of Presidential election).

28. (a) In order to remain focused on their assignment, Collation Officers are not allowed to make or receive telephone calls during collation. *(Phone calls during collation of results)*

(b) The Registration Area/Ward Collation Officer shall: *(Collation at RA/ Ward Level)*

(i) take delivery of the original copies of Forms EC 8A, EC8A(I), and EC8A(II) for the Presidential, Senatorial and the House of Representatives elections, respectively, including the EC 40H(I) and 40G;

(ii) take delivery of the original copies of Forms EC 8A and EC8A(I) for Governorship and the State Houses of Assembly elections, respectively;

(iii) receive the Smart Card Readers from the respective Presiding officers;

(iv) compare the number of voters verified by the Card Reader with the number of accredited voters and total votes cast for consistency;

(v) receive and consider if any, the reports of anomalies, adverse incidents, and equipment failure from the presiding officers including reports of where polls are either cancelled or not held;

279

(vi)   submit the Card Readers to the respective supervisory presiding officers (SPOs), in tamper-proof envelops;

(vii)  collate the votes entered in Forms EC 8A, EC 8A(I), and EC 8A(II) for Presidential, Senatorial and the House of Representatives elections, respectively;

(viii) collate the votes entered in Forms EC 8A and EC 8A(I) for Governorship and State Houses of Assembly elections, respectively;

(ix)   collate the votes entered in form EC8A and EC8A (1) for Area Council Chairman and Councillor;

(x)    add up the Polling Unit results to get the RA/Ward summary;

(xi)   enter the votes in both figures and words in the appropriate spaces in Forms EC 8B, EC 8B(I)and EC 8B(II) as the case may be; complete the forms as required, date and sign same and get the polling agents to countersign;

(xii)  completeForm EC 40G for Polling Units where election is cancelled or not held;

(xiii) distribute copies of each of the Form EC 8B or EC 8B (1) and EC 8B(II) to each polling agent and the Police;

(xiv)  take custody of the original copies of Forms EC 8B, EC 8B(I) and EC 8B (II) together with other materials, equipment and reports (if any) received from Presiding Officers at the election to the LGA Colation Centre; and

(xv)   Implement any result management procedure with the assistance of the RA Technical support (RATECH), where applicable.

(c)    Where there is a discrepancy between the verified figure and the total votes cast, the RA/Ward Collation officer shall:

(i)    review the figures against reports from the Polling Units;

(ii) request explanation(s) from the Presiding Officer(s) concerned, the circumstances of the inconsistency;

(iii) accept the result form if satisfied with the explanation(s); and

(iv) if not satisfied locate the point of discrepancy, resolve the discrepancy and request the Presiding Officer to endorse.

29. Where at a Polling Unit, accreditation and voting are to continue the following day on account of the non-availability of a required replacement Smart Card reader, the RA/ Ward Collation Officer shall:

*Collation at RA/Ward Level where Election extends to the following day in some PUs*

(i) inform the polling agents and stakeholders at the collation center of the situation;

(ii) collate the available results from the unaffected Polling Units;

(iii) on conclusion of (ii) above, proceed immediately to the LGA Collation Center where the results from (ii) above shall be saved until the following day, when the RA collation shall resume, including the results of the affected Polling Units; and

(iv) inform the LGA Collation Officer of the situation, who shall then proceed with the collation of the results of the unaffected RAs/Wards.

30. The Local Government/Area Council Collation Officer in-charge of the Presidential Election shall:

*Collation of Presidential Results at the LGA level*

(i) take delivery of all the originals copies of Forms EC 8B from the Registration Area/Ward Collation officers together with other materials and reports relating to the election including Form EC40(G) if any;

(ii) collate the results for the Presidential election by entering the votes in the original copy of Forms EC 8B into form EC 8C in figures and words.

(iii)   add up the RA/Ward results to get the LGA summary;

(iv)    cross-check the totals and entries in the EC 8C with the Collation Support and Result Verification System (CSRVS) secretariat where available;

(v)     announce loudly the votes scored by each party;

(vi)    sign, date and stamp the forms and request the polling agents to countersign;

(vii)   distribute copies of the forms to the polling agents and the Police.

(viii)  transfer the total number of registered voters of affected Polling Units where election was not held or were cancelled, from forms EC 40G into form EC 40G(I);

(ix)    complete form EC 40H(3) using form EC 40H (2); and

(x)     take the original copies of Forms EC 8C to the Presidential Collation Officer at the State Collation Centre together with other materials and reports relating to the election, including Form EC 40G(I).

31.   The State Collation Officer for the Presidential election shall:

Collation of Presidential Result at State Level

(i)     take delivery of the original copies of Forms EC 8C from the Local Government Area Collation Officers together with other materials and reports relating to the election including Form EC 40G (1);

(ii)    transfer the votes scored by each party from Forms EC 8C into Form EC 8D and enter the votes scored in both figures and words in the spaces provided;

(iii)   add up the LGA collated results to obtain the State summary;

(iv)    cross-check the totals and entries in the EC 8D with the CSRVS secretariat for computational accuracy;

(v)     transfer the total number of registered voters of affected Polling Units from Forms EC 40G(1) into form EC 40G(2), where elections were cancelled or not held in respect of all the LGAs.

(vi) announce loudly the votes scored by each party;

(vii) sign, date and stamp the form and request the polling agents to countersign;

(viii) distribute copies of forms EC 8D to polling agents and the Police;

(ix) complete EC 40H(4) using EC 40H(3);

(x) take the original copy of form EC 8D together with other materials and reports relating to the election which were returned by the Local Government Area Collation Officers to the National Collation Centre, in a tamper-proof envelope.

32. (a) The Chief Electoral Commissioner, who is the Returning Officer for the Presidential election, shall:

Collation of Presidential Result at National Level

(i) take delivery of the original copies of forms EC 8D from the state Collation Officers together with other materials and reports relating to the election including forms EC 40G(2), and EC40H(4) where applicable;

(ii) collate the votes scored by each party from forms EC8D received from state collation officers into form EC8D (A) and enter the votes scored by each party in both figures and words in the spaces provided;

(iii) add up the collated state results to obtain the national summary;

(iv) cross-check the totals and entries in the EC 8D(A) with the CSRVS secretariat for computational accuracy;

(v) transfer the number of registered voters of Polling Units where election was not held/cancelled for the respective states from EC 40G(2) into form EC 40G(3);

(vi) announce loudly the votes scored by eachparty;

(vii) sign, date and stamp the form, and request the polling agents present to countersign;

(viii) proceed to distribute copies of forms EC 8D(A) to polling agents and the Police;

   (ix)  compare the total number of voters affected in Form EC 40G(3) with the Margin of Win between the two leading candidates;

   (x)  if the margin of win is in excess of the figure recorded in form EC 40G(3), proceed to enter the scores of the candidates in form EC 8E for the declaration of the Presidential election result.

33.  (a) Where an election is declared null and void for over voting in line with Clause 23 of these Regulations and Guidelines and it is ascertained that the total registered voters in the affected Polling Units may affect the overall result of the election, another date shall be fixed for supplementary election in the affected Polling Units. *Supplementary elections*

(b)  Where the total number of registered voters in the affected Polling Units is less than the margin by which the leading candidate is ahead of the second candidate, indicating that the outcome of the election will not be affected by the supplementary election, the returning officer shall announce the result. *Announcement of result in spite of Supplementary Election*

(c)  Where an election is postponed as a result of serious breach of the peace or natural disasters or other emergencies in line with Section 26 of the Electoral Act, returns for the affected constituencies shall not be made until polls are taken in the affected Polling Units.

(d)  Where an election is postponed in line with Section 26 of the Electoral Act and it is ascertained that the total number of registered voters in the Polling Units affected by the postponement is less than the margin by which the leading candidate is ahead of the second candidate in the election, indicating that the result of the election will not be affected by the outcome of polls in the Polling Units affected by the postponement, the returning officer shall make a return for the election. *Making a return where elections are postponed*

(e)   Where the margin of lead between the two leading candidates in an election is NOT in excess of the total number of voters registered in Polling Units where elections are not held or voided in line with sections 26 and 53 of the Electoral Act, the returning officer shall decline to make a return until polls have taken place in the affected Polling Units and the results collated into the relevant forms for Declaration and Return. This is the Margin of Lead Principle and shall apply wherever necessary in making returns of all elections to which these Regulations and Guidelines apply.

*Margin of Lead Principle*

34.   (a) The Chief Electoral Commissioner and Returning Officer for the Presidential election shall complete Form EC 8E and return the candidate who:

(i)   has the majority of votes cast at the election; and

(ii)   has not less than one-quarter of the votes cast at the election in at least two-thirds of all the States in the Federation and the Federal Capital Territory, Abuja.

(b)   The Chief Electoral Commissioner and Returning Officer for the Presidential election shall then proceed to:

*Making a Return/ Declaration of Result for Presidential elections*

(i)   distribute copies of Form EC8E to polling agents or candidates of each party in the election and the Police; and

(ii)   complete the EC 40H (5) using the EC 40H (4)

(d)   Where no candidate meets the requirements of the majority of votes cast and the electoral two thirds, as provided in 34(a) (i) and (ii) above, a run-off election shall be organized by the Commission within 21 days in line with the provisions of Section 134 (2) to (5) of the 1999 Constitution as amended.

*Run – Off election for presidential Election.*

(e)   Where the margin of lead between the two leading candidates is not in excess of the total number of registered voters of the Polling Units where elections were not held or were cancelled in line with sections 26 and 53 of the Electoral Act, the returning officer shall decline to make a return until

*Margin of Lead Principle and Supplementary election indicated for Presidential election*

polls have taken place in the affected Polling Units and the results collated into a new Form EC 8D(A)and subsequently recorded into form EC 8E for Declaration and Return.

35. Where a Presidential election is uncontested, the Commission shall follow the procedure outlined in Section 133 of the 1999 Constitution (as Amended).

*Uncontested Presidential Election*

36. The Local Government/Area Council Collation Officer in-charge of Senatorial District Election shall:

*Collation of Senatorial District election result at LGA/Area Council level.*

(i) take delivery of all the original copies of forms EC 8B(I)from the Registration Area/Ward Collation Officers together with other materials and reports relating to the election including forms EC40(G)and the EC 40 H(2) if applicable;

(ii) collate the results for the Senatorial District election by entering the votes from forms EC 8B (I) into form EC 8C(I) in figures and words in the space provided;

(iii) add up the RA/Ward results to obtain the LGA summary;

(iv) cross-check the totals and entries in EC8C(I)with the CSRVS secretariat where available, for computational accuracy;

(v) announce loudly the votes scored by each party;

(vi) sign, date and stamp the forms and request the polling agents or candidates to countersign;

(vii) distribute copies of the forms to the polling agents or candidates and the Police;

(viii) transfer the total number of registered voters of Polling Units where election was not held/cancelled for the respective RAs from Forms EC 40G into form EC 40G (1);

(ix) complete the EC 40H(3) if applicable; and

(x) take the original copies of forms EC 8C(I) to the Senatorial District Collation/Returning Officer at the Senatorial District Collation Centre together with other materials and reports relating to the election, including form EC 40G(1).

37   (a) The Senatorial District Collation/Returning Officer for the Senatorial District election shall:

(i)   take delivery of the original copies of forms EC 8C(I) from the Local Government Area/Area Council Collation Officers together with other materials and reports relating to the election including form EC 40G (1);

(ii)   collate the results of the Senatorial District election by entering the votes in the original copies of forms EC 8C(I) into form EC 8D(I) and enter the votes scored in both figures and words in the spaces provided;

(iii)   add up the LGA results to obtain the Senatorial District summary;

(iv)   cross-check the totals and entries in the EC 8D(I) with the CSRVS Secretariat where available;

(v)   transfer the total number of registered voters of Polling Units where election was not held/cancelled for the respective LGAs from form EC 40G(I) into form EC 40G (2);

(vi)   announce loudly the votes scored by each party;

(vii)   sign, date and stamp the form and request the polling agents or candidates to countersign;

(viii) distribute copies of forms EC 8D(I) to polling agents or candidates and the Police;

(ix)   enter the score of each candidate into the declaration of result Form EC 8E(I) for the Senate and return as elected the candidate who scores the highest number of valid votes cast at the election;

(x)   distribute copies of form EC 8E(I) to polling agents and the Police;

(xi)   complete the EC 40H (4) if applicable; and

(xii)  submit to the Resident Electoral Commissioner, the original copies of forms EC 8D(I) and EC 8E(I) together with other materials relating to the election.

(b)     Where the margin of lead between the two leading candidates is not in excess of the total number of registered voters of the Polling Unit(s) where election was cancelled or not held in line with section 26 and 53 of the Electoral Act, the returning officer shall decline to make a return until polls have taken place in the affected Polling Unit(s) and the results incorporated into a new form EC 8D(I) and subsequently recorded into form EC8E(I)for Declaration and Return. *Supplementary election indicated for Senatorial District election*

38.     The Local Government/Area Council Collation Officer in-charge of Federal Constituency (House of Representatives) election shall: *Collation of Federal Constituency Election result at LGA/Area Council Level.*

(i)     take delivery of all the original copies of forms EC 8B(II)from the Registration Area/Ward Collation officers together with other materials and reports relating to the election including forms EC40(G)and EC 40H (I)if any;

(ii)    collate the results for the Federal Constituency (House of Representatives) election by entering the votes in the original copies of forms EC 8C(II) in figures and words in the space provided;

(iii)   add up the RA/Ward results to obtain the LGA summary;

(iv)    cross-check the totals and entries with the CSRVS secretariat where available;

(v)     announce loudly the votes scored by each party;

(vi)    sign, date and stamp the forms and request the polling agents to countersign;

(vii)   distribute copies of the forms to the polling agents and the Police;

(viii)  transfer the total number of registered voters of Polling Units where election was not held/cancelled for the respective RAs from Forms EC 40G into form EC 40G (1);

(ix)    complete the EC 40H (3) if applicable; and

(x)     submit the original copies of forms EC 8C(II) to the Federal Constituency (House of Representatives)

Collation/Returning Officer at the Federal Constituency Collation Centre together with other materials and reports relating to the election, including form EC 40G (1).

39. The Federal Constituency (House of Representatives) Collation/Returning Officer for the Federal Constituency election shall:

Collation and Declaration of Federal Constituency Election at Constituency level.

(i) take delivery of the original copies of forms EC 8C(II) from the Local Government Area Collation Officers together with other materials and reports relating to the election including form EC 40G (1);

(ii) collate the results of the Federal Constituency (House of Representatives) election by entering the votes in the original copies of forms EC 8C(II) into form EC 8D(II) and enter the votes scored in both figures and words in the spaces provided;

(iii) add up the LGA results to obtain the Federal Constituency (House of Representatives) summary;

(iv) cross-check the totals and entries in EC 8D(II) with the CSRVS secretariat where available;

(v) transfer the total number of registered voters of Polling Units where election was not held/cancelled from the respective LGAs from forms EC 40G(1) into form EC 40G(2);

(vi) announce loudly the votes scored by each party;

(vii) sign, date and stamp the form and request the polling agents to countersign;

(viii) distribute copies of forms EC 8D(II) to polling agents or candidates and the Police;

(ix) enter the score of each candidate into the declaration of result from EC 8E(II) for the Federal Constituency (House of Representatives) and return as elected the candidate who scores the highest number of valid votes cast at the Federal Constituency (House of Representatives) election;

(x)   distribute copies of form EC 8E(II) to polling agents or candidates and the Police;

(xi)  complete the EC 40H (4) if applicable; and

(xii) Submit to the Resident Electoral Commissioner the original copies of forms EC 8D(II) and EC 8E(II) together with other election materials.

(b)   Where the margin of lead between the two leading candidates is not in excess of the total number of registered voters of the Polling Unit(s) where election was cancelled or not held in line with section 26 and 53 of the Electoral Act, the returning officer shall decline to make a return until polls have taken place in the affected Polling Units and the results incorporated into a new form EC 8D(II) and subsequently recorded into form EC 8E(II) for Declaration and Return.

*Supplementary election indicated for Federal Constituency election.*

40.   The Local Government Area Collation Officer in-charge of Governorship Election shall:

*Collation of Governorship result at LGA Level*

(i)   take delivery of all the originals copies of forms EC 8B from the Registration Area/Ward Collation Officers together with other materials and reports relating to the election including the formsEC40(G) and EC 40H(2) (if any);

(ii)  collate the results for the Governorship election by entering the votes in the original form EC 8B into form EC 8C in figures and words;

(iii) add up the RA/Ward results to get the LGA summary;

(iv)  crosscheck the totals and entries in EC 8C with the CSRVS System Secretariat where available;

(v)   announce loudly the votes scored by each party;

(vi)  sign, date and stamp the forms and request the polling agents to countersign;

(vii) transfer the total number of registered voters of Polling Units where election was not held/cancelled for the respective RAs/Wards from Forms EC 40G into Form EC 40G(I);

(viii) distribute copies of the Form to the polling agents or candidates and the Police;

(ix) complete Form EC 40H (3) using EC 40H (2); and

(x) submit the original copy of form EC 8C to the Governorship Collation Officer at the State Collation Centre together with other materials and reports relating to the election, including forms EC 40G (1) and EC 40 H (3), where applicable.

41(a) The State Collation/Returning Officer for the Governorship election shall:

Collation and Declaration of Governorship Result

(i) take delivery of the original copies of form EC 8C from the Local Government Area/Area Council Collation Officers together with other materials and reports relating to the election including form EC 40G (1) and EC 40H (3) where available;

(ii) transfer the votes scored by each party from forms EC 8C into form EC 8D and enter the votes scoredin both words and figures in the spaces provided;

(iii) add up the LGA results to obtain the State summary;

(iv) crosscheck the totals of entries in form EC 8C with the CSRVS secretariat where available;

(v) transfer the total number of registered voters of Polling Units where election was not held/cancelled from forms EC 40G (1) into form EC 40G (2) in respect of all LGAs;

(vi) announce loudly the votes scored by each party;

(vii) sign, date and stamp the form and request the polling agents or candidates to countersign;

(viii)distribute copies of form EC 8D to polling agents and the Police;

(ix) compare the total number of voters on form EC40G (2) with the margin of win between the two leading candidates;

(x) if the margin of win is in excess of the figure recorded in form EC 40G (3), proceed to enter the scores of the candidates in form EC 8E for the declaration of the Governorship election result;

(b) The state collation/Returning officers for the Governorship election shall then complete Form EC 8E, sign, date, stamp and declare the result of the Governorship election and return the candidate who:

*Making a Return/ Declaration for Governorship election*

(i) has the majority of votes cast at the election;

(ii) has not less than one-quarter of the votes cast at the election in each of at least two-thirds of all the LGAs in the State;

(c) The state collation/Returning officer shall proceed to:

(i) distribute copies of Form EC 8E to polling agents or candidates of each party in the election and the Police;

(ii) complete the EC 40(H) using the EC 40 H (3);

(iii) submit to the State Resident Electoral Commissioner the original copy of Form EC 8D and the declaration of result Form (EC 8E) together with other election materials.

(d) Where no candidate meets the requirements of the majority of votes cast and the electoral two thirds, as provided in 41b (i) and (ii) above, a run-off election will be organized by the Commission within 21 days in line with the provisions of Section 179 (2) to (5) of the 1999 Constitution as amended.

*Run – Off election for governorship election*

(e) Where the margin of lead between the two leading candidates is not in excess of the total number of registered voters of the Polling Unit(s) where election was cancelled or not held in line with Sections 26 and 53 of the Electoral Act, the returning officer shall decline to make a return until polls have taken place in the affected Polling Unit(s) and the results incorporated into new form EC 8D and subsequently recorded into form EC 8E for

*Supplementary election indicated for governorship election.*

ABDULLAHI Y. SHEHU

42.  Where a Governorship election is uncontested, the Commission shall follow the procedure outlined in Section 179(1) of the 1999 Constitution (as Amended).

Uncontested Governorship Election

43(a) The LGA Collation Officer/Returning officer in-charge of State Constituency (House of Assembly) Election shall:

Collation and Declaration of State Constituency Election Result with one LGA

(i)   take delivery of the original copies of forms EC 8B(I) from RA/Ward Collation Officers together with other materials and reports relating to the election including form EC 40G(I) and EC 40H(2), where applicable;

(ii)  collate the results for the State Constituency (State House of Assembly) election by entering the votes in the original copies of forms EC 8B(I) into form EC 8C(I) in words and figures in the space provided;

(iii) add up the RA/Ward results to obtain the LGA summary;

(iv)  cross-check the totals of entries in EC 8C(I) with the CSRVS Secretariat, where available;

(v)   transfer the total number of registered voters of Polling Units where election was not held/cancelled for the respective RAs from forms EC 40G into form EC 40G (1) where applicable;

(vi)  announce loudly the votes scored by each party;

(vii) date, sign and stamp the forms and request the polling agents to countersign;

(viii) distribute duplicate copies of the form to the polling agents or candidates and the Police;

(ix)  enter the score of each candidate into form EC 8E(I) for the State Constituency (State House of Assembly) and return as elected the candidate who scores the highest number of valid votes cast at the State Constituency (State House of Assembly) election;

(x)   distribute copies of form EC 8E(I) to polling agents or candidates and the Police;

(xi)  complete where applicable, the EC40H (3) using the EC 40H (2);

293

(xii) submit the original copies of form EC 8C(I) to the State Constituency (State House of Assembly) Collation/Returning Officer at the State Constituency Collation Centre together with other materials and reports relating to the election, including form EC 40G (1) and EC 40H (3) where applicable.

(b) Where the margin of lead between the two leading candidates is not in excess of the total number of registered voters of the Polling Unit(s) where election was cancelled or not held in line with section 26 and 53 of the Electoral Act, the returning officer shall decline to make a return until polls have taken place in the affected Polling Unit(s) and the results incorporated into the new Form EC 8C(I) and subsequently recorded into form EC8E(I) for Declaration and Return;

*Supplementary election indicated for governorship election.*

44(a) The State Constituency Collation/Returning Officer for the State House of Assembly election comprising of more than one LGA shall:

*Collation of state constituency election results with more than one LGA.*

(i) take delivery of the original copies of forms EC 8C(I) from the LGA Collation Officers together with other materials and reports relating to the election including, where applicable forms EC 40G(1) and EC 40H(3) where applicable;

(ii) collate the results of the State House of Assembly election by entering the votes in the original copies of forms EC 8C(I) into form EC 8D(I) and enter the votes scored in both figures and words in the spaces provided;

(iii) add up the LGA results to obtain the State Constituency summary;

(iv) cross-check the totals with the CSRVS Secretariat where available;

(v) transfer the total number of registered voters of Polling Units where election was not held/cancelled for the respective LGA from forms EC 40G (1) into form EC 40G (2);

(vi) cross-check the entries in form EC 8D(I) and announce loudly the votes scored by each party;

(vii) sign, date and stamp the form and request the polling agents to countersign;

(viii) distribute copies of forms EC 8D(I) to polling agents or candidates and the Police;

(ix) enter the score of each candidate into form EC 8E(I) for the State House of Assembly and return as elected the candidate who scores the highest number of valid votes cast at the State Constituency election;

(x) distribute copies of form EC 8E(I) to polling agents or candidates and the Police;

(xi) complete where applicable, the EC 40H(4) using the EC 40H(2);

(xii) submit to the Electoral Officer the original copies of forms EC 8D(I) and form EC 8E(I) together with other election materials.

(b) Where the margin of lead between the two leading candidates is not in excess of the total number of registered voters of the Polling Unit(s) where election was cancelled or not held in line with Sections 26 and 53 of the Electoral Act, the Returning Officer shall decline to make a return until polls have taken place in the affected Polling Unit(s) and the results incorporated into the new form EC 8D(I) and subsequently recorded into form EC 8E(I) for Declaration and Return; — *Supplementary election indicated for State Constituency with more than one LGA*

45(a) The State constituency collation/Returning Officer for the State Constituency election comprising less than one LGA shall: — *Collation of State Constituency Election Result with less than one LGA.*

(i) take delivery of the original copies of forms EC 8B(I) from the RA/Ward Collation Officers together with other materials and reports relating to the election including Form EC 40G (1);

(ii) collate the results of the State House of Assembly election by entering the votes in the original copies of forms EC 8B(I) into form EC 8C(I) and enter the votes scored in both figures and words in the spaces provided;

(iii) add up the RA/Ward results to obtain the State Constituency summary;

(iv) cross-check the totals of entries with the CSRVS Secretariat where available;

(v) transfer the total number of registered voters of Polling Units where election was cancelled/not held from Forms EC 40G into Form EC 40G (1);

(vi) cross-check the entries in Form EC 8C(I) and announce loudly the votes scored by each party;

(vii) sign, date and stamp the form and request the polling agents to countersign;

(viii) distribute copies of Forms EC 8C(I) to polling agents or candidates and the Police;

(ix) enter the score of each candidate into form EC 8E(I) for the State House of Assembly and return as elected the candidate who scores the highest number of valid votes cast at the State Constituency election;

(x) distribute copies of form EC 8E (I) to polling agents or candidates and the Police;

(xi) complete where applicable, the EC 40H (3) using the EC 40H (2);

(xii) submit to the Electoral Officer the original copies of Forms EC 8C(I) and Form EC 8E(I) together with other Election materials.

(b) Where the margin of lead between the two leading candidates is not in excess of the total number of registered voters of the Polling Unit(s) where election was cancelled or not held in line with Sections 26 and 53 of the Electoral Act, the Returning Officer shall decline to make a return until polls have taken place in the affected Polling Unit(s) and the results incorporated into the new Form EC 8C(I) and subsequently recorded into Form EC 8E(I) for

Supplementary election indicated for State Constituency with less than one LGA

46   (a) Collation of Results and the Return of a winner to the office of the Chairman and Vice Chairman of an Area council of the FCT shall follow, with necessary modifications, the same procedure for the final collation of the governorship or presidential election.

Collation of FCT Area Council Elections

(b)   Collation of Results and Return of winner to the office of the Councillor of a Council Ward of an Area Council of the FCT shall follow, with necessary modifications, the same procedure for the final collation of the State Constituency seat of the House of Assembly of a state.

47   The following responses and procedures shall be used in managing the issues identified in this Clause during elections and collation of results, particularly in determining where supplementary elections may hold in line with the "Margin of Lead Principle" as in Schedule 1:

Managing the Margin of Lead Principle

(a)   Where the Commission is unable to deploy to Polling Units as a result of logistical challenges, a date for supplementary election shall be announced.

(b)   Where there is willful obstruction or resistance to deployment/ distribution of election materials, enter zero votes for the affected polling units and proceed.

(c)   Where there is voter resistance to the use of the SCR, enter zero votes for the affected Polling Units and proceed.

(d)   Where the use of the SCR is discontinued midway into the elections due to sustained malfunction and no replacement is available before 2 pm, a date for supplementary election shall be announced.

(e)   Where the Commission determines that violent disruptions occurred at a substantial number of Polling Units before announcement of result, a fresh date for election in the affected Polling Units shall be announced by the Commission.

(f)   Where a violent disruption occurs after announcement of results and ballot papers and result sheets are destroyed, regenerate the affected results from duplicate copies, fill new replacement result sheets with the approval of the Resident Electoral Commissioner and proceed with collation of result.

(g) Where result sheets are snatched or destroyed before they arrive at collation centres, regenerate the affected results from duplicate copies, fill new replacement result sheets with the approval of the Resident Electoral Commissioner and proceed with collation of result.

(h) Where balloting materials are still available or remaining after disruption at any stage of the election, proceed with available materials and conclude that stage of the election. However, where

(i) Where there are issues with results of a Voting Point (VP) such as over voting, treat the votes from the affected VP as rejected votes and proceed with the valid votes from other VPs of the Polling Unit.

48. The following shall be allowed access to the electoral material distribution centers, Polling Units, Polling Stations and Collation Centers: *Access to Polling Units and Collation Centers*

    (i) voters (at Polling Units only)

    (ii) INEC officials on election duty

    (iii) Security agents

    (iv) candidates or their accredited polling agents.

    (v) accredited journalists/media

    (vi) accredited domestic and foreign observers

49. Polling agents may: *Role of Polling Agents*

    (i) observe the distribution of election materials, conduct of accreditation, voting, counting of ballots and the collation and declaration of results;

    (ii) call the attention of an election official to any irregularities, but not interfere;

    (iii) counter sign the appropriate result forms at Polling Units and the appropriate results collation forms at Collation Centers.

    (iv) comply with lawful directives issued by or under the authority of INEC, and generally conduct themselves in an orderly manner.

50. Duly accredited election observers who are wearing the observer badges issued by the Commission for the election are entitled to:

(i) observe the process including the distribution of election materials, conduct of the voting, sorting and counting of ballots, collation of results and announcement and

(ii) call the attention of an election official to any irregularities, but shall not interfere; and

(iii) ask questions for clarification where necessary.

51. Security agents on election duty shall:

(i) provide security at the Polling Units'/polling stations and collation centers to ensure that the Polling Units, counting of ballots, collation and declaration of results are conducted without any disturbance;

(ii) take necessary measures to prevent violence or any activity that can threaten to disrupt the elections;

(iii) comply with any lawful directive(s) issued by or under the authority of INEC;

(iv) ensure the safety and security of all election personnel and materials by escorting and guarding the materials at all levels as appropriate;

(v) arrest on the instruction of the Presiding Officer or other INEC officials, any person(s) causing any disturbance or preventing the smooth conduct of proceedings at Polling Units/Stations and Collation Centers;

(vi) on the instruction of the Presiding Officer, stand at the end of the queue of voters at the Polling Unit at the official close of poll to prevent any person joining in;

(vii) escort the Presiding Officer and other election officials to deliver the election results, ballot boxes and other election materials safely to the RA/Ward Collation Centre; and

(viii) escort Collation Officers to deliver election results to the Returning Officer and subsequently to the Resident Electoral Commissioner or Electoral Officer, as the case may be, for the submission of election materials and results.

52. It shall be the responsibility of election officials at all levels to ensure the safe return of all election materials placed in their custody to designated locations after every election. Reverse logistics should be carefully monitored, and materials returned should be audited by the relevant units of the Commission. Reverse Logistics

These Regulations and Guidelines complement the provisions of the Constitution of the Federal Republic of Nigeria, 1999 (as amended) and the Electoral Act, 2010 (as amended).

DATED at Abuja this...*12th*..day of...*January*...2019

*Prof. Mahmood Yakubu*

**Prof. Mahmood Yakubu**
Chairman
INDEPENDENT NATIONAL ELECTORAL
COMMISSION

# Schedule 1

## MANAGEMENT OF THE MARGIN OF LEAD PRINCIPLE

(Response Scenarios)

In managing the Margin of Lead principle, a number of practical and effective field responses and result management techniques have been found effective in minimizing the impact of the adverse implication of "number of registered voter outstanding".

| | Adverse Factor | Required Response | Expected Outcome |
|---|---|---|---|
| 1 | Non-deployment at PU by the Commission due to logistics challenges | Announce a fresh date for the affected PU if necessary. | Supplementary election is indicated |
| 2 | Obstruction and Resistance to deployment/distribution | Enter zero votes and proceed | Conclusion of the process |
| 3 | Voter Resistance to use of IVAS (SCR) | Enter zero votes and proceed | Conclusion of the process |
| 4 | Mid-way discontinuation of the use of the SCR due to sustained malfunction | Request for replacement before 2pm. If no replacement arrives, a new date to continue the election is announced. | Supplementary election is indicated |
| 5 | Violent disruption at substantial number of PUs before announcement of result. | Commission shall announce a fresh date for the affected PU if necessary. | Supplementary election is indicated |
| 6 | Violent disruption after announcement of result including destruction of ballot papers and result forms. | Regenerate the affected results from duplicate copies, fill new replacement result sheets with the approval of the Resident Electoral Commissioner and proceed with collation of result. | Conclusion of the process |
| 7 | Snatching/Destruction of result forms en-route or at collation centres. | Regenerate the affected results from duplicate copies, fill new replacement result sheets with the approval of the Resident Electoral Commissioner and proceed with collation of result. | Conclusion of the process |
| 8 | Where ballot materials are still available or remaining after disruption. | Proceed with available materials and conclude. | Conclusion of the process |
| 9 | Where ballot materials are not available or remaining after disruption. | Commission shall announce a fresh date to conclude. | Supplementary election is indicated |
| 10 | Where there is a disruption at the Voting Point. | Treat as rejected votes and proceed | Conclusion of the process |

# List of abbreviations

ACAs Anti-Corruption Agencies

ACF Arewa Consultative Forum

ACJA Administration of Criminal Justice Act

CAN Action Congress of Nigeria

AfDB African Development Bank

AML/CFT Anti-Money Laundering and Counter Financing of Terrorism

ANC African National Congress

ANPP All Nigeria Peoples' Party

APC All Progressives' Congress

APGA All Peoples' Grand Alliance

AU African Union

BCD Bureau de Change

CBN Central Bank of Nigeria

CCB Code of Conduct Bureau

CCT Code of Conduct Tribunal

CDD Centre for Democracy and Development

CDI Chief of Defence Intelligence

CIA Central Intelligence Agency

CNN Cable Network News

CPC Congress for Progressives' Change

CSC Civil Service Commission

CSIB Corrupt Services Investigation Bureau (Singapore)

CSOs Civil Society Organizations

CUPP Coalition of United Political Parties

DG Director General

DSS Department of State Services

ECOWAS Economic Community of West African States

EFCC Economic and Financial Crimes commission

EMB Electoral Management Body

EU European Union

FCT Federal Capital Territory

FIRS Federal Inland Revenue Service

FIU Financial Intelligence Unit

FOI Freedom of Information

Forex/FX Foreign Exchange

FRA Fiscal Responsibility Act

FRN Federal Republic of Nigeria

GDP Gross Domestic Product

GIFMIS Government integrated Financial Management information System

GMD Group Managing Director

HCI Human Capital Index

ICPC Independent Corrupt Practices and Other Related offences Commission

IDCs Industrial Development Centres

IDPs Internally Displaced Persons

IGR Internally Generated Revenue

IGP Inspector General of Police

IMF International Monetary Fund

INEC Independent National Electoral Commission

IPSAS International public Sector Accounting Standards

IPPIS Integrated Personal Payroll Information System

ISSA International Strategic Studies Association

ISIS Islamic State of Iraq and the Levant

ISWAP Islamic State of West Africa province

JSC Justice of the Supreme Court

LFRN Laws of the Federal republic of Nigeria

LNG Liquefied Natural Gas

MAN Manufacturers' Association of Nigeria

MD Managing Director

MDAs Ministries, Departments and Agencies

MEND Movement for the Emancipation of the Niger Delta

MTN Mobile Telecommunication Nigeria

MW Megawatts

NACS National Anti-Corruption Strategy

NAMFREL National Citizens' Movement for Free Election (Philippines)

NASS National Assembly

NBS National Bureau of Statistics

NCE National Certificate of Education

NCS Nigeria Customs Service

NEITI Nigeria Extractive Industry Transparency Initiative

NJC National Judicial Council

NIA National intelligence Agency

NIMASA Nigeria Maritime Administration and Safety Authority

NITEL Nigeria Telecommunications

NNPC Nigeria National Petroleum Company

NPN National Party of Nigeria

NSCDC Nigeria Security and Civil Defence Corps

NSE Nigeria Stock Exchange

OGP Open Government Partnership

OPC Oodu'a People's Congress

PACAC Presidential Advisory Committee against Corruption

PDP People's Democratic Party

PEPs Politically Exposed Persons

PHCN Power Holding Company of Nigeria

PIB Petroleum Industry Bill

PICA Presidential Initiative on Continues Audit

PMB President Muhammadu Buhari

POCA Prevention of Corruption Act (Singapore)

PVC Permanent Voter's Card

SDP Social Democratic Party

SERAP Socio-Economic Rights and Accountability Project

SGF Secretary to the Government of the Federation

SIP Social Investment Programme

SMART Specific, Measurable, Achievable, Realistic and Time bound

SPPC Special Production and Processing Centres

SSS State Security Service

STEM Science, Technology, engineering and Mathematics

SWOT Strengths, Weaknesses, Opportunities and Threats

TETF Tertiary Education Tax Fund

TI Transparency International

TSA Treasury Single Account

UAE United Arab Emirates

UBEC Universal Basic Education Commission

UK United Kingdom

UN United Nations

UNCAC United Nations Convention against Corruption

USA United States of America

USD United States Dollar

USIP United States Institute of Peace

VAT Value Added Tax

WB World Bank

# References

Abati, Reuben (2016) 'Who Governs Nigeria', *The Guardian,* April 15, 2016.

Abubakar, Atiku (2016) 'Restructuring Nigeria for Greater National Integration and democratic Stability', Paper Presented at the Late General Hassan Usman Katsina Memorial Conference, Kaduna, Nigeria, July 30, 2016.

Adebowale, Yemi (2016) 'Reflections on Our Nation's Sliding Economy', *Thisday*, July 2, 2016.

Adibe, Jideofor (2016) 'Nation-Building: The Mandela and Nyerere Examples'.

Ajayi, A.T and Ojo, E.O. (2014) 'Democracy in Nigeria: Practice, Problems and Prospects', *Developing Country Studies,* Vol. 4. No. 2; ISSN 02225-0565 (Online)

Anya, Anya (2016) 'The Economy and You: Tales of the Unexpected', *Thisday,* July 10, 2016.

Breede, Christian (2012) 'The Challenge of Nation-Building: Insights from Aristotle', The Royal Military College of Canada.

Centre for Democracy and Development (CDD) (2016) 'NIGERIA: The Promise and Practice of Change – Citizens' Perception and Assessment of Buhari's Administration in the Last One Year.

Chiama, Paul (2015) 'Chronicling Nigeria's Transition since Independence', *Leadership*, May 1, 2015.

David, N. A., Manu, Y.A., and Musa, A. (2014) 'Elections, electoral Process and the Challenges of Democratization in Nigeria's Fourth Republic', *Research on Humanities and Social Sciences,* Vol. 4, No. 17, ISSN (online) 2225-0484; accessed through: www.iiste.org

Edevbie, David (2016) 'Stabilizing the Naira', Guest Columnist, *Thisday*, March 25, 2016.

Gambari, Ibrahim (2015) 'How To Make Nigeria Great Again', Leadership, October 8, 2015.

Gambari, Ibrahim (2008) 'The Challenges of Nation-Building', First Anniversary Lecture of the Mustapha Akanbi Foundation, Abuja, 7 February 2018,

Global Commission on Elections, Democracy and Security (2012) 'Deepening Democracy: A Strategy for Improving the Integrity of Elections Worldwide, September 2012.

Ibrahim, Jibrin (2018) '2019 Presidential Election: Predicting the Outcome', *Daily Trust,* Abuja. 31 December, 2018. P.8

Ibrahim, Jibrin (2016) 'What is the economic reform agenda?', *Daily Trust*, February 21, 2016.

Ishiekwene, Azubuike (2015) 'What is Possible In 100 Days', *Leadership*, April 17, 2015.

Jonathan, Ebele Goodluck (2018) *My Transition Hours,* Ezekiel Books, Kingwood, USA.

Kingibe, Babagana (2015) 'NIGERIA: Why change and how?' Daily Trust, Sunday, October 31, 2015.

Kolawole, Simon (2016) 'There Remaineth One More thing', *Thisdaylive*, June 19, 2016.

Kperogi, Farooq (2018) 'Electoral Law: 2019 Will be a Contest of rigging', Whatsapp post, December 8, 2018.

Kukah, Hassan Mathew (2014) 'To Heal a Fractured Nation', *Leadership,* November 24, 2014.

Mahmood, Abba (2016a) 'On The Journey So Far', *Leadership,* May 19, 2016.

...............(2016b) 'A Legacy Of Failure', Leadership, September 29, 2016.

Mahmood, Abba (2016c) 'A Crisis of Leadership', *Leadership*, December 24, 2016.

Momodou, Dele (2016) 'Time to Re-Write the APC Manifesto', *Thisday*, March 5, 2016.

Nda-Isaiah, Sam (2014:4) 'Moving Nigeria forward: lessons from Malaysia, Singapore, China and Dubai', First City People Monthly Lecture, Lagos, 17 August, 2014.

Obasanjo, Olusegun (2018) 'The way Out: A Clarion Call for Coalition for Nigeria Movement', Special Press Statement, Abeokuta, January 2018.

Obasanjo, O (2019) 'Points for Concern and Action', Abeokuta, 20 January 2019.

Okonjo-Iweala, Ngozi (2018) *Fighting Corruption is dangerous – The story Behind the Headlines,* MIT Press, Cambridge, Massachusetts, London, England.

Shehu, Abdullahi Y. (2016) 'The Fight against Corruption in Nigeria: Old Wine in a New Bottle', Keynote Presentation at a Two-Day Policy Roundtable on the Future of the Anti-Corruption Campaign in Nigeria, Organized by the Savannah Centre for Diplomacy, Democracy and Development, Abuja, 28 February – 1 March, 2018.

Shehu, AY (2015) *NIGERIA: The Way Through Corruption to the Well-being of a people,* National Open University of Nigeria Press, Lagos, Nigeria.

Shehu, AY (2013) 'Democracy, Good Governance and the Challenges of Development', Keynote Address to Elected Officials of Kogi State, Lokoja, Nigeria, 13 June, 2013.

Shittu, Wahab (2018) EFCC Convictions and the Role of the Judiciary', The Nigeria Lawyer, *Thisday*, December 24, 2018.

Soludo, Chukwuma Charles (2015) 'Can a New Buharinomics Save Nigeria?', 3rd Anniversary Lecture, African Heritage Institute, Enugu, November 19, 2015.

Usman, Bukar (2015) 'Leadership, Security and National Development', Lecture Delivered at the Faculty of Arts, Ahmadu Bello University, Zaria, on 20 January 2015.

Utomi, Pat (2015a) 'When the People Become Enemy Of The State', *Leadership*, February 16, 2015.

Utomi, Pat (2015b) 'The Issues The Campaign Forgot', *Leadership Newspaper,* March 23, 2015.

Uzomba, Victor (2016) 'Nigeria's Unending Woes', Daily Trust, July 2, 2016.

World Bank (2017) 'NIGERIA: Bi-Annual Economic Update', No. 1.

Yew, Lee Kuan (2000) *From Third world to First World - The Singapore story: 1965-2000,* HarperCollins Publishers, USA.

# Index

### P

### R

### S

## W

Wali, Mukhtari, 160

Wamako, Senator Aliyu, 156

Wilmot, Patrick, 200

World Bank, 46, 123, 126, 131, 148, 252

## Y

Yar'Adua, President Umaru, 55, 57, 82, 247

## Z

Zakari, Mrs Amina, 222

www.ingramcontent.com/pod-product-compliance
Lightning Source LLC
Chambersburg PA
CBHW030003290326
41934CB00005B/207